MW00628444

NUVOLARI

NUVOLARI

Christopher Hilton

First published in Great Britain in 2003 by
The Breedon Books Publishing Company Limited
Breedon House, 3 The Parker Centre,
Derby, DE21 4SZ.

ISBN 1 85983 349 7

Printed and bound by
Cromwell Press, Trowbridge, Wiltshire.

Contents

INTRODUCTION

NUVOLARI. This half a century later, even the name sounds an immortal compound of mastery, mythology and something approaching magnificent madness. It brings questions which demand to be answered in the present tense as well as the past. Who was this man and what exactly did he make racing cars do? Why, when the talk turns to Fangio and Moss, Clark and Stewart, Senna and Prost and Schumacher, does the little, lithe, leathery man have to be placed among them and, often enough, above them?

In a very real and enduring sense, Nuvolari was the first man in the history of motor racing to become what today we'd call an international superstar. If you are an habitual TV-viewer of the Grands Prix, captivated by the panorama of wealth and technology which the young gladiators fight over, *this* is where it really began: with the little feller.

He was born Tazio Giorgio Nuvolari on 16 November 1892 – two years before the first recorded motoring competition. In *that* sense, following the lineage from his birth to Schumacher today, we are covering the whole of motor racing history.

He was born in a small place called Castel D'Ario on the verdant and rural plain near the ancient city of Mantua – Mantova to an Italian – which, if you picture the top of Italy as a thigh, sits very approximately midway between Venice and Milan. As you approach it there is a cluster of four road signs mounted on two equidistant metal supports: 'CASTEL D'ARIO' in white on top; 'Birthplace of Tazio Nuvolari' in yellow beneath that; then a red and white circle, announcing a 50kph speed limit, on the left support and lower down. On the right support there's a square white sign – *ATTENZIONE* – threatening radar. He would surely not have approved.

His cousin Milada Nuvolari was stopped for speeding in 1996. She was then 84. 'Look at the name on my driving licence', she said to the policeman, 'what do you expect?'[1]

Tazio Nuvolari spent his whole life going as fast as he could and trying to go faster, sometimes during the Mille Miglia round-Italy race on just such roads as these through just such towns as these.

Castel D'Ario has a population of 4,000 today, and boasts a couple of restaurants, a square, and solid, stone buildings which are somehow ornate in the Italian way. It is a quiet place with a rural feel: solid, honest, locked into timelessness. Perhaps his restless spirit lingers in the long, shuttered house on the edge of the town where he was born – it, too, ornate and flanked by an orchard. Perhaps in this quietness and this timelessness lie clues to the mystery of what formed him, what drove him and why, this half a century later, the pilgrims still come to gaze at the house. But if the answers are here, nobody has found them yet – the mastery, mythology and madness have a wonderful quality of mystery woven into them.

Years later Nuvolari went to live in Mantua – 50,000 inhabitants there – and his name would become synonymous with the town: 'The Flying Mantuan', 'The Devil from Mantua' and so on.

Not surprisingly, the town has claimed him for its own. The Mayor, Gianfranco Burchiellaro, says that: 'without doubt 'Nivola' [his nickname] is the best-known Mantuan in the world. His courage as a driver, his triumphal ventures and sensational wins have kept the legend alive. The Tazio Nuvolari Museum[2] always attracts a lot of tourists from everywhere, particularly those from Germany, the United Kingdom, the US, Japan and Australia. When they come to Mantua they don't only want visit our monuments and palaces, they schedule a visit to the Museum where you can find mementoes, memorabilia, trophies and pictures of him.'

To an American (or Australian) the whole of Mantua must seem like a museum. As one city guide cryptically puts it, the city 'experienced a rebirth in the year 1000.' Here, too, is solid stone, but also a cluster of church spires, a panorama of slanting, red-tiled rooftops, a large pedestrian square with open-air restaurants arranged like beautiful decorations and in an adjacent, smaller, square a broad door set into one of the old stone walls.

If there are answers, they are through the door, along a hallway and into what ought properly to be called vaults because they house treasure. This is the Nuvolari Museum, a recreation of his life with virtually everything authentic – personal as well as racing – in it that the museum has been able to lay hands on. There is a lot. Here you feel very close to him. You *don't* feel that you have suspended common sense and think he might wander in himself at any moment. You *do* feel in his presence, or close to it. *This* is what he was and *this* is what he did.

In one of the vaults a video plays, on a loop, of his life and races. Rows of chairs face the screen and an elderly couple – Germans, no particular relevance to that – sit mesmerised. The commentary is in Italian but that doesn't matter because the pictures are international.[3] There's his bike racing in the early years, sometimes down dusty streets lined by trees; footage of a car race at Rome in 1927, his enormous Bugatti looming towards the camera as a battleship might; footage of the Italian Grand Prix in 1928, and the pit lane straight at Monza which looks hauntingly familiar; and so the video goes, for an hour and seven minutes.

Nuvolari. Mostly he comes to us in black and white photographs, where he is frozen in the act of pummelling and pounding racing cars, or standing beside them, face to the camera, sometimes smiling, mostly serious. He comes to us, still, in meagre quantities of flickering black and white film, and cumulatively it forms a mosaic of tantalising glimpses captured from the middle distance. The mosaic forms an overall impression: of a man exercising power.

As I've just said, when the talk turns to ultimate greatness – to timeless greatness, in fact – some usher Michael Schumacher forward and say it can't be consistently done any better. Some vault back across Ayrton Senna and Jimmy Clark to Juan-Manuel Fangio and say he is inviolate, whatever anybody else ever did, does or will do. Some are, still, in awe of Clark's simple sophistication, both in a car and out of it. Some will always see Senna as a godhead, capable of anything.

To reach the man from Castel D'Ario we have to vault back again from Fangio, across World War Two to an alien land, the 1930s. It is true: Nuvolari last competed in April 1950 and a month later the modern World Championship was born at Silverstone, Fangio (Alfa Romeo) on the front row. In a vague sense their careers overlapped – Fangio drove in South America before the war – but Nuvolari comes to us, still, from the 1930s and Fangio from the 1950s. They were photographed together before the start of the 1950 Mille Miglia and even then Fangio looked on the threshold of middle age, whereas Nuvolari's hair and facial structure betrayed a dignified descent – or ascent – into old age. They were contemporaries only in the sense that they happened to be alive at the same time.

I am not attempting here to make direct comparisons because, as everybody seems agreed, that can't be done. The vault is too big, the differences too many. I am only saying to make the vault is worth it to see what we find at the other end; to see why the little feller casts a giant shadow all the way to the present.

An American author, Ken Purdy,[4] fashioned his own judgement on Nuvolari into a challenge by asking 'who else' would ever compete for three decades, winning some 72 major races and 150 in total – with a mere 17 second places – and die in his own bed just three years after his final victory? The conclusion, and thus the question of ultimate greatness, 'really isn't arguable at all'.

But Purdy wrote this in 1954, while Fangio was in the process of winning his second World Championship. Purdy can have had no notion of what Fangio would do or become, never mind Clark caressing the Lotus in an astonishing economy of movement, or Senna redefining the art of the possible as if devil and deity rode with him at the same time, or Schumacher mastering all he surveyed across an immense, implacable decade of skill married to triumphant technology.

All we can do is use Purdy to eliminate all others up to Fangio. We shall be meeting these others, of course: Achille Varzi, who was Nuvolari's great rival; Rudolf Caracciola and Bernd Rosemeyer in the mighty German cars of the mid and late 1930s; the autocratic, enigmatic Manfred von Brauchitsch; and the well-bred Englishman Dick Seaman.

Nuvolari was quite unlike any of them, from Varzi to Schumacher. An almost maniacal lust to win – yes, something approaching madness

– gripped him and never let go. Maybe that was the Italian in him, maybe that was just him. If a slower car baulked him, he beat his fist against the side of his own car in rage and frustration. If his car caught fire near the finish of a race, as it did once in Monaco, he got out and tried to push it over the line. If, under his onslaught, a car began to break up, as it did in the 1948 Mille Miglia race, he ignored the bits falling off and drove on at maximum speed. Many people wondered about his more serious accidents and how – mentally – he accommodated them. Once when he was asked, he replied that 'some people might call them serious but, when racing, you cannot think of possible accidents.'

Maybe to him it was as simple as that.

He was, when he wanted to be, a hard man in what was supposed to be an era of camaraderie and chivalry among gentlemen racers. A fellow competitor, Piero Taruffi, has described how at a race at Monza 'I knew that Nuvolari would be a non-starter because he had other commitments, and so I asked if he would lend me the front axle assembly from his car; but typically, in his half brusque, half sarcastic way, he refused point-blank. I did not argue and left it at that.'[5]

There is a nice contradiction here, from Purdy, who insists that because racing was Nuvolari's life the prospect of it made him happy and as a race neared he was both amiable and cheerful.

Paul Pietsch, who raced against Nuvolari, told me: 'Socially he was a most normal man, rather quiet, but in a racing car he was furious! He would do things on a track which were naughty and potentially dangerous – he'd touch you. I must stress that he was not the only one who did this. Varzi did, too, and one or two of the others. It was rare, however, because conditions were so different. If you went off you were in among trees or walls or buildings – not like today when you can go off at 280kph, turn the car round and go back on again, continue in the race. We didn't think in those terms because we couldn't.' Pietsch, a German, started driving in 1932 and drove for the Auto Union team in 1935. His career lasted until 1952 and by then he had started a highly successful motoring magazine business.

Naughty? Nuvolari had a reputation for *needing* to win so badly that he would point to a competitor's tyre as he went past, indicating a puncture so that the competitor would naturally slow down.

Without question he had to be physically hard because the cars were brutal to handle with their solid axles and rock-like suspensions. More than that, the racing surfaces were often bruising – virtual shepherd's tracks in parts of the Mille Miglia race, for instance – and the races long. The Mille Miglia was, as in its name, a thousand miles on ordinary roads. In 1930 Nuvolari did it in 16 hours, averaging slightly over 100kph (62mph).

Today a Grand Prix is limited to two hours (in the wet) but otherwise lasts roughly an hour and a half. In Nuvolari's great year of 1933, these were his times: Grand Prix of Tripoli 2h 19m 51⅗s, the Eifel race at the Nürburgring 3h 0m, the Belgian Grand Prix 4h 9m, the Italian Grand Prix 2h 52m – and even Monaco in 1934 was 3h 33m. It was perhaps a different fitness, more akin to endurance than sprint, but even so remains astonishing. That year at Monaco he averaged 87kph (54mph) with kerbs, buildings, the harbour and spectators to miss rather than the protective Armco of today.

He comes to us, still, as a man who invented a whole new style of driving at speed and deployed it to defeat bigger, stronger, faster cars in races which – like the German Grand Prix in 1935 – are themselves touched by impossibility.

He comes to us, still, as a man who when asked wasn't he frightened of the racing and the racing cars replied 'do you expect to die in bed? Then how do you have the courage to get into it each night?' The mythology insists Nuvolari wanted to die in a car and not, as he did, in his own bed on 11 August 1953; the mythology also insists that he had some pact with the devil, whatever that may mean.

Pietsch did say: 'I know Nuvolari said he'd rather die in a car and I understand that. Just one moment and that's it: better than weeks, and maybe months or years, of living as a cripple.'

Certainly he feared no other driver, and that unites him with Fangio, Clark, Senna and Schumacher. They may, and did, respect other drivers (Fangio–Moss, for example, Senna–Prost, Schumacher–Senna) but fear: no. Nuvolari insisted that this lack of fear on his part was in no sense arrogance but rather a reflection of the confidence he had in himself.

He comes to us, always, as something of a stranger. We have already seen the hardness with Taruffi, the supposed amiability described by Purdy.

Another American author, Brock Yates[6], writes that Nuvolari raced with 'a wild wardrobe, often choosing knickers[7] and argyle knee socks.' A Briton who drove against him, T.P. Cholmondeley Tapper[8], wrote that Nuvolari 'invariably wore a sleeveless leather jerkin and a white helmet, and always his lucky charm, a small golden tortoise dangling from a chain round his neck.'

Whether these two descriptions represent another contradiction is not at all clear, but they do emphasise how great the differences really are between Nuvolari and Fangio, never mind Schumacher and his flame-resistant overalls, his flame-resistant gloves and his crash helmet which, I suppose, would withstand a jet plane striking it a glancing blow.

If genius is attention to detail, Nuvolari qualified easily. Although he dressed in a way which was probably the equivalent of casual chic then, he could present himself impeccably if the occasion demanded that. He made his own travel arrangements, using detailed telegrams. He packed his own suitcases. Evidently he had some 30 keys and knew what each was for.

It wasn't done to talk about money among the gentleman racers but Nuvolari liked it, went out to get it and got it. We shall see. One estimate (Purdy) has placed his annual earnings at $25,000 to $75,000 a year. Such figures must be approached as symbolic rather than statements as accurate as income tax returns. We do not know where they come from or how they translate from then to now. We can say with confidence that in the 1930s they represented very good money indeed.

Motor racing was largely the province of wealthy amateurs and money was rarely discussed. The professionals did their own deals with factories. René Dreyfus says that in the early 1930s Bugatti offered him 60 dollars a month and, later, that Nuvolari was paid twice as much. We know that when Nuvolari won the Vanderbilt Cup in America the prize money went to Enzo Ferrari, the team owner.

We know that Nuvolari was careful with money. Two of his expense claims survive – for the Avus and Eifel races of 1934 – and everything is itemised in detail. The Eifel claim comprises 30 items, set out day by day, and embraces such things as petrol, garage parking, phone calls to Maserati and breakfast.

We also know that the Mercedes and Auto Union teams paid their drivers well enough that Dick Seaman needed an agent – a thing unheard of at the time. We know that Auto Union still owed Nuvolari money when the war began. We know that there was prize money (£250 for winning the Donington Grand Prix), while the Mercedes archives record the prize money in the races they contested. In sum, the financial aspect was as haphazard as racing itself and would remain so until long after the war.

Nuvolari comes to us, too, as a man of superstition. When travelling abroad, he never booked return tickets. His tortoise mascot, hung round his neck, became extremely famous and he never raced without it. He 'considered his greatest aid to good fortune was to embrace a little hunchback friend of his before a race, and for some time this pathetically ill-formed midget of a man accompanied him from race to race.'[9] There are black and white photographs of the hunchback, wearing jacket and collar and tie, his face slightly distorted. He was, evidently, welcomed by organisers and other drivers as well.

And the magnificent madness? Here is Nuvolari discussing the aftermath of a crash in practice for a race at Turin on 18 April 1937 which he described as 'just an accident'.

> *'But your health,' you will say, 'you must have had an awful shaking, besides the cracked ribs.' My friends, it is a matter of philosophy. I was able to review quite quietly every incident in my racing career, and the accident was wonderful. Now I know that my blood is in fine condition. My wounds healed up rapidly. My appetite was formidable all the time I was in bed. Isn't that remarkable? Now I know how strong I am!* And I drove at Tripoli on May 9th! [author's roman]

In recreating the life of any sportsman from any time up to the 1930s the historian faces many pressing problems. The first of them centres round what does not exist. With Nuvolari, specifically, there is an almost complete absence of his own words during his career. The quotation above about Turin is something of a rarity. Journalists scarcely quoted drivers until the 1960s, and not always even then. Nuvolari rarely had a microphone thrust into his face, nor the tight phalanx of tape recorders pressed towards his mouth. He did not know the obligatory and choreographed walkabout for sponsors, nor the endless and repetitive mandatory press conferences. That is why he is still something of a stranger to us. I have made full use of some of the interviews he did give and the insights into his personality that they offer. They are all we have.

The second problem is the sources which a historian must rely on and work with. Companies like DaimlerChrysler (that's Mercedes) keep archives, so a real picture can be gained of what the Mercedes team did in the 1930s. Newspapers and magazines – especially the specialist weeklies and monthlies – based their coverage on factual reporting, but, pre-TV, the journalists could only write about what they could see with their own eyes. By definition at Monaco, for example, that was only a fragment of the circuit – and it was the same at Le Mans, the Nürburgring, the Mille Miglia and Ards in Northern Ireland. Most of the incidents in the race – not just crashes, but overtaking and so on – would have to be recreated afterwards, and that depended on the acumen and diligence of the reporter as well as the accuracy of recall of those he talked to. It is quite common to find a specific incident described in three contradictory ways in three contemporary publications.

I don't want to be pedantic about all this but it does seem important because so many of Nuvolari's races were highly dramatic and don't need either inaccuracy or embellishment to help them. If you have admired Schumacher's mastery of the modern machine, thrilled to Senna's ability to create masterpieces from nothing; if you're a little older and watched in awe as Clark subjugated the old, dangerous Spa; if you're a little older than that and marvelled at Stirling Moss's versatility or Fangio's fantastic finesse, these experiences are very much alive for you.

Very few can do that with Nuvolari. Too long ago. Anyone of 20 seeing his astonishing triumph at the Nürburgring in 1935 would today be in their late 80s.

I have presented Nuvolari through the medium of his great races so that, albeit at one remove, they are as much alive to you as anything Fangio or Schumacher has done. To sustain that it *must* be accurate or, if there are ambiguities which cannot be resolved, these must be clearly indicated.

Film coverage, which might bring the whole thing alive, tends to be clips shot for newsreels. It is why Nuvolari comes to us only in the flickering images from the middle distance – even at the heart of the treasure chest, in the video in the museum.

In theory the most valuable sources ought to be the biographies and autobiographies of the people involved, but they are surprisingly few and must be treated with extreme caution. Let me give an example. In his book *Speed was my Life,* the Mercedes team manager Alfred Neubauer set out to demonstrate the rivalry between Nuvolari and Varzi:

> *A typical clash took place at Alessandria in 1930 for the Bordino Cup. Although one Mercedes had been entered privately, the race was really between the blue Bugattis and the red Alfa Romeos. Before long, two of the Alfa Romeos had pulled well away from the rest of the field. For ten laps under a blazing sun Varzi chased Nuvolari round the circular course. Then in the second last lap Varzi made a desperate bid for the lead. Yard by yard he reduced the gap...*

And more in the same vein, all the way to a gripping grandstand finish. Then you look up the race in the authoritative reference *When Nuvolari Raced.*[10] The Alessandria race was on 20 April 1930 and Nuvolari retired on the first lap with engine failure. Perhaps Neubauer meant another year. Well, in 1931 Nuvolari retired on lap 10 with a broken differential, didn't compete in 1932; and in 1933 – when Nuvolari won – Varzi didn't compete. In 1934 Nuvolari retired on lap 2 when the car overturned.

Neubauer also wrote a colourful (and utterly fanciful) account of the infamous 1933 race in Tripoli which was supposedly fixed, and it has provided the foundation for virtually every subsequent rendition. (I have chosen that word carefully.) An American researcher, Don Capps, went back to the primary sources and uncovered the truth. His recreation appeared on the Atlas F1 website (www.atlasf1.com) and I'm grateful to him as well as Biranit Goren, who runs the site, for permission to use it. Capps kindly read my chapter when I'd finished it. Meanwhile William Boddy, MBE and founder editor of *Motor Sport,* was happy to go back down memory lane to describe how he wrote a feature article in the 1960s which planted the seeds of doubt in Capps's mind. Betty Sheldon played a leading role in inspiring Capps, and I am grateful to her and Paul for permission to quote from their *Record of Grand Prix and Voiturette Racing*.

I am further grateful to Capps because he gave me an intriguing interview about his reasons for investigating the race and how he did it, and sent valuable background for the Vanderbilt Cup race of 1936. He steered me to Mark Steigerwald, Reference Librarian at the International Motor Racing Research Centre in Watkins Glen, and he enabled me to get in contact with Joel E. Finn, whose authoritative *American Road Racing – the 1930s* I wanted to quote from. Thanks to Finn for agreeing, and providing a lovely anecdote.

Nuvolari's life story is littered with examples of not letting the facts spoil a good story and one book on him, by Count Johnny Lurani[11], is completely unreliable. How many generations of readers have accepted every word? I have used Lurani with extreme caution and, within the text, I've included specific examples of how unreliable he was.

This study of Nuvolari is centred, as I've said, around a recreation of his great races and I have chosen them to try and demonstrate both his personal range and that of his career. It is why the Mille Miglia is in as well as Monaco, the 24 hours of Le Mans as well as the sand-blown spaces of Tripoli, the lanes of Ulster as well as the Nürburgring roller coaster, the pretzel-shaped Roosevelt Raceway on Long Island and the cobbled streets of Belgrade. Incidentally, I've used a device which I've called 'intermezzos' between the races to continue his career from one great race to the next. These have not been done slavishly or exhaustively; more, they are to link the races, keep the narrative moving and broaden the whole picture.

Despite those such as Neubauer and Lurani, there *are* a whole variety of sources which cumulatively do help. I pay my dues to them below. Nuvolari expressed himself through the races: they were his only medium of articulation, no words necessary.

Away from this, his life moved from the ordinary – a rural existence, a happy marriage – to the tragic, because both his sons died before he did and he himself died painfully, and before his three score years and ten.

I am indebted to Paul Pietsch and Hans Ruesch[12] for granting me interviews. As drivers who competed against Nuvolari their memories are particularly valuable. I'm particularly grateful to Ruesch for lending me the last copy of a book he wrote called *The Racers* (Ballantine Books, New York, 1953) where the leading figures of the 1930s are given pseudonyms. Nuvolari, for some reason, is called Dell'Oro and Ruesch said: 'Whenever you see him, that's exactly Nuvolari!'

I am equally indebted to two other interviewees: Jabby Crombac, who saw Nuvolari and has been close to Grand Prix racing for 50 years; and Neil Eason Gibson, who met Nuvolari, has studied his career and lent many photographs from his collection which have not been published before. I am particularly grateful for that.

There is a full bibliography at the end of the book but I want to pay immediate tribute to two titles which were always at my elbow: *When Nuvolari Raced* by Valerio Moretti (Autocritica Edizioni, Milan and Veloce Publishing plc, Dorset) which can, I think, be regarded as the definitive work of thumbnail sketches of every Nuvolari race from 1920 to 1950; and *Racing the Silver Arrows* by Chris Nixon (Osprey Publishing Limited, 1986). I'm grateful to Nixon for permission to quote.

The specialist motoring press covered the races in detail and, while they didn't probe too deeply into many aspects of what they were watching, they didn't fall back on invention and do provide a bedrock of information: *The Autocar*, *The Motor* and *Motor Sport*. Thanks to Eric Verdon-Roe, chairman of Haymarket Autosport Publications, for permission to quote from all three.

As Italian sources I have consulted the newspapers *Gazzetta dello Sport* and *Corriere della Sera* extensively. The book *Nuvolari* by Aldo Santini was full of solid information while a video, *Over the Limit Part 2, Portraits of Great Italian Racing Drivers* (Warwick Video, written by Pino Allievi) was illuminating.

Doug Nye helped with the mystery of the Monaco finish in 1933 when Nuvolari tried to push his car over the line and passed me on to the film-maker David Weguelin, whose labours shed comforting light. His video *Racing Mercedes Part 2* (Motorfilms) was also invaluable (© Bill Mason Films/David Weguelin Productions 2001).

DaimlerChrysler, in the guise of Mercedes, allowed me to explore and exploit their archives at Stuttgart, and that was an enormous help in chapters seven and nine.

The April 1968 issue of the German magazine *Motor Revue* contained a detailed description of the 1935 German Grand Prix. The former owner of the Eifeler Hof Hotel in Adenau, although ill and in a home, provided fascinating details about Nuvolari and the other drivers who habitually stayed there for the Grand Prix.

In recreating the Ards race of 1933, I also consulted – and have quoted from – the *Belfast Telegraph, Ireland's Saturday Night* and *The Chronicle (Ards)*. Thanks to David Neeley, Editorial Executive, *Belfast Telegraph* for permission to quote from the former and Stephen Dunwoody for permission to quote from the latter. Pam Ellis of *Ards Tourism* was kind enough to send me maps, background information, a lovely little anecdote and a video, *Strictly T.T. The R.A.C. Tourist Trophy Race 1928–1936* (Spence Brothers Productions, 1994) – a superb piece of historical recreation itself, and invaluable.

Corriere della Sera covered the 1936 Vanderbilt Cup race on Long Island from an Italian perspective and also the Mille Miglia races of 1930 and 1948. Sharon Gavitt of the New York State Library in Albany, NY, dug out the relevant cuttings in the New York papers for the Vanderbilt, and had them photocopied and sent over. They add, I hope, a racy (pun intended) flavour to that chapter.

I have used extracts from an interview Nuvolari gave to *Sports Illustrated* in New York in 1937 and I am grateful to Nigel Roebuck for lending me a photocopy of it as well as an interview he did with René Dreyfus. Roebuck also allowed me to raid his library, provided many invaluable suggestions and drew on his vast experience whenever I needed it. He also fought – and won – a protracted battle against his new fax machine. I mention this because all victories over technology should be celebrated as much as Nuvolari's own victories over machinery.

Eoin Young hunted through his own archives to find some Nuvolari correspondence. I have used several of these letters because they carry with them intimacy and immediacy.

Dominic of the archives at *L'Equipe* in Paris dug out race reports from the 1930s, photocopied them and sent them at high speed. They were extremely useful in filling in many details and, like so much else, have a wonderful period feel to them. I am grateful to Jerome Bureau and Caroline Beauchamps of *L'Equipe* for permission to quote.

Between them, Jean-Claude Virfeu and Laurence Coriton of *Ouest-France* got to me a working copy of that newspaper's 1933 Le Mans coverage, *et pour ça, merci, mes braves!* A special word, also, to Georges and Elizabeth Lecomte who originally put me in touch with Virfeu.

I thank Mark Hughes, editorial director of Haynes, for permission to quote from three G.T. Foulis titles, *Grand Prix Driver* by Hermann Lang, *Amateur Racing Driver* by T.P. Cholmondeley Tapper, and *A Racing Driver's World* by Rudolf Caracciola.

Brock Yates was good enough to allow me to plunder his classic *Enzo Ferrari: The Man and the Machine,* and I did. I am much in his debt.

Clive Richardson, who runs Audi's in-house magazine in Britain, sent an evocative video, *The Silver Arrows from Zwickau* (Audi), and introduced me to valuable contacts at Audi.

Two other videos gave their precious glimpses: *The History of Motor Racing Volume Two* (Shell/Duke Marketing) and *Donington* by Neville Hay.

Amanda Gadeselli translated a great deal of Italian and provided social background; Birgit Kubisch in Berlin and Inge Donnell in Britain translated a great deal of German, just like that. All three often had to work with imperfect photocopies of material from the 1930s and did a terrific job. So *grazie* and *danke schön.*

Before we begin, we must also confront the potentially tricky business of miles and kilometres. The main weight of the book concerns the 1930s, when Britain, its white Commonwealth and the United States used imperial measures (except on very rare occasions) while, naturally, the continental countries used the metric system. As a consequence, the former expressed distance in miles and speed in miles per hour, the latter in kilometres and kilometres per hour. Throughout I give both because that's the era we're in now. If the original source was in miles I add the metric equivalent in brackets; if in kilometres, I add the imperial equivalent in brackets. Look if you want. Don't if you don't.

And yes, on top of this the US gallon was (and is) different from the UK gallon. You will be happy to know I have studiously ignored this and very cleverly called all gallons gallons.

1

Pact with the Devil?

ARTURO Nuvolari, born 1863, has a stern, emotionless face in photographs but we can't read too much into that. Invariably people in Victorian photographs posed in such a way, rigid in their formality.

Although his son Tazio's early portraits were the same, familiarity with being photographed increased and he seems to have become thoroughly at ease with it. You could easily construct a gallery of Tazio smiling his toothy smile, casually leaning against cars, chatting to people, gesticulating.

Arturo, his father, was a farmer of means and a bike racer (and Arturo's brother, Giuseppe, was a bike racer, too). If Arturo comes to us from the great silence with the facial solemnity of an undertaker, Tazio's face positively bubbles down the decades and you san see how, in Brock Yates's description, 'he drove like a madman, crashing often and flogging his cars as if they were recalcitrant beasts of burden. He was, in the argot of the day, the classic *garabaldino* – a driver with the slashing, all-out style of a winner; a charger who drove with such abandon that rumours spread through the crowds that he was haunted by a death wish or, like Paganini[1], had a pact with the devil.'

Tazio Nuvolari was born, as we have seen, at Castel D'Ario on 16 November 1892 at 9 o'clock in the morning, to Arturo and Emma Elisa Zorzi. He was their fourth child. A sister, Artura, had been born in 1887 and a brother, Arturo, in 1888. Maria came along in 1890, and was followed by Tazio in 1892. Another sister, Carolina, completed the family in 1898. According to Lurani (who inevitably claims Tazio was the first-born), the mother favoured Artura while the father favoured Nuvolari because he was so slight that he probably wouldn't live long.

The forces which shaped Nuvolari are themselves mysterious because they are unknown, although the fact that father and uncle were bike riders – Giuseppe achieved international standard – meant that Nuvolari was brought up in a 'sporting atmosphere'.[2] At eight, he was given his first bike. He cycled to elementary school in Castel D'Ario's[3] main square. The classroom was on the ground floor. Evidently Nuvolari propped the bike against the wall outside and, when lessons were over, could jump from the window straight into the saddle.[4] Perhaps here is the very first example, not of the Nuvolari mystery, but of the Nuvolari myth. To vault straight on to the saddle from above has to be painful and, if the landing goes even a little bit astray, much worse than that.

More likely he lowered himself with the fluid dexterity of a gymnast, making sure that his hands reached the handlebars to redistribute his body weight before his bottom hit the saddle. Without reading too much into any of this, it does suggest that he had abnormally good balance. This is clearly something you are born with but Nuvolari had it to such an extent that, in time,[5] he was able to take racing cars round circuits in flat-out power slides, and develop four-wheel drift, 'an exquisitely balanced slide that was eventually adopted by every fast driver in the world.'

Lurani writes about Nuvolari's ability as a horseman even before he was a teenager, and explains that he rode without saddle or bridle. What makes this plausible is the balance.

At 13 he got his first motorbike, from his uncle Giuseppe. It was a fateful moment. Within days he felt he had mastered it[6] and Moretti recounts the tale of how Artura was waiting for evening shoes from Mantua and Nuvolari set off to get them. When he emerged from the shoemaker's a policeman was waiting and wanted to see his licence. Nuvolari explained that it was his uncle's motorbike and he was pushing it home. He began to push it, 'quickened the pace', jumped on and rode away.

That same year uncle Giuseppe took him to see his first motor race, at the large town of Brescia some 60km north of Mantua. It must have been another fateful moment. We must assume that the 13-year-old could not have imagined that one day a great race – the Mille Miglia – would start and finish in this town, or that what he would do in it would entrance and excite the whole of Italy.

Motor racing had begun in rudimentary form in 1894, became more refined by 1897 and by the turn of the century was recognisable to modern eyes. Racing began in France but spread quickly enough. In these early years all comers – even motorcycles – could enter and the races themselves were domestic, most run from town to town. The first race on a circuit was held in 1899, and a major turning point came in 1900 when races were run to a specific formula (the Gordon Bennett races). They led to the first Grand Prix, held in France in 1906.

The race which Giuseppe and Nuvolari went to see, on 10 September 1905, was called *Il Coppa Florio* and was over three laps of rough roads – 500 kilometres (311 miles) – and attracted a strong entry of 22, several from France. The great drivers of the day were in it, including Vincenzo Lancia (we all know what he went on to make). There were various makes of car, five by the Societa Aninima Fabbrica di Automobili–Torino (FIAT to you) and four by Mercedes.

Paul Sheldon[7] writes that there were three control points but the administration of the race was not well handled, 'making it very difficult to appreciate who was in the lead at any given time, especially as the battle was quite a close one.' A driver called Carlo Raggio, an amateur in an Itala car, won it by almost 10 minutes with a time of 4 hours 46 minutes 47.4 seconds (65.13mph/104.8kph). A French driver, Victor Hemery, thought he had won and reacted with great anger when he was informed that he hadn't.

Did Nuvolari witness this? Did he see that motor racing was about many things, including passion?

Anyway, as Sheldon points out, 'the life of a top driver was now busy and many of the ones here would go straight away to finalise their plans for making the great voyage to America.' That would be for the Vanderbilt Cup, 13 days after Brescia. The Vanderbilt, on Long Island, had been first run the year before and continued until 1916. It was revived in 1936. By then, the little 13-year-old would be 44. He would make what was still a great voyage, and win the Vanderbilt easily. The Americans were scarcely able to believe what he could make a car do.

Giuseppe was a motor car dealer and when Nuvolari finished his schooling he joined him, but in 1913 he was called up to do his military service. Later that year he was sent on indefinite leave, but when Italy entered World War One in 1915 he was called up again.[8] He drove an ambulance and, mythology insists, had a crash when the steering failed. This is the first recorded incident of a Nuvolari crash (although Lurani says he'd fallen off a horse years before, and if it's true that would have been the first of them).

Nuvolari seems to have had a very *Italian* military career: the initial call-up in March 1913, the indefinite leave eight months later, the recall in 1915, a discharge in September 1915 after the crash, marriage to girlfriend Carolina on 10 November 1917, birth of their son Giorgio in 1918 and then the call up again in February 1919. He was discharged forever in August 1919 on the grounds of ill health, having been diagnosed with suspected tuberculosis.

In 1920, while making a living selling cars in Mantua, he took out a competitive motorbike licence and made his debut at Cremona on 20 June. He didn't finish, though why has vanished into the mists of time. Lurani describes how Carolina sensed that Nuvolari *needed* the racing and decided to give her unconditional support. By today's standards, of course, he was impossibly old – 28 – to be embarking on a career which would seem to demand an accumulation of experience; and in any case after Cremona he did not race again until Verona the following year, in a time trial for cars which he won.

There seems little doubt that Nuvolari intended to compete much earlier, because he initially took out a competitive licence in 1915. Then the war came. That he had the licence then strongly implies that Carolina knew what she was getting when she married him.

Nor, the war over, could he go racing immediately, because racing didn't restart until 1920. He competed on a more or less regular basis through the early 1920s, but not 'in earnest'[9] until 1923. Far from being instantly and intuitively brilliant, he was short of money, short of top-class machines and short of race successes. He came through this by willpower. He *had* to keep on because racing was his lifeblood. On 13 May he finished second at Parma in a hillclimb. The winner was a fastidious man, 'chilly, aloof, [the] well-born son of a textile magnate from near Milan.'[10] He was called Achille Varzi and his rivalry with Nuvolari would last right up to World War Two. It was of such an intensity that there is only one accurate historical parallel, between Senna and Alain Prost – and that, of course, was only in cars and only lasted six seasons. Nuvolari and Varzi fought their duels both on bikes and in cars.

The turning point for Nuvolari's career came on 1 June 1923 when he won a bike race at Busto Arsizio, a town 35 kilometres from Milan, defeating strong opposition. He was invited to join the Indian team and become a works rider. The Indian is not perhaps a familiar name to followers of Formula 1 racing, especially these days, but in the 1920s it was a major American bike company.

A man called Oscar Hedstrom was 'probably the first American to incorporate an internal combustion engine with a bicycle.'[11] In 1899 he 'produced his first motorised bicycle'. With a man called George Hendee, they founded Indian in 1901, based in Massachusetts. The 600cc Indian Scout (1920) and the 1000cc Indian Chief (1922) were best-sellers. Now, however, they were being challenged by Harley-Davidson and getting Nuvolari represented – or would come to represent – a coup.

According to Moretti, however, it might all have gone wrong in his first race for Indian when his team leader, Amedeo Ruggeri, had a puncture and Nuvolari struck out for victory. Fortunately (!) he had a puncture himself, which allowed Ruggeri to get ahead again.

Nuvolari's contract was not renewed for 1924 and his thoughts began to turn towards cars. On 29 May he drove at Ravenna against Enzo Ferrari and a photograph of it survives, Ferrari already a portly man standing to one side of the car with a hand on it, Nuvolari, goggles on his forehead, leaning on the car from the other side.

By now Nuvolari had a reputation as a fiery rider who adored a challenge. Motorbikes were what he did, and he rode frequently throughout 1924 and 1925 – the year when he signed for the Bianchi company, then 'one of the most prestigious businesses in Italy'.[12] The 350cc Bianchi was a superb motorbike and Nuvolari proved to be virtually unbeatable on it.

We have reached the land of legend.

On 26 July the French car Grand Prix was run at Montlhéry and a very famous Italian driver, Antonio Ascari, drove an Alfa Romeo in it. The race had a rolling start and Ascari seized the lead. On lap 11 he broke the lap record and when he pitted four laps later held a lead of seven minutes. He was told he could ease back the pace but he indignantly refused:

> *While saying this he munched a* Zabaglione *(an egg-flip with Marsala wine), threw two bananas into the cockpit next to what he called his 'Oriental Commodities' – thermos of champagne and water, and a fire extinguisher – resting on the racing mechanic's empty seat. Then he climbed back in himself and, having lost only two minutes, resumed his lead.*[13]

Rain began to fall on lap 20 and on lap 23, as it would seem, he still had not eased off the pace. 'Apparently he misjudged the slight, long left-hander which breaks the otherwise near straight return'[14] from out in the country. He struck a post, the car went into a slide and rolled twice. He was thrown out but the car struck him. He died on the way to hospital.

The Italian Grand Prix was on 6 September. Non-motor racing people, I am sure, find the immediate and dispassionate search for a replacement callous, but that is the way it is, now as then. Alfa Romeo needed to find a driver. They tested several candidates at Monza and, as it happened, Bianchi were testing there that day, too – their next big race was the Grand Prix des Nations, also at Monza, on 13 September. Whether Alfa Romeo intended to test Nuvolari as well, or whether he thrust himself upon them, is unclear. We do know that Nuvolari drove it last and crashed heavily. He was taken to hospital. He had failed the test and that might have had profound consequences for his career in cars at the highest level.

Vittorio Jano, a brilliant designer poached by Alfa Romeo from Fiat,[15] 'considered Nuvolari beyond the fringe, a madman intent only on wrecking himself and the cars he battered. In the mid-1920s the senior engineer had used his considerable influence at Alfa Romeo to prevent Nuvolari from being hired for the factory team, although it was acknowledged that he possessed enormous talent. He was in his mid-thirties, but Jano still insisted on referring to Nuvolari as "the boy", a pointed barb at his alleged immaturity, and a nickname the engineer used even after Nuvolari had reached the very pinnacle of the sport.'

Did the Monza crash simply reinforce this?

Naturally Nuvolari discharged himself, went by taxi to Bianchi in Milan and assured them he would be in the Grand Prix des Nations. He was. He needed strapping and padding, and a cushion on his stomach for when he leant forward. The received wisdom – that he had his legs in plaster – is inaccurate. The mechanics did have to lift him on to the bike and felt that if he crashed he'd clearly kill himself. *He* felt he had so much padding he'd bounce. A rainstorm made the organisers cut the race distance by a hundred kilometres and that helped him, but even so he won it nicely enough.

Meanwhile Bianchi, seeing clearly what they had in Nuvolari, made him sign a new contract which stipulated that he only race Bianchis. He did that until midway through 1927 when he drove Bugattis as well, although Bianchi took some persuading to agree to this. The balance of Nuvolari's career was shifting.

He drove a Bugatti in the 1928 Tripoli Grand Prix, which he won (Varzi third) and two weeks later he took on the Mille Miglia. To the student of motor racing we are at last among familiar names and places. In 1928 Nuvolari and Varzi formed a partnership with Bugatti, but it was 'uneasy' and the 'rivalry became intolerable for both'.[16] Varzi used family money to buy an Alfa Romeo. Curiously, they had seldom actually raced against each other on bikes. The full intensity of their rivalry would be in cars.

By 1929 Nuvolari was in Alfa Romeos – and Enzo Ferrari was, one way or another, a moving force there, had been for years. In 1930 Nuvolari, who had run his own team for a while, joined Scuderia Ferrari.

The great years and the great races were at hand.

2

Light and Darkness

Mille Miglia 1930

THAT Saturday morning was hot enough to cover the town of Brescia in a haze. The sun loomed behind it, ghostly, threatening perhaps to break through and burn the haze away. April is a cleansing month along the northern Italian plain which stretches from Turin near the French border to Venice on the Adriatic but already – well before 11 o'clock – the air was drowsy. The activity was not.

On a broad, straight street some halfway between Brescia's centre and its outskirts – an imposing street of stone buildings with a line of trees in the distance – the starting area had been closed to the public by barricades and an 'imposing gateway of canvas and wood. Black-shirted Facisti soldiers in field grey, smartly-uniformed policemen and gendarmes in swallow-tailed coats, cocked hats and much silver braid, kept all trespassers severely away from the select enclosure.'[1] Well, severely in an Italian way because down one side stretched a café where people sat sipping aperitifs.

There had been 143 entries for the 1930 Mille Miglia, the fourth running of the event, and of these 134 had materialised (it was the first total of more than 100). Nuvolari was in a works Alfa Romeo with Gianbattista Guidotti – who subsequently ran Alfa Romeo – as co-

MILLE MIGLIA, 1930
1,018 miles (1,638km)

driver. That did not mean what it said. Nuvolari, of course, would drive the whole way. Varzi also had an Alfa. There was an intriguing entry, too. Rudolf Caracciola, a young German of infinite promise, had a powerful Mercedes and, although he hadn't driven the event before and didn't know the roads that mattered not at all. He was using it as a trial run[2] for 1931. Maserati fielded the experienced Luigi Arcangeli. And then there was Giuseppi Campari, twice winner and the favourite to win again, in an Alfa Romeo.

They all prepared to cover 1,000 miles from Brescia down one side of the Italian boot to Rome and back up the other side, finishing at Brescia on the Sunday. Over the rough roads of the era, across mountains and passes as high as 3,000ft, through towns and villages with thousands upon thousands of unprotected spectators at the roadside, the winner would average over 100kph. The event was, by definition, absurdly dangerous and during the practice two pedestrians had been killed. A driver might have died too, when his car struck a cart bearing stone and it cascaded all over him, but he survived and his car was rebuilt in time to take its place among the other 133 that Saturday morning.

The Mille Miglia was not a race but a time trial, with cars starting at intervals from 11.00am. The slowest went first: up to number 92 at intervals of a minute then thereafter at 30 seconds so that, evidently, 'late starters would not be handicapped in the event of fog being encountered in the Monti Cimini district'.[3]

> *At 11 o'clock precisely there was a fanfare of trumpets and the yellow-bearded chief of the Italian Militia arrived. He stood very solemnly with a black and white flag poised over the radiator [of the first car].[4] Then in a moment charged with drama he lifted the flag in homage to the memory of Count Brilli-Peri, one of Italy's greatest drivers who lost his life a week previously practising for the Grand Prix of Tripoli. A bugle call, resembling the Last Post, rang out and then, as if calling the roll, the officer called in a clear voice* Gastone Brilli-Peri *and with one voice the multitude thundered the reply* Present! *It was a thrilling, heart-tearing moment. We replaced our hats, the flag lifted, dropped again, and the race had begun.*

This first car accelerated along the road from the starting area, rounded a bend and was out on to the Cremona road: Cremona being the first big town on the route, 50 kilometres away.

The 1930 Mille Miglia comes to us, truly, in the flickering images from the middle distance. Here is Varzi, wearing a tartan-patterned cap, goggles over his forehead, sitting in his car smoking. He looks suddenly self-conscious as the camera closes on his face.

Here is the starter with the flag. He holds it vertical, hesitates, lowers it in a swift, downward threshing motion and then raises his right hand, waves that in a semi-salute to the car he has just released: '*good luck!*' People stand beside him on the lip of the pavement and in unison their gazes swivel to track the progress of the departing car. It is a square sort of vehicle, solid in its symmetry, and it accelerates towards the left-hand bend. A knot of spectators stand on either side of the road under a web of telegraph poles. There's a house on the right, as square as the car passing it, the same solid symmetry. As the car rounds the corner towards Cremona it stirs a little dust.

The last of the 1100cc cars was gone by exactly 12.00pm and with that the luncheon interval, to last one hour, was declared. Officials and the remaining drivers went off to eat while a 'seething mass of cyclists and pedestrians'[5] came on to the Cremona road and milled about. Count Lurani now drove *The Motor's* correspondent out to the edge of a small place called Manerbio, some 25 kilometres south of Brescia, where 'there is an S-bend followed by a quarter-mile straight and a wicked right-angle turn over a long iron bridge'. They waited for the fast men to set off and prepared themselves for some 'thrilling cornering'. They were not to be disappointed.

At 1.00pm sharp, the Cremona road was cleared and the first car in the 1500cc class was sent off.[6] Varzi was on his way at 1.12pm and Nuvolari at 1.22pm. This represented a huge tactical disadvantage for Varzi because, however hard he drove, he wouldn't know where Nuvolari was, whereas all Nuvolari needed to do was gain on Varzi to the point where he could see him – even in the far distance – and provided the gap was less than ten minutes he would win. Campari was so popular that he was given a special send-off by members of the Italian parliament.

At Manerbio, one 3000cc car was:

... incredibly fast on the corner, yet very straight. The hundreds of peasants – young girls, children and old women amongst them – backed nervously from the edge of the road as he went past. Varzi was without doubt the finest exponent of cornering. He took the perilous, dusty S-bend extremely fast yet with never a sign of a skid and roared off amid tremendous applause. Through the clouds of dust came Caracciola, the champion of Germany, in his low, white Mercedes. Then the pretty Princess Colonna came by amidst considerable applause...[7]

Near Cremona, a driver called Cerri in a 1750cc Alfa Romeo found himself being overtaken and kept over to the right. The surface was dusty and and the Alfa Romeo skidded, knocking down and killing a young lad. Cerri retired immediately, but that did not obscure or mitigate the risks of high-speed cars on ordinary roads.

The whole of Italy seemed to be looking on, lining the roadside, clustering on the kerb, sitting on milestones and bridges. Cyclists pedalled carelessly about the roads while some of the fastest cars in the world shot by at anything up to 130mph (210kph). Children ran about happily, only retiring to the edge of the road when a bugle call heralded the approach of another car. The cars ran wheel to wheel down a long, straight stretch, obscuring the whole landscape in a cloud of dust. In the towns and cities the cars tore through narrow lanes composed of close-packed men, women and children, polishing their wings, as it were, on the spectators' stomachs.[8]

The *Autocar's* Continental Correspondent, W.F. Bradley, caught that, too.

Running over level, dusty roads, often with a stream of water on each side, the competitors made their way through village after village, with the natives safely ensconced in doorways, at windows, on ledges, in the trees or, occasionally, in the more important centres, behind a rope or protected by a flimsy hoarding.

The roads were not closed to ordinary traffic; no orders had been issued from headquarters forbidding citizens to drive or walk on the highway, and we saw no posters with instructions to the population. Instead, the newspapers had made an appeal to the sporting spirit and the discipline of the people, and the way in which that appeal had been met was most amazing. It was stated that thirty thousand unpaid helpers were guarding the highway, but one was hardly aware of their presence.

After Cremona they ran towards Parma. There was a straight section of road about 15 miles long just outside Cremona and here speeds increased: the world 10-kilometre record had been set on it the year before. At Parma the streets were crowded. After Parma they were on the 'the perfectly surfaced highway'[9] to Bologna, 97 kilometres away.

The *Autocar's* correspondent, in Count Lurani's Lancia – itself a fast car – was 'anxious to see the real performers, which we knew were bearing down on us at a mad pace.' A driver called Baconin Borzacchini had averaged 79mph (127kph) from Brescia to Bologna the year before and several of them (including doubtless Nuvolari) had vowed to beat it. 'A few miles outside Bologna we waited for them. Campari was the first to go by, having passed seven cars. Then came Balestrero's O.M.,[10] obviously not so fast, because this driver was among those who had been passed by Campari. Varzi gave a wonderful impression of speed, as did also Nuvolari... but undoubtedly the greatest impression was created by Caracciola, driving the big Mercedes, and having Werner by his side. The two Germans knew that everything depended upon getting as far ahead as possible on these long straight stretches.'

At Bologna the order was Arcangeli, Nuvolari, Varzi and Caracciola. Arcangeli had equalled the 1929 time from Brescia, 90 minutes, and that – of course – equalled the average speed, 79mph; Nuvolari was a fraction of a second slower, Varzi and Caracciola one minute off the pace. Arcangeli had reportedly made leading into the town a point of honour because it was where his Maserati was made.

The timekeepers there sat at a table on the pavement beside a barber's shop so that people having their hair cut could watch what was happening through the mirrors. At a bedroom window above this, 'a black-haired damsel missed no details of each car's arrival; a tramcar rumbled ponderously by from time to time, or was stopped by much waving of flags if a racing car was in sight.'[11] In fact, the tram drivers were quite content to wait and watch for so long that they had to be waved on. One young man was thrown from a tram – under braking? – and landed in the arms of an official who was poised to wave a flag energetically. The crowd loved that and burst into laughter. The young man recovered much faster than the official and, no doubt sensing trouble, fled.

The Autocar described the procedure at Bologna:

> *No time was lost. Before a car had come to a standstill some official jumped on the running board, grabbed the log book, stamped it, patted or embraced the driver according to the degree of intimacy or enthusiasm, then waved one of a dozen yellow flags, signifying 'go ahead and do your best'. It was a strange mixture of grim determination on the part of the drivers, of overflowing enthusiasm on the part of the officials, and of effervescent gaiety among the spectators. One very good idea for checking the cars was a seven-star lead disc attached to the steering column at the end of a yard of flexible cable. This disc had to be punched at seven control stations around the circuit.*

A timekeeper sat at a table on the roadside, with advertising hoardings behind him, while officials – each wearing hats and coats – milled about ready to do their job.

Nuvolari had been flagged to a halt. The co-driver handled the formalities. Both men had their goggles on their foreheads, and both seemed to be wearing heavy jerkins. As Nuvolari accelerated away he nodded his head – *OK* – to something an official had said or signalled. He took the car to a junction a few yards away and as he turned left he instinctively looked the other way to see if anything was coming. Then he followed the road across tramlines, moved past a gaggle of spectators and was gone.

From Bologna the cars turned south towards Florence, 105 kilometres away, and immediately the plain gave way to the mountains for the first time. Their average speeds were now sharply reduced: the roads through the mountains were steep, narrow and tortuous.

In these mountains some teams had set up pits by the ruins of a mediaeval castle overlooking the Raticosa Pass. This pass, about halfway between Bologna and Florence, was 3,200ft (975m) above sea level and one of the highest points in the Appenines. The pits were on the ancient road to Rome, 'winding along a ridgeway and a hilltop'.[12] It was treacherous terrain, so ancient that it was little more than a sort of traditional pathway which had evolved, not been deliberately designed. There was a drop, then another climb to the Futa Pass at 3,000ft, but after that it was mostly downhill with much 'tricky corner work' towards Florence.

It caught out Arcangeli who had fading brakes and crashed. Although he wasn't badly injured he was taken to hospital, and Nuvolari took the lead. It caught out Campari, who, coming round a bend at high speed, was confronted by a parked car. In avoiding it he went off the road and although he, too, was largely uninjured, he decided to slow his pace. One report suggests Campari may have been deceived by dust thrown up from another competitor and that, going off, he slightly bent an axle. From here on he would play what was described as a waiting game.

Count Lurani produced his most vivid prose to describe Nuvolari at work, claiming that he induced something approaching terror in Guidotti by the way he cornered. He had Guidotti 'huddled' in his seat 'desperately' hanging on. He also had Guidotti pointing out hazards in the distance – level-crossings or carts – but Nuvolari had already seen them. Conditions inside the car, however, were not spartan.

> *Under the dashboard in the centre a thermos flask had been fitted, complete with two little rubber tubes. From these tubes the two companions from time to time sucked very sweet tea, while Guidotti handed Tazio an occasional orange or piece of barley sugar. [There was] plenty of dust, which Nuvolari and Guidotti swallowed involuntarily. The air was cold and bracing.*[13]

Near Florence, a Count called Vinci hit a stone post – they lined Italian roads – and his Alfa Romeo crashed at speed. His co-driver, Benini, was killed instantly.

W.F. Bradley wrote in *The Autocar* that the Bologna-Florence leg 'really brought out the peculiar skill of the Italian drivers. The most brilliant work was done by Nuvolari.'

He reached Florence in 2 hours 53 minutes, averaging 67.7mph (108kph), *on elapsed time* from Varzi (one minute behind) with Campari third (a minute after Varzi). The mountains had slowed Caracciola.

They kept going south, to a small place called Poggibonsi where Nuvolari still led, his average down to 65.2mph (104kph).

The positions *on the road* were Campari still second, Varzi fifth and Caracciola eighth. Between Florence and Rome, a distance of some 240 kilometres, Varzi quickened his pace and took the lead.

Lurani claims that 'from Florence to Poggibonsi, while a lazy lukewarm sun was rising [it was in fact early evening], Varzi made his expected effort. He had learned that his team companion was in first place... at Poggibonsi the Galliatese [Varzi was from the northern town of Galliate] was leading both on the road and on time. Guidotti had goose-pimples every time Nuvolari, in order not to lose a fraction of a second, passed another competitor or some innocuous motorist (or worse still an ox wagon) to the right or left with complete disregard for the highway code.'

Varzi entered Rome – 605 kilometres from Brescia – having averaged 64.8mph (104kph) for 5 hours 48 minutes. He had broken all records by 20 minutes. Caracciola's plight worsened because as the roads became difficult he dropped further and further back. He was a full 30 minutes behind the leader at Rome.

Lurani claims that 'with a screech of brakes Nuvolari arrived at the Rome control, but did not stop completely. An official stamped his book as he went by accelerating fast in second, accompanied by the enthusiastic roar of the crowd. He showed no signs of exhaustion.'[14]

Dusk was gathering. Somewhere after the cars turned north-east from Rome, and it is not at all clear where, Nuvolari struck back and the positions settled like that: Nuvolari, Varzi and Campari. Darkness fell and they were on an awkward, hilly, winding road. The lights on the Mercedes must have been defective because twice they failed and

Caracciola went off. He was involved in a private duel with fellow Italian Pietro Ghersi (Alfa Romeo) and this duel lasted an estimated 250 miles. The darkness claimed its victims with drivers misjudging corners and going off, but nobody was seriously hurt.

They ran up towards the distant Adriatic, through the town of Terni and then Perugia, where Alfa Romeo had a pit and made their cars stop for new tyres as a precaution. They ran on, to Ancona on the shores of the Adriatic – the average speed now down to 59mph (94kph) – and then along the shoreline to Rimini. The road was level here and the average speed began to creep up.

Throughout the night spectators thronged at the roadside and many brandished torches to see the cars more clearly – and help the drivers see the road ahead. What the spectators saw was a titanic struggle between Nuvolari and Varzi, Campari still watching and waiting. They turned inland towards Bologna again, and still the average speed crept up. They reached Bologna at about midnight: Nuvolari, Varzi, Campari, then Caracciola, profiting from the level roads, fourth although still 45 minutes behind the leader. Bologna

> *... presented a scene of feverish activity. Depots for fuel, oil, tyres, etc, were arranged at the side of the street, and an unlimited number of helpers was allowed. As the drivers drew up in the brilliantly lit control they were led blinking to wash and refresh themselves. Here Sig. Jano, the active head of the Alfa Romeo concern, handled his precious team.*[15]

Jano did more. He was so concerned that Nuvolari, Varzi and Campari would race each other to destruction that he decided to deceive Varzi by telling him he was, in fact, leading and Nuvolari was second. Varzi, hampered by that 10 minute start, could scarcely know the real gap back to Nuvolari and, as it seems, believed what Jano told him. And Jano went further: 'you can', he told Varzi, 'ease off a little'. Nor did Jano confine himself to Varzi. 'Nuvolari was compelled to rest for several minutes at Bologna in order to calm him down and persuade him to drive a little slower.'[16]

Nuvolari would say later that 'the hardest part was when Signor Jano locked me up in a room at Bologna, compelled me to rest for five minutes or more and had me washed and fed. I was in such a frenzy to get off that I almost fought with the pit attendants. I was much too excited to listen to the arguments that I had the race in the hollow of my hand and could afford to take it easy.'

They ran on, north-east again towards the town of Ferrara, and went through that at real speed at 2.20am, Varzi ahead *on the road* but Nuvolari within six minutes of him – giving Nuvolari a lead of four minutes *on elapsed time*. At Padua, with only 112 miles (180km) to go, Nuvolari had gained two more minutes. They ran north to Treviso, ran further north on the contorting roads to the small town of Feltre – Nuvolari now three minutes behind – and between there and Treviso, Varzi and Nuvolari had precisely the same times. Nuvolari had held his two minutes. Campari was a minute slower here.

They ran down on to the Venetian plain again through another small town, Bassano, and 'the old-world cities of Vicenza and Verona [Nuvolari one minute behind], roaring over perfect highways before dawn. All the interest lay in the fight between Nuvolari and Varzi, and in estimating how much Caracciola could improve his position now that the roads had become in his favour.'[17]

What happened next entered motor racing history as the supreme example of Nuvolari's skill, and it became revered. In simple terms, Nuvolari drew up some distance behind Varzi, switched his headlights off so that Varzi wouldn't see him approaching, drove blind and overtook him.

The reality is much messier.

Lurani claims that 'Varzi had his book stamped at the last control point, where he learnt that he had an advantage of two minutes; a lead which he expected to hold quite easily, as his adversary had an engine of only equal power. Nuvolari also learnt at the Venetian control point of the distance separating them, and went full out in a frightening manner. He took the bends without easing the throttle, with his characteristic touch of the brakes, and poor Guidotti was in a cold sweat.'

Lurani further claims that 'it was dark again' – but this was the night: it had been dark the whole time. At the 'far end of a straight' Nuvolari saw Varzi's rear lights – and Varzi, 'ignorant of what was happening,' assumed he was still in the lead, although perhaps not by much. Later, at the town of Peschiera on the run-in to Brescia and the finish, Nuvolari switched off his headlights. Guidotti gazed at him 'stupefied', fired a question – '*why?*' – but Nuvolari 'did not deign to answer. The car ran into the darkness outside the town, where Nuvolari was guided solely by the lights on Varzi's Alfa. He had taken the bend with a gigantic skid that had raised a black cloud. How he could see the road even with the small red lights blinking in front of him baffles belief.'

Lurani's account baffles belief, too. He says that Nuvolari, 'with a flick of the steering-wheel, overtook Varzi on the left.'

Brock Yates has reconstructed a much more plausible and authentic account.[18] He points out that the incident has been 'immortalised', not only in motor racing history, but also in 'historical references' and Ruesch's film *The Racers* with Kirk Douglas.

Yates recapitulates the folklore: Nuvolari switched his headlights off and 'stalked' Varzi just before dawn, 'lulling his rival into thinking he was holding an easy lead. Then, with the finish in sight, it is said, Nuvolari sped up and passed a shocked Varzi for the victory. This was clearly not the case.'

Yates reiterates that, throughout, Nuvolari had the advantage of starting 10 minutes behind Varzi and 'therefore could determine his rival's progress at each control or fuel stop. Worse yet, Varzi lost time with two punctured tires [sic][19] south of Bologna and as he headed for the finish he surely knew he was behind.' Moreover, speaking after the race, Varzi said that 'he and his riding mechanic, [Carlo] Canavesi, sighted Nuvolari's distinctive triple-headlight 1750 Alfa Romeo at least 120 miles from the finish and knew then they had lost.'

The evidence is more compelling than that. A journalist interviewed Guidotti, who confirmed that Nuvolari switched the headlights off but 'only for a minute or so, as they moved up on Varzi.' Both knew where the other was, Guidotti added, but Nuvolari switched the headlights off 'hoping to deceive Varzi into thinking he had stopped.'

Why, Yates muses, would Nuvolari have bothered to do that? After all, he was assured of victory and needed only to follow Varzi to the finish. Surely it was 'Nuvolari's fiery, prideful urge to shame his rival by passing him before the finish' which made him do it: deceive Varzi who would slacken his pace before he realised what was going on, and then it would be too late.

Giovanni Canestrini, who worked for the famous Italian daily sports paper *Gazzetta dello Sport,* suggests that on the bends between Feltre and Bassano Nuvolari 'switched off his headlights to avoid being singled out by Varzi and to surprise Varzi.' Canestrini points out that a lot of things have been written about this race which are not true, and tells the story from Varzi's point of view. Varzi had recognised the Alfa Romeo because of the car's 'unique shape' and *saw* Nuvolari switch his lights off.

Varzi said to Canavesi 'it's *him'* – meaning Nuvolari. Varzi decided it would be pointless to react because his 10-minute advantage was gone. This was around 5.20 in the morning – just at sunrise, making the switching off of the lights irrelevant.

Guidotti would remember 'I was sitting beside Nuvolari and Varzi was in front of us, having set a storming pace from Bologna. Incredibly Nuvolari caught up with Varzi near Verona. We saw him in front of us and then I had an idea. We switched off our headlights, giving Varzi the impression that we had problems. He slowed down, thinking that he could win easily. We shot past him and very sportingly he moved over to let us.'

Perhaps the folklore can now be rationalised from all these versions. Nuvolari switched his lights off – it was dawn, anyway – to deceive Varzi, not knowing that Varzi had already seen him. Nuvolari came up and Varzi, knowing the race was lost whatever he did, moved over.

There is no doubt that somewhere out there, in this dawn, Nuvolari did overtake him. (One report suggests it was in the final 10 kilometres and Varzi was understandably enraged when he realised Nuvolari was on him, and knew that there was no time left to fashion a response. This is nonsense because Varzi's response would have involved pulling back the 10-minute stagger in 10 kilometres!)

What Varzi intended to say to Jano does not seem to have been recorded.

Long before, the 'gigantic crowd which had surged all night before the great scoring board' in the middle of Brescia moved to the Via Venezia, where the race would end. In the distance came 'the musical roar of an exhaust.'[20]

Dawn broke as we waited for them. The early morning chatter of the birds was silenced, the electric lights were switched out, and a thousand faces were turned eastward in the hope of catching sight of one of the champions down the long straight road. At about a quarter to six Nuvolari rushed up, brought his most healthy-sounding Alfa Romeo to a standstill, was surrounded by officials, and then was hurried out of the way because the exhaust of another car could be heard in the distance. The second arrival was Varzi.[21]

Nuvolari had covered the 1,000 miles[22] in 16 hours 18 minutes, 59⅖ seconds; Varzi in 16 hours 29 minutes and 51 seconds. If you build in the 10-minute stagger, Varzi came in *on the road* some 51⅗ seconds behind Nuvolari – and that after a wild and wonderful run over almost half of Italy. Nuvolari had averaged 62.4mph (100.4kph), destroying all records. He had improved on Campari's 1929 time by one hour and 45 minutes (Campari averaging 89.67kph). Nor did the pace of progress end there. By definition, Varzi was also ahead of the old record having finished so close to Nuvolari, and Campari had beaten his own time by an hour and five minutes.

Ironically, as Nuvolari and Varzi had arrived, rain fell and the finish area became the final, and very slippery, test for all the rest of the competitors.

Campari... pulled up with a stern, almost sullen, expression, forty-one minutes after the winner. There was a belief that Caracciola might gain something on the last leg of the course, but after the first three Alfa Romeos there came Ghersi's Alfa Romeo, and Bassi's O.M., all ahead of the Mercedes, which finished sixth. Indeed, among the first seven cars the only visible damage was a slightly bent rear mudguard on the Mercedes.[23]

Nuvolari was mobbed by happy spectators and hoisted high. The moment comes to us with a certain restrained dignity: half a dozen men, in the obligatory hats and coats, surround the slight figure of Nuvolari, in overalls, and as they hoist him they turn towards the camera, their faces locked into a formal pose.

In that era, the human touches which make great events come alive were not reported at all or kept firmly in the background. Few journalists sought to find out what the drivers themselves thought, or got them to explore the reasons for success and failure. It leads to many silences. For example, the reference by Brock Yates to Varzi suffering two punctures is the only one I have come across. *The Motor's* reporter, by-lined only as Our Special Representative, did however go seeking when it was all over and his words demand to be reproduced.

> *When some of the applause had died down and Tazio Nuvolari was seated in the café at the finishing point, surrounded by a group of admirers, we succeeded in evading the watchful eye of the gendarmes and crossed the finishing enclosure to offer our congratulations.*
>
> *We found a young man, sunburnt, dirty and with the dust of 30 provinces of Italy still matting his eyebrows and lying deep in the wrinkles about his eyes and mouth. He looked remarkably fresh; indeed one would have thought that he had not done anything more strenuous than participating in a 24-hour reliability trial.*
>
> *'It was a good race and from Rome onwards I never had any doubt that I should win. The car was wonderful and never gave me a moment's trouble. I could have driven it much faster had I wished to do so.'*
>
> *Nuvolari then went on to tell us of the extraordinary good service given by the new buttressed Pirelli tyres. He used the same front tyres throughout the race and the rear tyres, which looked absolutely unworn at the finish, were only changed purely as a precaution.*

One Italian report,[24] quoted in *When Nuvolari Raced,* says Nuvolari used the least petrol, fewer tyres and had the least brake wear of all the competitors, which 'suggests his driving was the most stylistically correct'. *The Motor* reported:

> *Varzi... was almost inarticulate with rage when we sought him out. [Lurani, absurdly, says that Varzi took the defeat philosophically.] He was furious because all along the route*

> *and at every control he had been told that he was leading. He was in fact the first of the fast cars to arrive from Rome onwards but was not actually leading on a time basis because Nuvolari, who started ten minutes behind him, was fast catching him up. However, thinking that he was leading by a very comfortable margin, he slackened his speed so as to nurse the engine over the last 100 miles or more. He was horrified suddenly to find Nuvolari on his heels.*
>
> *Campari arrived looking thoroughly fed up. He would not say much except that he was bitterly disappointed at not winning and he seemed almost in tears.*

Bradley wrote:

> *Although not particularly well known to the English public, Varzi and Nuvolari have both been active in races and competitions for the past six years. Nuvolari first came into prominence in 1924 when he won on the Garda circuit. For a time he was Alfa Romeo reserve driver, and his greatest successes have been at Rome, Tripoli, and Monza. It is interesting to note that both Varzi and Nuvolari are motor cycle riders, the former being attached to Sunbeam, and the latter to Bianchi. They seem to alternate between cars and two-wheelers.*

From this moment on, the English public and many others would at least begin to know the names. They would never forget them.

The result:

Nuvolari/Guidotti	16h 18m 59⅖s (100.45kph/62.4mph)
Varzi/Canavesi	16h 29m 51s
Campari/Marinoni	16h 30m 53⅗s
Ghersi/Cortese	17h 61m 31s
Bassi/Gazzabini	17h 8m 34⅖s
Caracciola/Werner	17h 20m 17⅖s

Intermezzo

To emphasise the aspect of growing reputations abroad, both Nuvolari and Varzi competed in the Tourist Trophy round the Ards circuit, Belfast, in August 1930 and Alfred Neubauer, himself poised to become mythological as the Mercedes team manager until 1955, recounts a strange anecdote about Ards, where Nuvolari, Campari and Varzi were the first three finishers.[25]

Neubauer wrote of the 'private war' between Varzi and Nuvolari, which had 'reached a new pitch of intensity.' The 'bitter struggle' had exacted such a 'heavy toll' from the two men and their cars that the Italian Government became 'incensed'.

Neubauer was at Ards, and after the race spoke with the Alfa Romeo racing manager, Aldo Giovannini (Jano was in fact an engineer, not team manager), a 'small, volatile man with laughing brown eyes.' Giovannini was obviously not happy and Neubauer wondered why.

Giovannini 'fished a crumpled telegram from his pocket' and showed it to Neubauer. (That Neubauer couldn't read Italian is not mentioned. Perhaps Giovannini translated – if he could speak German, of course.) The telegram was from the Italian State Secretary and ordered Varzi and Nuvolari to overcome their personal 'ambitions' for the greater good of Italy, presumably meaning that if they were winning easily in Alfa Romeos they should nurse their cars home to ensure victory rather than race each other to destruction.

That a State Secretary should understand so little of racing drivers and their mentality is astonishing enough, even at a time when political extremism – Fascism in Italy, Nazism in Germany – was poised to cast a long shadow over everything. That any Italian should, after the 1930 Mille Miglia, understand so little of Tazio Nuvolari and the tempest within him is even more astonishing. Anyway, Giovannini recounted that neither man cared in the least about the telegram and added: 'I hate to think what might happen if this goes on much longer. They'll end up trying to kill one another.'

The strange and contradictory relationship between Nuvolari and Varzi will be explored later in the book. Here I want to try and assess the impact that the Mille Miglia victory had on the perception of Nuvolari. He had been competing for 10 years, from his first and only race in 1920. He had not competed outside Italy until the Penya Rhin car race at Barcelona in 1923; he'd ridden the Bianchi at Stuttgart in 1926 and Geneva in 1927; he'd driven in the 1928 Tripoli Grand Prix and won it, but the race was not – despite its name – a major one.

Cumulatively these forgotten races were nothing like enough to build a reputation on, particularly before the instant and immense communications industry began to cover just about everything that moved anywhere. *The Motor's* coverage of the 1930 Mille Miglia was introduced by this paragraph:

> *The accompanying report was telephoned from Milan by our special representative, and, owing to co-operation with the* Daily Mail *and* Daily Mirror *Phototelegraphy Service, we are able to present our readers with actual photographs of the event, including the winner finishing and being 'chaired'.*

You can feel the sense of wonder, and rightly so. To broaden that, into the 1950s certain areas of Britain did not yet have television and the only way to see film of current events was at cinemas which showed newsreels; into the 1970s wired cricket photographs from Australia were so poor in quality that retouching artists were required. Moreover, in the 1930s travel abroad was for the upper and middle classes only, and even then a rarity. Italy was a long way away and Nuvolari a distant name, if that. Hence Bradley's phrase about him not being particularly well known.

Within three years of the Mille Miglia he would have changed that completely, and done it on a monumental scale. The races on the calendar everybody *had* heard of – Monaco and Le Mans – fell to him and, in the nature of the man and the events, dramatically. It may well be, too, that the distance fed the legend and enhanced the myth. There can be no such mystique about Michael Schumacher because he is there in the corner of your living room 16 or 17 races a season, not to mention qualifying.

What Nuvolari could not do was retain the Mille Miglia in 1931. Caracciola won it in the Mercedes, profiting from the recce of 1930, while Nuvolari and Arcangeli limped along in the new Alfa Romeo 2300s, which ate tyres: Nuvolari had to change *ten* on the out leg to Rome, where 'miraculously'[26] he led.

Neubauer was poised to give one of his virtuoso performances. Caracciola, he wrote, knew that although he'd passed the Alfa Romeos of Nuvolari and Campari he was 'still behind them on time' because they had started after him.[27]

Neubauer sat with Caracciola's wife Charly in Brescia, learning of Caracciola's problem and recovery over the loudspeakers. It 'left us limp and trembling.' A subsequent announcement said that the first driver to reach Rome was Nuvolari.

'Charly had tears in her eyes. I felt as if someone had hit me hard in the solar plexus. And all around us was wild jubilation. Champagne corks popped like machine-gun bullets. The Alfa Romeo racing manager Giovannini kissed an elderly woman, who promptly fainted with excitement. And the noise in the crowded market-place outside was indescribable.'

Neubauer discovered, however, that Caracciola was only two minutes behind. When Caracciola reached the plains the power of the Mercedes came fully into play and he won it decisively, Nuvolari falling away to ninth.

Later that summer Piero Taruffi – a young man destined to become a pillar of motor sport – 'drove a good race on Montenero circuit, where I encountered all the top drivers of the day, including Nuvolari, [Louis] Chiron, [Luigi] Fagioli, Campari and Varzi, who finished in that order while I came in eighth. This was my first proper race on a tricky circuit against big-time opposition.

'My main interest was in watching Nuvolari and Varzi, whom I had admired in their motorcycling days. They were still just as different in temperament, and still as equally matched: the former acrobatic and daring, the latter deadly accurate and self-possessed. Nuvolari, the maestro of over-the-limit motoring, delighted the crowds with his wizardry, while Varzi, cornering like a white line, used to leave many spectators almost indifferent. Even the experts timing the two men through a corner, though, found it hard to say which was the better.'[28]

3

On Every Street

Monaco 1932

'THE TRAMLINES had been removed and part of the circuit resurfaced, but practice speeds were not particularly fast during Thursday,' wrote David Hodges in *The Monaco Grand Prix*.[1]

There's a nice period feel to that paragraph, although the tramlines surely cannot have been removed to make the ride easier for Grand Prix drivers, and anyway from the following day to the race everything got faster and faster.

Monaco then was recognisably as it is today, no matter how much building has been done. Expensive boats rode at anchor in the harbour and expensive houses – not so tall as these days – had small balconies which allowed perfect views of the boats. The absence of sky-scraper apartment blocks would, however, have revealed sudden and unexpected vistas to the modern eye. As the cars moved up the hill after Ste Devote corner you could see *all* the hillside behind them. Monte Carlo had the feel of a large French town nestled into the rocks beside the Mediterranean. Today it feels like something quite different, a very prosperous vertical community with its own style and its own identity.

The basic configuration of the circuit was the same, because altering it in any fundamental way would involve demolishing very, very expensive properties. There were differences, of course: the pits sat

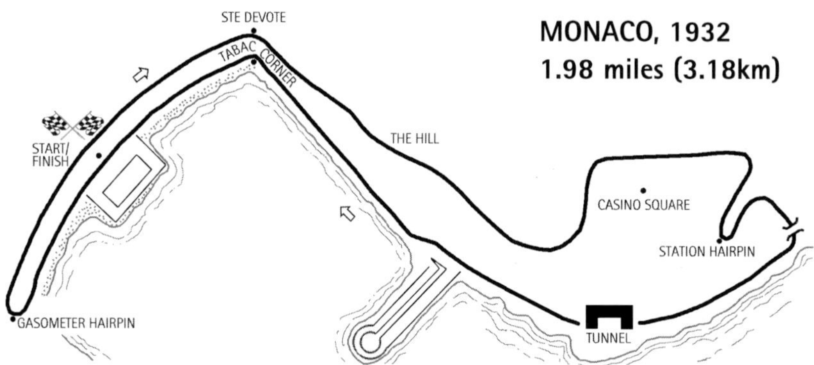

directly behind where they are now, the tunnel wasn't the same – that area has been redeveloped – and, most striking of all, Armco did not exist. No protection was offered except along the harbour, where sandbags were laid. Incidentally, with the removal of the tram lines had gone cobbles, too, and – surely for the drivers – a special non-skid surface laid.

To this, in April, came the racers and this time the dominance of the Bugattis would be challenged. Nuvolari, Campari and Borzacchini had Alfas, and so did Caracciola (not as a member of the team but as a semi-independent who was close to the factory but had bought his own car), Philippe Etancelin and Goffredo Zehender. Maserati fielded Fagioli, René Dreyfus and Ruggeri. The Bugattis might still be formidable, however: nine drivers had them, including Varzi and a Monegasque, Louis Chiron.

Nuvolari had not driven in the race before.

On the Friday the speeds did increase, Borzacchini doing 2m 4.8s, Varzi a second slower. It increased again on the Saturday, when Chiron was quickest with 2m 4s.

> *The final day of the runners learning the circuit permitted some first class performances, like the lap of Chiron, which corresponds to an average speed of more than 92kph. Afterwards, we saw 2m 5s for the veteran Campari, always a danger; then 2m 6s for Etancelin, Dreyfus and Varzi. The time of 2m 7s was achieved by Borzacchini, Nuvolari, Caracciola,* [Marcel] *Lehoux, Williams* [of him, more in a moment] *and Zehender.*

And here we are more perplexed than ever: ten men can win, and are as close to each other as it is possible to imagine.[2]

However, according to Hodges, 'only one of the fastest drivers [Etancelin] was lucky in the draw positions for grid positions, the rest being distributed among the slower men with Chiron on the second row.' Nuvolari was on the fourth, Varzi on the fifth alongside Caracciola. Grid:

Ruggeri (Maserati)	Etancelin (Alfa Romeo)	Williams (Bugatti)
Czaikowski (Bugatti)	Campari (Alfa Romeo)	Chiron (Bugatti)
Dreyfus (Maserati)	Borzacchini (Alfa Romeo)	Lehoux (Bugatti)
Zanelli (National)	Nuvolari (Alfa Romeo)	Bouriat (Bugatti)
Howe (Bugatti)	Caracciola (Alfa Romeo)	Varzi (Bugatti)
Fagioli (Maserati)	Zehender (Alfa Romeo)	Divo (Bugatti)

At 7.00 that Friday evening a chauffeur drove a Rolls-Royce to a 'leading Monte Carlo garage'.[3] The chairman of the race's organisers, a Monsieur Dureste, saw it and thought it would be perfect to open the circuit with before the race. He already had a celebrity to drive it, Sir Malcolm Campbell.[4] Dureste approached the owner, asked if he would be kind enough to lend it to Campbell and the owner said yes.

Sunday was clear and fine at first but clouded over before the race began. Campbell was loudly applauded as he toured the circuit and, as he did that, the cars were brought to the grid. At 1.30pm the starter, positioned in the road facing the cars but about 30 yards from them – enough to scamper out of the way – raised and lowered his flag. A driver known as Williams – a British ex-patriot, William Grover, who raced under French colours – seized the lead from Chiron as they went up the hill towards Casino Square.

The pack of cars, pug-nosed, firm-jawed, came up the hill in a rush and a roar, churning a vast, rolling cloud of dust, those at the back boring into it like spectres.

Somewhere between Casino and the exit to the tunnel Chiron overtook Grover: the tunnel was then a dark place, lit only by a necklace of centre lights, and instinctively drivers leant their heads to the right as they negotiated its curve.

Chiron came down from the tunnel to the chicane, where a white hip-high wall faced him. Here the drivers shifted their weight almost like side-car passengers, manhandling their cars left, brushing close to the wall, twisting right.

Chiron came onto the quayside, a stone wall at his left elbow, and crossed the line to complete the opening lap (of 100) slightly over four seconds ahead. Bugattis filled the first three positions.

The corner today known as La Rascasse (it means scorpion fish, incidentally, whatever they are) – the twist right-right into the pits or the start–finish straight – was then a traffic island with trees on it and some sandbags at its apex where three or four policemen stood in front of a hut. That made the corner 180 degrees and the cars went as near to the apex as they could, almost heaving like boats in a swell as they came out of it and felt for the power. It was known as the Gasometer hairpin.

Chiron sensed that he must force his Bugatti clear of the field and build a substantial cushion so that when Nuvolari had fought his way through the pack he – Chiron – would be too far away to be caught. Chiron extended his lead over Williams by a second a lap, and it went out from 7 to 8 and then to 9 seconds.

> *How that boy Chiron is driving. Lap by lap he pulls away from the others until, after a dozen rounds of the circuit, he is swinging round the little tobacco store on the foreshore* [still known as Tabac today] *as Williams is emerging from the tunnel. The drawing of positions has not favoured Nuvolari, because it placed him in the middle of the pack at the start, and it takes him four laps to get into fifth place. On his fifth*

lap Ruggeri stops with a broken super-charger and Nuvolari, bare-armed, in a yellow sweater, gets fourth.[5]

On the sixth lap Chiron broke the record (set at 2m 7s by Dreyfus in 1930), with 2m 5s.

Nuvolari overtakes Lehoux [lap 8] and Williams [lap 9], but his Alfa Romeo is still a long way behind Chiron's Bugatti.[6]

On this ninth lap, Chiron was in among the back-markers and into lap 10 led Nuvolari by 17 seconds, Varzi was fifth and 24 seconds behind Chiron, while Caracciola was eighth at 32 seconds behind:

Chiron	21m 10s
Nuvolari	21m 27s
Williams	21m 29s
Lehoux	21m 33s
Varzi	21m 34s
Borzacchini	21m 39s

During the tenth lap Varzi moved up to third. Jano, seeing Chiron in among the back-markers, waved to his four drivers to accelerate. Evidently these were pre-arranged tactics, presumably once the draw for the grid had been made. Certainly Bradley in *The Autocar* felt that Nuvolari had been 'expecting this' because the 17-second gap began to 'diminish by a few seconds' each lap.

Nuvolari lowered the record on lap 12, by one second, but in 10 laps 'gained only one second on Chiron, who clearly had responded. During the same period Varzi gained three, on lap 19 cutting the record to 2 minutes 2 seconds.'[7] Moreover, *Motor Sport* wrote that 'Chiron no longer increased his lead over Nuvolari but on the other hand Nuvolari could not reduce the lead between them, try as he might.'

On lap 20 Chiron led by 16 seconds:

Chiron	41m 59s
Nuvolari	42m 15s
Varzi	42m 20s
Williams	42m 36s
Borzacchini	42m 38s
Caracciola	42m 39s

Somehow Nuvolari did accelerate so that by lap 25 he was within five seconds of Chiron.

> *With stop watches and by eye, we follow the dark, wiry Italian as he closes up on the Monegasque [Chiron] yard by yard. Unless Chiron can find a little more speed Nuvolari will catch him. And the Italian is driving beautifully; the way he takes that left-hand turn from the pier [today's chicane] to the foreshore, close in, not losing an inch of ground, whereas some of the others are wide out and almost hitting the sandbags, is just one indication of his masterly manner.*[8]

On lap 29 Nuvolari had the gap down to three seconds and, next lap, Chiron strained too hard to hold him off. He was lapping two slower cars and one of them, the Bugatti driven by the Polish Count Czaikowski, he reached at the Station hairpin (today the Grand Hotel hairpin, the horse-shoe between Mirabeau and Portier). The Count would not move aside and Chiron had to follow him through the tunnel.

At the chicane after the tunnel, Chiron went to the left and his hubcap touched a sandbag – he said himself the car swerved and struck the footpath, where the sandbags were. A voice over the loudspeakers shouted 'he's over!'

The Bugatti rolled three times, throwing Chiron out, and came to rest facing the wrong way, having hit the sandbags hard enough to scatter them. He had a deep cut on the forehead, his lower jaw was injured and he was bruised.

By reflex Nuvolari missed him – and the Bugatti. The crowd did not know Chiron had escaped so lightly because they'd:

> *... only seen their favourite placed on a stretcher, lowered into a white motor boat and taken across the harbour to a waiting ambulance on the opposite pier. Presently a doctor stands up prominently and twists his hands in a suggestive and reassuring manner.*[9]

Nuvolari was in the lead but Varzi hunted him and was now closing:

one report suggests the gap was down to a couple of seconds but almost certainly it was more, because at 30 laps:

Nuvolari	1h 2m 55s
Varzi	1h 3m 1s
Borzacchini	1h 3m 28s
Caracciola	1h 3m 36s

Ten laps later Nuvolari's lead was 28 seconds but Varzi would not be beaten and mounted a charge, gaining and gaining. Borzacchini went with him and on the 47th lap was no more than 13 seconds from Varzi, Caracciola holding fourth. At half-distance, 50 laps:

Nuvolari	1h 45m 6s
Varzi	1h 45m 23s
Borzacchini	1h 45m 40s
Caracciola	1h 45m 49s

Soon enough Caracciola was right on Borzacchini and they engaged in a tight duel. However, Borzacchini 'repeatedly points to his off rear tyre'[10] and then pitted for a new wheel, making Caracciola third – and that became second on lap 57 when Varzi was forced to retire: the rear axle had broken.

> *Chiron out, it was the set-to between Nuvolari and Varzi. Six seconds separated them at that moment. Nuvolari needed twenty laps to increase that to 17 seconds. During more than a hundred kilometres the two drivers competed with audacity and precision, making everyone marvel at their sureness. Then Varzi had to stop.*[11]

Jano immediately signalled Nuvolari to slow down. The reasoning was that with Caracciola in another Alfa Romeo now in second place and Borzacchini third, team orders would apply. Fagioli in the Maserati could scarcely pose a threat. At lap 60:

Nuvolari	2h 6m 20s
Caracciola	2h 6m 50s
Borzacchini	2h 6m 58s
Fagioli	2h 7m 27s

Now Caracciola joined battle with Nuvolari. It was, Caracciola would judge, a 'very difficult race. Nuvolari... put on a speed that was almost murderous on the long, tortuous course. I had got off to a bad start and was in the middle of the field, but with each lap I worked my way forward until, finally, I was second.

'There is an unwritten rule among drivers of the same calibre: if two from the same team are ahead they are not to compete with each other, but the one who had the lead after the halfway stage was to drive home to victory. The rule exists for the benefit of the firm for which the driver starts, because if the second man forces the pace too much there is the danger of overstraining the engines and both cars may fail, making the company the real loser.

'The rule is a time-honoured one and professional drivers consider it etiquette to stick to it. However, young, ambitious drivers often violate it. I was following Nuvolari's red car and noticed that, with each second, I was coming closer.'[12]

Between laps 60 and 70:

> *The interest was now on the 'match' between Nuvolari and Caracciola. The latter gained some seconds every lap and wasn't more, at a certain moment, than nine seconds from the leader.*[13]

Borzacchini began to fall away because at lap 70:

Nuvolari	2h 27m 54s
Caracciola	2h 28m 3s
Borzacchini	2h 28m 38s

Still Caracciola attacked. Borzacchini was forced to make a brief pit stop, allowing Fagioli up to third, and at lap 80:

Nuvolari	2h 49m 5s
Caracciola	2h 49m 13s
Fagioli	2h 50m 20s

When the gap was down to five seconds Nuvolari's 'signs to his pit become increasingly agitated. The pit staff were somewhat perplexed, failing to realise that as the pace had not been accurately foreseen, Nuvolari's tanks were practically dry.'[14]

Bradley wrote that an 'interesting' place to watch was at the hairpin opposite the gas works (La Rascasse) where you could stand so close that you could almost touch the cars.

Nuvolari talks to himself. Naturally the words cannot be heard above the noise of the exhaust, but his lips can be seen moving, and one can imagine the full-throated words they are emitting.

As the end of the race approaches he becomes excited, hitting the side of the car with his right hand, gesticulating – not to the spectators, because he is blind to all that is outside himself and his car. His fuel supply is very low. Perhaps he is beseeching Madonna that it may last to the end.

The order at 90 laps:

Nuvolari	3h 10m 27s
Caracciola	3h 10m 34s
Fagioli	3h 12m 14s

Giovannini, reflecting after the race, said that Nuvolari had enough time in hand over Fagioli to have stopped for fuel and still won, reasoning that Caracciola would have 'waited' for Nuvolari although, as Hodges points out, observing team orders at that moment would have 'seemed to the crowd an outrageous fix.'

Nor do Giovannini's views necessarily reflect what Caracciola would have done. Caracciola was 'slowly gaining ground every lap'[15] and the gap went down from 7 to 5 seconds on a lap. Just then Caracciola came upon Zehender, running several laps down, but at a point on the circuit where overtaking was impossible because it was so windy. Caracciola had to follow him and any real chance of catching Nuvolari was gone. But Caracciola kept on – hard.

Bradley described a 'fine struggle' during the final 15 minutes – translating to the final six or seven laps.

They are less than three seconds apart and driving in entirely different manners. The former [Nuvolari] gives the impression of a jockey whipping a tired horse, and the latter of a man making a fast run for the pleasure of the thing.

During the last lap Caracciola 'was so close that I could look into his [Nuvolari's] car. He had slowed down considerably and we were driving side-by-side, almost wheel-to-wheel. I saw him shifting with nervous, hasty gestures. Apparently his fuel line was fouled, or else he had to switch over to the reserve tank. I thought quickly: I was not part of the team. They had rejected me. I had no obligations toward the Alfa people. If I got Nuvolari now no one could reproach me. Of course, it would be fairer if I let him keep the lead. I slowed down. While driving by I glanced at the stands. The people were jumping to their feet and shouting. Then came the finish line...'[16]

The man with the flag – in four squares, two black and two white – stood at the left hand side of the track. As Nuvolari approached, the flag was held up like a stiff-arm salute – that rigidity, that angle – and the man made a scooping motion with his free arm: *'you've done it, you've done it!'* Caracciola is at this instant powering past a slower car. Now he passes the flag which has been lowered a little.

Nuvolari crossed the line at 3 hours 32 minutes 25⅕ seconds, Caracciola a couple of seconds after him. Nuvolari seems to have stopped straight away – perhaps fearing he lacked enough fuel for a slowing-down lap – and was 'immediately' presented with a bouquet of flowers from the Rolls-Royce which Campbell had driven.

'When I got out of my car there were jeers and whistles of contempt from the spectators,' Caracciola wrote. 'They felt betrayed, assuming that I had made a deal with Nuvolari. I left the car and went over to the pits... I felt miserable. After all, it was the first time the public had hailed me with jeers.'

Giovannini said 'that was decent of you' and asked Caracciola if he'd like to become a member of the Alfa Romeo team.

The result:

Nuvolari	100 laps, 3h 32m 25⅕s
Caracciola	100 laps, 3h 32m 28s
Fagioli	100 laps, 3h 34m 43s
Howe	98 laps
Zehender	96 laps
Lehoux	95 laps*
Fastest lap:	Varzi 2m 2s (58.31mph/93.836kph)

* *L'Equipe* has Lehoux fifth on 95 laps and Williams sixth, also on 95 laps.

The world was, truly, a more gentlemanly place then. The day after the race, while the stands were being taken down, a reception was held at 11.00 in the morning by the *Automobile Club de Monaco* in honour of the drivers. A roll call of notables and, it appears, all the drivers attended. No doubt it would have been very bad form to have left the night before, never mind *during* the race – which modern drivers have been known to do when they have broken down.

Afterwards they all made their way to the Monte-Carlo Beach – I assume it was an hotel – where a luncheon was held, followed inevitably by speeches of effusive thanks to just about everybody. A telegram was read out from Malcolm Campbell congratulating Nuvolari and giving a history of the Grand Prix. Nobody seemed quite sure why Campbell telegrammed this history and no doubt with the sun shining, the food good and the wine flowing, they didn't mind. The name of Williams was applauded as having been a model driver during the whole race. There were general expressions of get-well-soon to Chiron, and then they all went away – when they were ready, and at their own pace.

* * * * *

Intermezzo

A central theme of this book is the relationship between Nuvolari and Varzi, both personally and professionally. A proper judgement is extremely elusive because we are discussing an era when personal feelings, especially controversial ones, were rarely if ever revealed. As a general rule, people grinned and bore it, whatever it was. Worse, the contemporary sources are often contradictory. Before we reach that I want to quote Paul Pietsch, who'll give us a scene-setter.

> *The relationship between drivers was very good – better than today because there is so much money in it now – and it was a more polite era, anyway. Of course we knew there were exceptions: the aristocratic Manfred von Brauchitsch and Hermann Lang, for example. Lang came from the mechanics and took some years to be accepted. Nuvolari and Varzi? It was*

proper, not warm, and when they got on the track it was normal between racers: they both wanted to win. I can't say if Varzi believed he was better than Nuvolari. Maybe he did but he wasn't! Varzi was very good, very fast, but Nuvolari was a bit faster. Why? Because he was. It's like asking why Senna was faster than Prost and Mansell, why Clark was faster than Graham Hill.

The relationship between Nuvolari and Varzi has been described as a 'bitter rivalry' so obvious that you couldn't miss it whenever they raced against each other. The man making this claim, T.P. Cholmondeley-Tapper,[17] was a contemporary racer so he had seen it for himself.

Both, he says, were excellent drivers of course and both had 'the fierce singleness of purpose that seemed to characterise the Italian motor racer'. He expanded on the comparison, claiming they were about the same age. (They weren't: Nuvolari was born in 1892, Varzi in 1904.) He was more accurate when he said both had started their careers as bike riders and 'both at one time had been official drivers for Alfa Romeo, until, at the end of the 1930 season, Varzi was forced to leave the team because of his quarrels with Nuvolari'. Cholmondeley-Tapper describes Varzi as 'sullen, unapproachable.'

How personal the rivalry was – meaning that the two men disliked each other – is, I repeat, much harder to penetrate. Chris Nixon in *Racing the Silver Arrows* says that early on 'in spite of their budding rivalry on the race track, Achille and Tazio became good friends off it and used to meet socially quite often'. Certainly they were separated by temperament, on track at least. Varzi calculated, Nuvolari was literally driven by a host of demons. Moreover, given the competitive nature of *any* driver, and superimposing that on the natural ferocity of Nuvolari and Varzi to dominate, it may well be that neither man could tolerate someone of almost equal stature in their presence on the same race track so, with an inevitable logic, Nuvolari was the sworn enemy of Varzi and Varzi was the sworn enemy of Nuvolari. If Varzi hadn't existed and someone else had risen to challenge Nuvolari, no doubt the situation would have been just the same.

René Dreyfus[18] would say that there was always a distance between himself and Varzi, whom he found 'aloof'. Varzi, he went on, was always immaculately dressed and everything had to be just so, down to the creases in his driving clothes. These clothes were specially made for him – at the time such a rare thing as to be worth commenting on.

By contrast, Dreyfus found Nuvolari to be a 'phenomenon' and unique in at least one aspect. While every other driver began with the urge to drive competitively and then painstakingly had to learn the art of how to do it, Nuvolari was born to it and the painstaking part was entirely eliminated. *He could simply do it.* This was built around his instincts and 'uncanny' reflexes.

Dreyfus went further, emphasising that fame had not altered the essential Nuvolari: he remained modest, approachable, warm and great fun to be with – unlike Varzi.

Beyond question, the rivalry extended out from the track. As Peter Stevenson relates,[19] when 'Varzi had a blue silk driving suit custom-made for him, he took the precaution of paying the tailor extra to keep Nuvolari from finding out about it. But Nuvolari's spies were everywhere, and after paying the tailor twice the price, Nuvolari showed up in blue silk as well. On the track the rivalry was less trivial, reaching a point where both drivers were wrecking an alarming number of Italian cars trying to outdo each other and requiring a telegram from Mussolini to stop.' The Neubauer story we have already heard, in fact.

Neubauer insists that 'but for the famous Italian journalist, Giovanni Canestrini, the enmity between Varzi and Nuvolari might have ended in disaster'. Evidently Canestrini organised for the two men to meet at the roadside near Bergamo in 1932 or 1933, where Canestrini told them the facts of life. 'He pointed out that not only were they losing their good name, they were taking risks which could easily end in one or other of them being killed – if not both'. Nuvolari, who seems to have had an unusually keen eye for financial matters, pointed out that because they were driving each other to destruction as well as distraction, they weren't finishing races and they weren't getting the prize money they ought to have done. Maybe it all turned on that. Nuvolari did not need Canestrini or any other human being on the planet to lecture him on whether he could kill himself. He already knew that better than any other human being on the planet. One must assume Varzi of the calculating mind had calculated that too.

If Neubauer is to be believed, they shook hands and the rivalry altered in tone, the 'bitterness and the enmity' gone. There's a modern echo to this: Ayrton Senna and Alain Prost, whose feuding tore into the fabric of Grand Prix racing across the late 1980s and early 1990s. The reconciliation began in a press conference after an Italian Grand Prix, when a journalist asked 'How long is this going to go on?'

Certainly Varzi has been quoted as saying[20] that the 'so-called' personal rivalry was a myth. 'The newspapers have printed so many incredible stories about the so-called rivalry. Nothing could be more untrue, more absurd, more spiteful. Something exists between Tazio and me which may seem almost paradoxical but which can be called brotherly friendship, mutual respect.'

To show how Varzi thought, Taruffi[21] explains that he was a master at 'slipstreaming', which he'd learned as a bike rider. 'Races are very often won by riders who sweep past their opponent with momentum gained while using the suction created by the latter's machine. Varzi demonstrated this in the motor car Grand Prix of Tripoli which he won in 1933, 1934 and 1936, swishing into the lead right on the line, to beat Nuvolari, Moll and Stuck respectively. His total margin in the three races combined was barely five seconds. Just one more illustration of that calculating temperament of his which, even in races with huge prize money at stake, prevented his exerting more than the minimum effort necessary to win.'

These references to Tripoli are slightly out of sequence – the next chapter is about the 1933 race, and any reference to the close finish in it remains controversial (although we may be finally facing the truth about that). We shall see. The general point is made, however, and the contrast between the two men drawn even sharper.

Nuvolari could play the showman working a crowd when he wanted. Once upon a time, during a race at Turin, his steering wheel came off but he continued round for a couple of laps 'frantically' brandishing the wheel in his right hand as he went. According to Taruffi, this 'sent the crowd into ecstasies' – as, naturally, it would: Nuvolari can do the impossible *and we are watching him do it.* The explanation, of course, was more prosaic. He was still able to steer 'by means of a single fixed spoke forming part of the column itself.' The car had a steering wheel that 'hinged out of the way on this spoke to give more room for drivers getting in and out, and in Nuvolari's car the hinge had broken.'[22]

Nuvolari could play the hard man when he wanted, devil take the hindmost. Some few weeks after the victory at Monte Carlo he was at Rheims for the Grand Prix of France as part of the three-man Alfa Romeo assault. Caracciola and Borzacchini were the others.

We have variants of what happened before the race.

Evidently Jano had decided to allow either Caracciola or Borzacchini to win if it turned out that the Alfa Romeos could win it. Nuvolari listened 'gravely'.

A second variant has Taruffi describing how 'apparently Alfa had decided, for reasons commercial or political, that the race should be won by Caracciola. Nuvolari accepted this order beforehand but once the race started he drove like a man possessed, Caracciola trailing behind.' Jano 'kept frantically waving the conventional red flag to slow him down.'

Another[23] says Jano 'wanted the three cars to cross the finish line together.' This contemporary report adds 'when the three Alfa Romeos rounded the final bend before the finishing line, Jano signalled to Nuvolari to slow down and wait for Caracciola and Borzacchini who were not far behind.' This would give Jano the triple finish 'but Nuvolari did not understand the signal and finished slightly ahead of his colleagues'.

Paradoxically, the times do not seem to have survived because it was a five-hour race. After five hours Nuvolari had covered 461 miles, Borzacchini 461.35...

There are, too, slight variants of the aftermath. One says that when Jano confronted Nuvolari he replied 'oh well... you see, I had green sun goggles and the flag looked green to me.' (Green was the flag meaning '*go flat out!*')[24] Nuvolari has also been quoted as enquiring 'was that a red flag? I had on green glasses, and I thought it meant go faster.'

The next race was the German Grand Prix at the Nürburgring. Moretti[25] has described how 'for commercial reasons' Alfa Romeo wanted the German Caracciola to win but Nuvolari 'was not listening'. The fact that he finished second to Caracciola has led to all manner of speculation, although it does seem he was driving as lustily as he could and Caracciola was better on the day.

That Jano sought to orchestrate two races in succession, each involving someone of Nuvolari's temperament, seems extremely curious. It also has a modern ring to it, especially the overtones of business before pleasure. Whether it all happened so in the summer of 1932, or exactly what did happen, is not at all clear, but you'll be reading more of it in Chapter Five.

Another time, according to Purdy, Nuvolari 'refused to stop after a collision with Wimille brought out the black flag for him. The judges had mistakenly decided that he had deliberately hit the other car. Afterwards, when they disqualified him, he said: 'What is the black flag to me? I am interested in one flag: the checkered [sic] flag.'

Just before we reach the next great race – Monaco, 1933 – it's worth pausing to reflect that Nuvolari was now at the peak of his powers. After Monaco he won the Targa Florio, the Grand Prix of France at Rheims and was second in the German Grand Prix to Caracciola, as we have seen. Moving into 1933 he won the Mille Miglia. That might qualify as one of his great races, too, but we already have two Mille Miglias (1930, 1948) and anyway he was in such form that once Manfred von Brauchitsch (Mercedes) dropped out the only interest was whether Nuvolari would beat the winner's average speed of the year before. He didn't. For once in his life he put prudence before passion.

Two weeks later he was in Monaco.

4

Duel to Destruction

Monaco 1933

THERE is a famous phrase about never having 'the girl, the money and the fame' all at the same moment. This describes how life doesn't simplify itself into a great, perfect finale. Sometimes motor racing contradicts this. There are so many variables in play at any given moment in any race that even *quite* close finishes are comparatively rare, but when the variables do come together and stay together you get very close to the girl, the money and the fame.

The variables came together at 1.30 on a sunny afternoon in Monaco and stayed together for almost three and a half hours. That they broke apart on the climactic last lap makes the finale imperfect but the race itself genuinely epic. No other phrase will do.

Practice, held between 6.00 and 7.00am on the Thursday, Friday and Saturday, suggested that the Bugattis and Alfa Romeos were evenly paced. This was potentially important because for the first time in Grand Prix history the grid would be determined by the fastest practice times rather than a draw. Even so, of the 19 entries no more than 11 took part on this Thursday.

Nuvolari had an Alfa Romeo, Varzi a Bugatti.

Chiron and Caracciola had Alfas, too, and evidently they'd formed a 'partnership'[1], because Chiron was driving his car for the first time so

Caracciola showed him round. They both did 2m 3s (57.83mph/93.0kph) and that was only a second from Varzi's lap record, set the previous year. Nuvolari, meanwhile, crashed at Ste Devote – he hit a barrier – in what David Hodges[2] describes as a 'very erratic session'. Nuvolari managed 11 laps but his best time was a second off Chiron, and so was Borzacchini. Nuvolari's car was so badly damaged that repairs took until the Sunday.

> *Normal procedures: traffic prohibited from 5.30 in the morning and, at 6.00, the competitors could go out on the track for an hour in front of several thousand spectators. The practice is always followed by a big crowd. Sullen weather, sky overcast, signs of rain.*
>
> *Among the new arrivals, we saw this morning the two Maseratis of Raymond Sommer and of Zehender, which were awaited with curiosity. The Englishmen Lord Howe and Birkin equally made their appearance.*[3]

On this second day Caracciola crashed heavily. On the way down to the quay 'I wanted to slow down. I braked, but the brake did not hold.' In fact, it only worked on one front wheel and 'the car skidded towards the stone parapet that separated the bend from the precipice… I was aware that I could not make the bend at 80 and I was going over 100 kilometres an hour, perhaps even faster. I held to the right where the stone wall reared steeply up. It was better to crash into the stone than to fall over the parapet into the sea below.'[4]

The car struck the wall and came to rest. Caracciola heard a screeching sound – Chiron hard on the brakes to miss him. As Chiron passed he shouted 'I'll send the mechanics.'[5]

Caracciola felt a 'ferocious' pain' in his leg as if it was being 'slashed by hot, glowing knives.' Two people ran into a tobacconists nearby and brought back a chair. They carried him up the street and into the shop. His thigh was smashed and he wouldn't race again for a year.

Chiron's time from the day before was still worth provisional pole at the end of this second day. Nuvolari had been out in Eugenio Siena's car – he was a junior member of the team – but could only manage 2m 7s.

You will recall that Nuvolari had an accident in which his car, particularly, suffered – to the point where it needed important repairs. Now, for practice this morning, Nuvolari used Siena's race car. The latter waits for another car from Italy, and if not he won't compete. In that case the number of competitors will be reduced to 17.[6]

Up until the third day, some drivers and teams might have been hiding their hand. The session was 'more animated than the ones before.'

All the competitors were on the circuit except Etancelin, and I ask you to believe there were some beautiful struggles which make us think that tomorrow we will be attending an ardently disputed race. Varzi and Dreyfus, using the same car in relays, covered a total of thirty laps. It was Varzi who was fastest of all.[7]

He took pole with 2m 2s, thus equalling his own record. Chiron's 2m 3s put him alongside, Borzacchini next to Chiron. Nuvolari managed 2m 4s.

At last, Nuvolari did a clever lap in 2m 7s. Having done a lap yesterday of 2m 4s, he was now certain to find himself on the second row, alongside Philippe Etancelin. Yesterday Nuvolari used Siena's car and Siena's withdrawal from the race was announced. But the car in which Nuvolari had his accident has been repaired and Siena will be able to drive it. Thus, the Ferrari team will be complete, with Nuvolari, Borzacchini, [Count Carlo] Trossi and Siena.[8]

Enzo Ferrari had been close to Alfa Romeo for years, selling and racing them. When he set up his own team in 1929 Alfa Romeo was a major sponsor, offering discounted racing cars and other services.

The first three rows of the grid:

Borzacchini	Chiron	Varzi
(Alfa Romeo)	(Alfa Romeo)	(Bugatti)

Dreyfus (Bugatti)	Etancelin (Alfa Romeo)	Nuvolari (Alfa Romeo)
Lehoux (Bugatti)	Wimille (Alfa Romeo)	Fagioli (Maserati)

After practice on Saturday the cars were subjected to a mild form of scrutineering, the chief concern being the legibility of the number and whether the exhaust outlets might be so located as to raise dust. All cars were also equipped with huge vacuum flasks with rubber tubing, so permitting the drivers to take refreshment.[9]

The race was due to start at 1.30pm but the grandstands were full long before this and 'thousands of people were peering down from the cliffs and from the windows of the houses on the terraces high above the course. It was a sunny, colourful scene.'[10]

From 9 o'clock, the first spectators arrived and took their place on the Monaco rock. From moment to moment the traffic increased, bringing thousands of tourists. In the port, yachts and motor boats were numerous, and made natural grandstands. From 12.30 the first drivers arrived and took over the refuelling area which had been set aside for them. During this time, the grandstands filled rapidly. They were full half an hour before the start. It was the same at the windows of the hotels, on the rock and the square. Discipline is severe because the track is completely clear. Soon the loudspeakers announced the names of the drivers.[11]

The starter held the flag and the engines revving sounded to *L'Equipe*'s reporter like the roaring of fierce lions. When it fell – it was 1.33pm – Varzi, accelerating hard, took the lead immediately. Borzacchini moved across on Chiron to get behind Varzi. Nuvolari was fourth.

Round Ste Devote corner Varzi, Borzacchini and Lehoux were slightly ahead of the pack, which they led screaming up the hill to Casino. As they emerged from the tunnel down to the quayside Varzi was seen to be [still] in the lead.[12]

The order was unchanged although *The Autocar's* correspondent wrote that Nuvolari was in second place from the start and, emerging from the tunnel, was 'close behind' and this despite 'a violent skid at the bottom of the station hill, causing [the car] to jump on to the footpath'. By lap three Nuvolari was up into second place and on lap four

... as a mighty roar goes up from the crowd Nuvolari, in his rather stained yellow jersey, is seen to flash past Varzi on the hill leading to the Casino.[13]

It was the beginning one of the most intense struggles ever witnessed.[14] Nuvolari held the lead for three laps before Varzi took it from him; Varzi held it for two before Nuvolari took it off him. At lap 10:

Nuvolari	21m 12s
Varzi	21m 13s
Borzacchini	21m 17s
Lehoux	21m 19s
Etancelin	21m 21s
Dreyfus	21m 30s

Varzi retook the lead on lap 13 and lost it on lap 17, then regained it on lap 19. The cars were never more than 20 yards apart and sometimes as close as six inches. At lap 20:

Varzi	42m 26s
Nuvolari	42m 27s
Borzacchini	42m 29s
Lehoux	42m 30s
Etancelin	42m 31s
Fagioli	42m 48s

Nuvolari would lead 66 laps and Varzi 34. Nuvolari retook it on lap 23 and held it until lap 29 – Wimille out, brakes – then lost it for the next two. Interestingly, on that 29th lap Etancelin had increased his speed enough to get past Borzacchini and begin to move on the two leaders. *L'Equipe* reported that lap after lap the pace did not slacken; 'on the contrary, they were run with an unparalleled animation.' At lap 30:

Varzi	1h 3m 23s
Nuvolari	1h 3m 24s
Etancelin	1h 3m 25s
Borzacchini	1h 3m 30s
Fagioli	1h 3m 47s
Dreyfus	1h 4m 3s

On lap 31 Nuvolari, Varzi and Etancelin all did 2m 3s and had shed Borzacchini. Nuvolari regained the lead on lap 32 and a lap later Varzi equalled the lap record. On lap 36 Nuvolari and Varzi lapped Trossi, who wouldn't let Etancelin through. Once he had got by, Etancelin accelerated furiously to try and close the gap. On that lap Varzi equalled the record a second time, and on lap 37 did it again. Then he forged to the front. That was the 39th lap. Etancelin

> *... was driving magnificently, but just when it looked as if he might actually pass the two Italians he took the bend coming on to the quayside slightly too fast, turned completely round and hit the sandbags while at about the same time Nuvolari went over the pavement just after coming out of the tunnel.*[15]

Etancelin spun down the track for 50 yards and, when the car had come to rest, jumped out and inspected the car for damage, found none and jumped back in again. He had lost some 45 seconds. By lap 40 Nuvolari had regained the lead.

Nuvolari	1h 23m 57s
Varzi	1h 23m 58s
Borzacchini	1h 24m 21s
Etancelin	1h 24m 42s

Borzacchini had regained third place because of Etancelin's spin. He was 23 seconds behind the leaders and Etancelin 44 – nothing, with 60 laps still to run.

The battle intensified but the two leaders couldn't break each other and, more than that, at half distance only 30 seconds separated the first four. Etancelin had broken the lap record with 2m 1s, an average speed of 58.7mph (94.6kph), and was moving on the leaders again. On lap 48 Howe's Bugatti went out with a rear axle failure. At 50 laps:

Varzi	1h 44m 48s
Nuvolari	1h 44m 49s
Borzacchini	1h 45m 9s
Etancelin	1h 45m 18s

Fleetingly the crowd could think that – at last – the race order had settled. However Etancelin got past Borzacchini on lap 55 but, as it would seem, took Borzacchini with him because both caught the two leaders and they ran together, like a pack hunting. At 60 laps:

Nuvolari	2h 5m 39s
Varzi	2h 5m 40s
Etancelin	2h 5m 41s
Borzacchini	2h 5m 42s

On lap 61 Fagioli went out with a magneto problem. On lap 65 Etancelin went out as he mounted a direct assault on Varzi. His transmission failed.

The Autocar caught the detail of the spectacle and the mood of the moment beautifully. 'The best place to watch this scrap is at the gasworks hairpin. Here, on the footpath, behind the white-washed sandbags, one is so close to the drivers that it is possible to see their lips move and to read the words they are uttering.

'Varzi, Nuvolari and Etancelin approach this bend in a compact group. They are so close that Nuvolari's dumb-iron[16] overlaps Varzi's tail. Etancelin is three lengths behind. He swings his Alfa round the bend, grits his teeth in a manner which indicates "now I am going to get these two", accelerates, slips into third and – slows down. A differential shaft has broken! He free-wheels into the pits, only a short distance away, and after jumping out of the car finds that both his hands are a mass of blisters.'

Borzacchini's engine sounded as if it had a problem and he fell away from the two leaders. At 70 laps:

Nuvolari	2h 26m 3s
Varzi	2h 26m 4s
Borzacchini	2h 26m 16s

The pace was 'killing' (*The Autocar*). Their report summed up quite how much killing there had been. 'Howe's and Birkin's cars are in the cemetery. Zehender's right foot is in blisters, and he has had to stop to put on heavier-soled shoes; Fagioli has had trouble with defective fuel flow, followed by a magneto which refuses to do its duty. Brakes and plugs have held Williams back. Chiron's car does not appear to be very happy.'

On lap 71 Falchetto's Bugatti went out with a back axle failure.

A great cheer went up when Varzi got past Nuvolari again 'just after they had passed the stands bonnet to bonnet when pulling over to get by Zehender.'[17] Nuvolari had led 21 consecutive laps, the longest sequence in the race. At 80 laps:

Varzi	2h 46m 47s
Nuvolari	2h 46m 48s
Borzacchini	2h 47m 4s

Nuvolari retook Varzi on lap 82 and now – at last – the race seemed settled because at 90 laps:

Nuvolari	3h 7m 23s
Varzi	3h 7m 27s
Borzacchini	3h 7m 39s

That gap of four seconds, so meagre and inconsequential in most other races, might have seemed crucial here. Borzacchini held third but at this pace he must have seemed like a long, long way out of it. Nuvolari led from lap 82 to lap 97 – Varzi was baulked when he was lapping Laszlo Hartmann, 'one of the slowest cars in the race'.[18] On lap 98:

... as Nuvolari and Varzi come into the hairpin, just as they had done for those preceeding laps, Varzi, six inches astern, slips into second gear, presses on the accelerator, and shoots his Bugatti past the Alfa. But Nuvolari has slightly higher speed and on the hill to the Casino his car flashes past the Bugatti.[19]

They were on lap 99 and Nuvolari led into the final lap – 100 – towards the perfect finale: the girl, the money and the fame.

On the climb to the Casino for the last time, Varzi held on to third [gear], stretching his engine to the limit and risking all at over 7000rpm to take the lead. Nuvolari held him...[20]

Nuvolari was also in third gear, was also taking the engine to its maximum. At this point the full extent of the drama had overwhelmed some of the reporters trying to cover the race. They did not have television, of course, and as a consequence when the cars were out of sight they could not know what was happening – and reconstruction afterwards would be even more problematic. Who to ask, and how – in this intensity – would they remember?

The Autocar had Varzi going past Nuvolari somewhere on the rise to Casino. *The Motor* implies that Nuvolari led to Casino Square. Hodges has Varzi 'risking all' to take the lead. On balance, it seems that Varzi did do the overtaking on the hill up to Casino.

> *When Nuvolari, hard pressed by his rival, held the revs at more than seven thousand an oil pipe broke and the hot oil was directed on the exhaust pipe. As he passes in front of the Hotel de Paris the car is signalled to be on fire; but Nuvolari refuses to stop. He races down the station hill... (The Autocar)*

> *Then came the last lap. And like a scenario too well conceived, the denouement exploded, sublime, tragic. On the incline, towards the Casino, Varzi attacked ferociously. And he overtook at the same instant that we saw the Alfa Romeo spitting black smoke, a little smoke which rose towards the blue and red banners of the Principality. It was its soul which was flying away. (L'Equipe)*

> *The crowd at the stand, not knowing of Nuvolari's misfortune, had their eyes glued on the exit from the tunnel. Who would appear first? A low blue car shot into view. 'Varzi!' But where was Nuvolari? He emerged from the tunnel slowly, and appeared to be sitting on the tail of the car with his feet on the seat and smoke was pouring from the bonnet. (The Motor)*

> *Nuvolari reaches the seashore. Men with fire extinguishers try to stop him, but he cannot be stopped. The engine fails. Just*

after the turn on to the Quay the car can run no longer on impetus. Nuvolari stands up in his seat, jumps out of the car and pushes. (The Autocar)

The Bugatti had conserved more forces, more life. Varzi, freed from the cares of the battle, crossed the line. We saw, coming slowly, the Italian car [Alfa Romeo] under which were flames and Nuvolari, girdled in yellow, drove standing on his seat to avoid being burnt. Then, because the track rose a little, the car stopped and the little driver – a devil in this hell – jumped to the ground and began pushing towards the final goal. And he smiled sadly, politely, at the crowd who acclaimed him and looked out for Borzacchini. He smiled again at Varzi, who [came past] finishing his slowing down lap, a cigarette in his lips. (L'Equipe)

And Nuvolari pushed onwards. The reporters, already as intoxicated as the crowd, were no longer thinking like reporters. One report says the Alfa Romeo stopped 'five hundred metres from the finish,' suggesting Nuvolari pushed it that distance. *The Autocar* says that he arrived 'exhausted at his pits. Despite his protests, someone opens the bonnet and uses a fire extinguisher. In the excitement Nuvolari forgets to push his car just those few yards to the actual finish.' *The Motor* said Nuvolari did reach the finishing line 'but only by outside aid, and was disqualified for receiving assistance.'

To make any sort of sense of this is extremely difficult, and for a most surprising reason. It is not at all clear where the finishing line actually was, and the authenticity of the mythology of 'The Push' rests on that.

In 1933 the pits were facing the harbour approximately where the swimming pool is today and it is possible the race started there, too. There is moving film of the finish and it is obviously elsewhere: in fact somewhere up an incline. If you have watched a Monaco Grand Prix on television, you know that the harbour front is flat, the turn at La Rascasse (then the Gasometer hairpin) is a slight rise and the start–finish straight essentially level. The incline starts after Ste Devote. However, contemporary film strongly suggests that today's start–finish was an incline – gentle, but a definite incline – then and, perhaps, has since been levelled a bit.

Where does that leave The Push?[20] The most likely explanation is that Nuvolari emerged from the tunnel and went downhill through the chicane, the car's impetus carrying it forward even if the engine had failed. Somewhere after that the car stopped and the mythology began. He got out and pushed. A photograph of him doing this shows the verdant traffic island on his right, so the harbour must have been on his left. He was still on the waterfront and going slowly towards the pits. He reached them, a mechanic assisted him in whatever way, and he was disqualified.

To reach the line he'd have had to continue past the pits, round Gasometer – somehow heaving the heavy car up the slight gradient there – and along today's start–finish straight at least. It is unimaginable that he did anything like this – if he had, as the mythology insists, got to or near the line itself – *no* film or photographs of him round Gasometer was taken, and no reporter mentioned it. Nuvolari pushing and steering round Gasometer, with the gendarmes at the hut stolidly watching, would have been one of the great motor sporting images: it would be in this book and plenty of others, too. Nor is it conceivable that the newsreels got Varzi crossing the finishing line but didn't bother with Nuvolari and The Push as he literally heaved into view.

I believe the whole afternoon produced something like mass hysteria as it climaxed, and in an era when reporters had a limited view – physically, not metaphorically – the hysteria demanded that he had pushed a fiery car to the line, and they obeyed the hysteria. That he did not may diminish the reporters but it hardly diminishes the man, the afternoon or this quite astonishing race.

The result:

Varzi	3h 27m 49.4s (56.45mph/91.80kph)
Borzacchini	3h 39m 49.4s
Dreyfus	99 laps
Chiron	97 laps
Trossi	97 laps
Zehender	94 laps

(Nuvolari disqualified, 99 laps)

Intermezzo

You can construct an argument that Nuvolari's most prolific season was 1933: prolific in the sense that of the 10 races I've chosen, the year contains four. Monaco had been 23 April and he raced only once more – at Alessandria (where he won) – before he sailed across the Mediterranean for a race which, as I've said, remains highly controversial. It is the second of the 1933 harvest – Tripoli.

The Old Master at Marseilles in 1946, racing because that was all he knew. The years are taking their toll. *(Neil Eason Gibson)*

The town where he was born in 1892, complete with a warning to speeding motorists. *(Author)*

Fading splendour: the house where he was born. *(Author)*

From here he would become famed and celebrated for two decades. Here he is in the 1935 French Grand Prix at Montlhéry, his Alfa Romeo already in the lead. *(Neil Eason Gibson)*

At the Steering Wheel Club in London with, on the left as we look, Alberto Ascari. *(Neil Eason Gibson)*

Tazio and Carolina in his office at home in Mantua. It also looks like a trophy room. *(Neil Eason Gibson)*

The Raticosa Pass. Its raw and terrifying aspects have been smoothed away by a modern road and its smooth tarmac. *(Author)*

You have to imagine what this section of the Mille Miglia looked like in the 1930s. *(Author)*

The 1933 Mille Miglia, Nuvolari at the wheel of his Alfa Romeo, Decimo Compagnoni the co-driver. *(Alfa Romeo)*

A man and his cars. Nuvolari in the Auto Union Type D – with which he won Donington and Belgrade. *(Neil Eason Gibson)*

Victory at Le Mans with Raymond Sommer in 1933. Nuvolari looking imperious in the Alfa Romeo Tipo 8C. *(Neil Eason Gibson)*

Paul Pietsch, who went on to a successful career in publishing – motor sport! *(Paul Pietsch)*

Manfred von Brauchitsch: action at the Nürburgring and a classical pose. *(Mercedes Benz)*

Rudolf Caracciola who, it seemed, didn't care for the Nazis at all giving the stiff arm salute which haunted so many after the war. *(Mercedes Benz)*

Among friends and enemies. Nuvolari at the German Grand Prix in 1937, where he took his Alfa Romeo to fourth overall. *(Neil Eason Gibson)*

Possibly a unique photograph, taken by Nuvolari himself at Tripoli in 1937. The driver is Raymond Sommer.

5

Honour Among 'Thieves'

Tripoli 1933

The Grand Prix of Tripoli was a repetition of the Monaco race in that it produced another terrific struggle for premier honours between Varzi (Bugatti) and Nuvolari (Alfa Romeo). It was also notable for the splendid fight put up by Sir Henry Birkin.

Birkin immediately took the lead followed by Nuvolari, Campari, Varzi, Fagioli. At the fifth lap Campari held an advantage of 9 secs over Birkin who in turn was 7 secs ahead of Nuvolari and 48 secs in front Varzi.

By lap ten Nuvolari was second and only 100 yards behind Campari. Campari pitted for fuel on lap 14, Nuvolari leading.

Half distance: Nuvolari 1h 9m, Birkin 1h 9m 10s, Varzi 1h 9m 19s.

A lap later Birkin pitted for fuel and ran fifth.

Next Campari was virtually out of the race – he lost 15 mins for repairs to his oil tank.

At 20 laps Nuvolari led Varzi by 18s but the positions were reversed five laps later, Varzi's advantage being 20 secs. With four laps to go Nuvolari was within a few yards of his rival, and on the 29th lap he attempted, unsuccessfully, to pass Varzi, who won by one-tenth of a second.

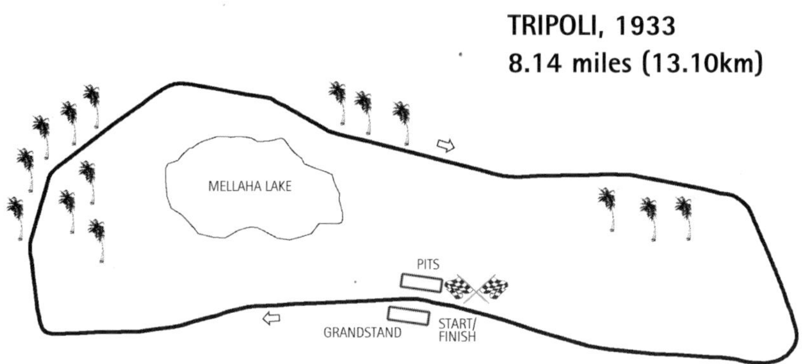

This is *The Motor's* report, slightly edited. You could not even glimpse the undercurrents which had flowed round the fast and sand-blown 13-kilometre Mellaha circuit near Tripoli, Libya, that day; could scarcely deduce that this would become, some two and a half decades later, arguably the most notorious motor race of all.

Listen to Nuvolari[1] gazing back on it some four years later. 'You can believe me when I tell you that smart work at the pits is important to a racing driver. I will never forget the finish of the Tripoli Grand Prix in 1933. Varzi was driving a Bugatti and I had an Alfa. The race was for 390 kilometers and I lost to Varzi by one fifth of a second! Just imagine it: over a race that took 2 hours and 20 minutes! Only one second less at a pit stop and I would have been first! But then I was defeated by a great driver.'

The received wisdom is – or was until comparatively recently – that Nuvolari was talking absolute nonsense because the seventh Grand Prix of Tripoli, on 7 May 1933, was fixed, and he was perfectly well aware of that because he had been part of the fix. Moreover, everybody knew the truth – had known it, in fact, since the week after the race, because *L'Auto Italiana*[2] in their issue of 20 May, wrote: 'Nuvolari was duly beaten in this race by Varzi but many people, without knowing the reason, did not really believe in this defeat. On the one hand, it is ridiculous to think that the two drivers had agreed a 'fiddle' yet, on the other, it is true that the two drivers (and Borzacchini, who retired) had made a pact with three holders of their [lottery] tickets.'

This is the point to stop the narrative and find its true context, which moves between three distinct levels: the obvious one, that any fixed race is offensive ethically and morally; the legendary one, which *claims* that the race was fixed; and the elusive one, which is what actually happened.

A most curious thing, to deal with the first level. Motor sport has always involved money (by definition cars are made by it and run on it, then there's start money, prize money and money to be made through it). In theory this should have brought endemic corruption, and the history of motor sport ought to be riddled with dubious races – something made effortlessly easy because any car can go slowly or stop, and the driver simply point to unprovable mechanical problems. The curiosity is that this seems almost never to have happened. There must be many reasons for this, but surely the most powerful is the driver's own desire to win. If he doesn't have that, what is he doing in such an egotistical, macho and dangerous activity, anyway? Ron Dennis once remarked, quietly but accurately, that if it ever came to it the modern drivers would drive without pay because they need to drive to be alive.

Note, also, the convulsion in 2002 when, as they were entitled to do, Ferrari made Rubens Barrichello slow at the Austrian Grand Prix for Michael Schumacher to win. This was widely portrayed as a hammer-blow to the credibility of Grand Prix racing, even though it was within the rules and had been done to varying degrees many times before by other teams. For a team to insist it has the right to control its employees as it wishes is quite different from drivers from different teams, or different teams themselves, deciding the result in advance. I repeat: this is all but unknown, going as far back as you like.

It is why Tripoli remains notorious.

The second level was created by Alfred Neubauer who, in *Speed Was My Life* (first published in German in 1958, English language edition 1960), wrote a most evocative account of Tripoli, complete with descriptions of the people, even dialogue between some of them and a vivacious account of the race, blow-by-blow, as Neubauer explained that it was fixed and elaborated on how it had been done. All this appeared at the end of a chapter called 'Melodrama and Tragedy', and it occupied some four and a half pages – 2,000 words. These pages became the accepted version of Tripoli and many subsequent historians built upon them, so that cumulatively this *was* what happened.

Neubauer was not at Tripoli, but this doesn't seem to have made people question the veracity of his account, not least because – as we've just seen in *L'Auto Italiana* – clearly something subterranean *had* been going on. Neubauer confirmed that, expanded on it and, because he had been at the centre of motor sport from the 1920s, you could reasonably assume that people had confided such things in him. You could assume with equal reason that someone of his integrity and attention to detail (as a team manager with Mercedes) wouldn't distort, embellish and ultimately fictionalise something so important to motor racing history. It was also important to the reputations of three men – Nuvolari, Varzi and Borzacchini – who were all dead in 1958 and could neither defend themselves nor contradict the fiction.

The third level is provided by an American, Don Capps, a motor racing historian in the accepted sense of that term. Something about Tripoli gnawed at him and niggled him but he had a full time job elsewhere and 'you can't put your finger on it because it's not an issue that you really have time to look at.' The gnawing was that 'it didn't track, it didn't fit with what we know about Nuvolari.' The gnawing became more intense and he found time to have a look. He moved past the accepted 'facts' and the statistics – 'statistics are wonderful but what's important is what lies behind all that, what's the story. Until Neubauer, nobody even discussed the race – there is virtually nothing prior to 1958 or 1959 then all of a sudden you have a string of articles and they are all variations on Neubauer, with wonderful fantasies.' Capps started 'looking at it from a different point of view because my training is as an historian and also a research scientist, and that makes you question things.' I have devoted an extensive footnote[3] to an interview with Capps, and you can find his own recreation of Tripoli on the Atlas F1 website (http://www.atlasf1.com). In the simplest terms, he has rewritten history and in doing so has written the notoriety out of the race. I have leant very heavily on what he has done.

Libya was an Italian Protectorate and, as it would seem, the Fascist dictator Benito Mussolini, who had seized power in 1922, wanted to make Tripoli the centre of a North African empire. Evidently Mussolini thought motor racing a way of promoting Italian prestige and the attractions of Libya, not to mention a way of raising money. A 26.2-kilometre circuit was built at Mellaha, round a salt lake of that name, in 1925. It was technically unchallenging and, worse, slow. The races there, run until 1930, were not a financial success. That 1930 race had the 'deadly combination of a small field – 12 cars on the grid, a small crowd, and the death of a very popular driver, Gastone Brilli-Peri'.[4] (It was the same Brilli-Peri whose memory had been honoured at the start of the 1930 Mille Miglia.)

The president of Auto Club di Tripoli, Egidio Sforzini, managed to get Italian government money to build a proper race track, 8.14 miles long and fast. The new track has been described as luxurious – formal gardens, a giant white cantilever-roofed grandstand[5] facing modern pits with a tower above them showing the leaderboard. It had a distinctly imposed, colonial, clean feel to it.

It inevitably attracted the attention of Giovanni Canestrini of *La Gazzetta dello Sport* – who we've already met.[6] Canestrini began to ponder the success of the Irish Sweepstakes, which raised huge sums of money on horse races, and wondered if something similar couldn't be done for a race at Tripoli. Canestrini contacted Sforzini and put the idea to him, based on a race in the spring of 1933. Canestrini also approached the governor, Emilio de Bono, who was enthusiastic, and so was Augusto Turati, secretary to the Fascist Party.[7] Eventually Mussolini gave his approval and the King of Italy, Vittorio Emanuele III, signed a decree authorising it on 13 August 1932. It would be called a Lottery Of The Millions and tickets went on sale that winter.

The tickets bore a drawing of a racing car, its rear wheel forming an O – coloured for some reason green – in the middle of the ticket itself. Above the car was printed 'LOTTERIA DI TRIPOLI'. To the left of the green wheel was printed 'Serial', followed by a letter, and to the right the ticket's individual number. Across the bottom, again left and right, were 'DODICI LIRE' and 'LIRE DODICI' – 12 lire. The ticket looked such an innocent thing, a visually pleasant marriage of the dramatic and the utilitarian.

The lottery worked to a simple format. The tickets were sold all over Italy up to 16 April 1933, three weeks before the race. Then 30 would be drawn, one for each of the starters. If you drew the driver who went on to win the race you got 3,370,376 lire, if second

2,000,000 and third 1,000,000. These were potent sums at a time when an Italian would have been happy to earn 1,000 lire a month.

The lottery was a triumph, raising around 15,000,000 lire – that's over a million tickets. The prize money for the competing teams was 550,000 lire, and when you add that to the three lottery winners – 6,000,000 lire – you're still a long way short of the 15,000,000 lire. What happened to the difference? Capps says that 'the money left after the prizes and administration costs was supposed to [partially] offset the costs of the colony, which represented a negative cash flow nearly the whole time the Italians controlled it. For many reasons, the colony never attracted [a viable] number of immigrants from Italy or produced the anticipated riches in minerals or agriculture.'

The counterfoils of the tickets were taken to Tripoli for the draw on Saturday 29 April. The 30 winners were notified by telegram and told which driver they had drawn.

That day Nuvolari apparently contacted Canestrini 'about a meeting'.[8] Nuvolari was at Alessandria practising for a race the following day, as were Varzi and Borzacchini. (Varzi wouldn't be allowed to compete because he had entered too late.) Canestrini was there, too. The four men met, although Canestrini claimed they only talked about the travel arrangements to Libya. 'However, Varzi said that the only topic discussed was the race the next weekend in Tripoli and the lottery'.[9]

The plot thickened.

A meeting was arranged in Rome between Canestrini, the three drivers and the three lottery winners who had drawn *them*. Evidently on the grid at Alessandria Nuvolari pointed his finger at Canestrini, which has been taken to mean *'don't forget the meeting!'*

It took place on the Monday evening, at the Massimo D'Azeglio hotel near the Termini station. Canestrini was there as a 'neutral party who could arrange the terms to avoid any conflict with the regulations'.[10] This is of central importance and one which, as far as I am aware, had not been widely discussed before Capps got hold of it.

The meeting wasn't, he says, in any sense secret because an Italian magazine reported it *and* 'someone had approached Pietro Ghersi with an offer of 1,000,000 lire if he won the race. Others have Tim Birkin being offered either 70,000 or 100,000 lire by his ticket holder if he won the race.' All are agreed that Birkin did not involve himself.

Whatever, in the Massimo D'Azeglio an agreement was reached (and put in writing) that if Nuvolari, Varzi or Borzacchini won the race, the 3,000,000 would be divided equally among the six. If they also finished second and third, those amounts would be added to the total and divided. The plan minimised the risk of outright loss but 'the important outcome of the meeting was that there was to be no pre-arrangement in the document as to the outcome of the race.'[11] In other words, it wasn't a 'fix' because it did not stipulate who would win. There was nothing to prevent the three racing each other as hard as they wished, and equally no guarantee that another driver altogether wouldn't win.

So far, so good.

Yates claims that Enzo Ferrari must have known what was afoot because 'all of his drivers were participants' but there is 'no concrete proof.' Yates also claims Campari and Chiron were in on it. Yates further claims that because Birkin had been quick in qualifying he represented an outside danger for the fix. To remove even that, a late ruling was made: one mechanic had to service one car. Birkin and Campari had Maseratis but shared a mechanic. He would now work on Campari's car while Birkin had to hire a local, who turned out to be a 'hopeless drunk'.[12] Birkin would be hobbled by the new regulation: at his pit stop he'd have to put fuel in and change the tyres himself. Under the legend propagated by Neubauer, it has always been easy to construct a giant conspiracy.

When the drivers and lottery winners gathered in Tripoli, the word was out and some of the drivers were not happy about it. Campari and Fagioli, according to Capps, were 'especially hostile' to Varzi and Nuvolari, and were determined to destroy the arrangement by winning the race themselves. Birkin felt the same.

The grid:

Cussini (Maserati)	Bianchi (Maserati)	Nuvolari (Alfa Romeo)	Premoli (Maserati)
Varzi (Bugatti)	Fagioli (Maserati)	Gazzabini (Alfa Romeo)	Birkin (Maserati)

Pratesi (Alfa Romeo)	Glusti (Not known)	Balestrero (Alfa Romeo)	Battaglia (Alfa Romeo)
Battilana (Alfa Romeo)	Matrullo (Maserati)	Borzacchini (Alfa Romeo)	Gazzangia (Bugatti)
Zehender (Maserati)	Barbieri (Maserati)	Castelbarco (Alfa Romeo)	Campari (Maserati)
Biondetti (Maserati)	Moradel (Talbot)	Corsi (Maserati)	Hartmann (Bugatti)
Cucinotta (Talbot)	Ferrari* (Bugatti)	Taruffi (Alfa Romeo)	Tadini (Alfa Romeo)
	Ghersi (Alfa Romeo)	Pellegrini (Alfa Romeo)	

(*Gerolamo Ferrari, no relation to Enzo)

Varzi knew that Campari and other drivers were relying on the intense competition he had with Nuvolari: that Nuvolari, driven by the demons, would forget all about the arrangement and they'd crash or break down. 'According to Canestrini, Varzi approached him on the morning of the race about his concerns.'[13]

Canestrini would say: 'We went together to Nuvolari's room, where he was already dressed for the race, and I explained Varzi's worries.'[14] Nuvolari now said: 'Let's toss to see which of us should win, if we are ahead at the end of the race.' Canestrini took out a silver coin, and Nuvolari chose 'heads'. The coin came down tails. Nuvolari accepted that the race would go to Varzi. (Borzacchini was not aware of this development.) It is *this* spin of the coin, *if it happened,* which shifted the arrangement into a fix.

Don Capps says 'ah, the coins business. It doesn't feel right. If you can bet on anything, it's that Nuvolari was going to try and win any motor race he was in. He was a very focused man. The coin business just does not track at all. It's just too pat, and nothing in here was pat. I don't think the coin toss happened, although something like that might have been talked about. It's part of the wonderful myth. If you look at the race there was no coin toss there.'

By this, Capps means that if you study the race itself there is no suggestion that Varzi and Nuvolari were doing anything but racing each other full out. More than that, it seems highly improbable that a man of Varzi's pride would go to Nuvolari's room and risk a refusal that Nuvolari would have anything to do with it. It seems equally improbable that Nuvolari would agree to forfeit a race in advance when he had no reason to do so – in financial terms, winning or losing to Varzi made no difference. And gifting a race to *Varzi* contradicts everything we know about Nuvolari as a man and a racing driver – no, it *violates* everything we know.

A hot day, and the crowd which came looked entirely European and colonial. The place wasn't Africa at all: women in full skirts, stoles and broad-rimmed fashionable hats, some wearing coats; men in jackets and ties and hats, some in suits. Even the soldiers on guard, locked in the stand easy position – their rifle butts on the ground, the barrels tilted forward by the right hand – were held by European discipline.

On the grid, people milled around as they did – and as they do – on grids, while Varzi leant over the engine of his car, smoking and talking quietly to a mechanic. Nuvolari in his jumper accompanied his car as it was pushed to its place on the grid, his left hand resting on the bodywork – a lover's gesture. Dignitaries, one wearing a waistcoat, talked nearby.

Far away, the Libyans watched. They wore white robes and white head-scarves. A camera panned across some of them and their faces betrayed curiosity. The camera panned on, across the people in the grandstand: whatever high society in Tripoli might have been, here it was, manicured, confident, well-dressed, at ease with itself. That was in *their* faces. The crowd was a large one, many, many thousands.

The flags of a dozen nations fluttered in a sudden stir of a breeze.

At the start a mechanic was still working on one car. The others – accelerating at quite different speeds as the power came on – went past him and travelled along the length of the grandstand. They moved towards the first corner a couple of hundred yards away. The horizon – near and far – was decorated by palm trees, at places so tall and close together that they formed a kind of shade: their shadows fell full across the track and the sun licked the cars, taking their shadows on to the track, too. The drivers were unprotected both from the tree trunks and the white stones set at intervals to mark where the rim of the track was.

Completing lap one, Birkin led from Nuvolari, Campari third. Next lap Campari led. Varzi was 'nursing' his Bugatti because it was only on seven cylinders: a mechanic had overfilled the sump. Varzi reasoned that as the oil level fell the problem would correct itself.

At 14 laps Campari pitted. His oil tank had to be roped into place. Yates, proponent of the giant conspiracy, writes 'then the farce began. Campari cruised into the pits and began a fuelling stop that consumed about the time required to fill the tanks of a... tri-motor bomber.'

Campari needed further repairs a few laps later and eventually retired. Contradicting Yates, Capps writes: 'Campari did not give up easily. His efforts to win were obviously stirred by his anger towards Varzi and Nuvolari.'

Another retirement has fed the great conspiracy theory: that of Borzacchini. Nixon writes that his 'Alfa was clearly slowing drastically, although it sounded perfectly healthy. It slowed even more drastically when Borzacchini drove it into an oil drum marking the side of the road, before hobbling to the pits with a burst tyre, where he promptly retired!'[15]

Nixon is one of the most accurate and respected motor racing historians but it may be here that, once you have the idea of the great conspiracy in your thoughts, ordinary incidents seem to fit that pattern. *If* the coin toss did happen, Borzacchini was unaware of it. He was bound only by the original agreement, which had no problem with him winning. Why then would he deliberately drive into an oil drum? *If* for some inexplicable reason he did feel a need to withdraw from the race, why didn't he coast into the pits with one of the unprovable mechanical problems I mentioned earlier?

Birkin pitted and, changing wheels and refuelling himself, burnt his arm on the hot exhaust pipe.[16]

Nuvolari led from Varzi and Zehender, Birkin fourth. Nuvolari, however, had to pit (on lap 23) for fuel, something Varzi wouldn't have to do because the Bugatti had an extra tank. In context Nuvolari's stop was quick, some 20 seconds, but of course much longer because he had to slow to enter the pits and accelerate away. When he emerged Varzi was in the lead. Nuvolari went after him and began to catch him, not least because Varzi was having problems switching over to the spare fuel tank.

One report has Canestrini positioned on a corner waving to the two leaders not to forget the agreement. Canestrini would recount how both drivers were 'shouting and making gestures at each other.' Neither took any notice of *his* gestures and neither slowed.

Does this sound like two men obeying the toss of a coin?

Into the last lap they were side-by-side but Varzi had the advantage into the last corner and won it by 0.2 of a second: Varzi 2h 19m 51.4s (an average speed of 104.7mph/168.4kph), Nuvolari 2h 19m 51.6s.

As Capps says, *if* the finishing line had been a little further on Nuvolari would have won it; and, bearing in mind Nuvolari's earlier words, four years later he was still regretting that his pit stop hadn't been one second quicker to give him the race.

You can argue that Nuvolari might have backed off, however fractionally, towards the very end to give it to Varzi but, again, why should he?

Neubauer's fiction is a wondrous thing at this point. With 'a mile and a half to go' he has Nuvolari 'throwing anxious glances over his shoulder' – a strange thing to be doing since Varzi, leading, was in front of him. Then on the home straight Nuvolari slowed and stopped. 'Nuvolari climbed out of the car and stood in the middle of the track, wringing his hands.' He shouted that he'd run out of fuel and mechanics 'rushed' from the pits with cans. As this was going on, Varzi and Chiron were both 'crawling' – a strange thing to be happening since Chiron was not present in Tripoli. Neubauer is now into a great denouement: Nuvolari 'joined in this fantastic slow-motion finish.'

The contemporary reports make no mention of anything like this. In fact, one which appeared the week after speaks about Nuvolari's 'unforgettable pursuit' from his pit stop and suggests Nuvolari was 'morally' the victor because he'd caught Varzi and so nearly got past him to the line.

Capps says that 'all those in the syndicate made a tidy profit from the affair and got on with life.'

Piero Taruffi, who finished fifth at Tripoli, wrote (in 1964)[17] a refined version. 'To increase their chances of success the three conspirators promised verbally to cut other drivers in on the deal provided they held back; a number of them agreed, and although they kept their word no money was ever distributed and strong feelings prevailed for a number of years between the "welshers" and their victims. The most bitter about it was Luigi Fagioli, who used to threaten the defaulters before every race.'

It seems most likely that the arrangement spawned a thousand rumours at the time, and Taruffi heard many of them. There is no independent evidence whatsoever, including the race coverage, that any driver held back; he offers no examination of how involving other drivers would disturb the division of the prize money or how it would now be distributed; he does not touch upon the delicate matter that the original arrangement was not illegal but offering money to other drivers to go slowly clearly would have been fraud; and this is the only reference I have seen to Fagioli berating the 'defaulters'. Has Taruffi misinterpreted Fagioli's noisy displeasure at the 'arrangement' and deduced that Fagioli must have been involved?

The fact that Taruffi claims this, no matter how unsupported and unlikely, does however bear out the idea that all talk of race fixing is virtually unknown. That is why Tripoli has exercised a fascination which remains almost morbid to this day.

The Motor carried a nice little postscript. 'A lottery was held in connection with the Tripoli Grand Prix and six residents of the Riviera town of Imperia (Italy) were lucky enough to draw Sir Henry Birkin. By finishing third, "Tim" has brought a fortune of £2,250 [in 1933 – a real fortune] to the shareholders in the ticket, and as a result the leading townsfolk are having a special gold medal struck for him.'

Alas, Birkin, a wealthy lace manufacturer, began to feel unwell on the boat journey home, his burnt arm bandaged. One source[18] says he actually burnt his arm in practice for the Tripoli race, touching the exhaust pipe 'while reaching into the cockpit for his cigarette lighter.' He was admitted to hospital with septicaemia (blood poisoning) and died on 22 June. However, W.O. Bentley (of Bentley cars) claimed that it wasn't the burn but a mosquito bite in Libya which 'related back to malaria he had picked up in Palestine during World War One.'

There's a much sadder postscript. Borzacchini, who needed the money more than Varzi and Nuvolari to protect his family's future, died at Monza in September during the Italian Grand Prix, and so did Campari.

The result:

Varzi	2h 19m 51.4s (104.7mph/168.4kph)
Nuvolari	2h 19m 51.6s
Birkin	2h 21m 23.2s
Battilana	2h 21m 57.0s
Taruffi	2h 23m 57.8s
Balestrero	2h 23m 59.0s

6

Soap Opera

Le Mans 1933

RAYMOND Sommer had the money to go racing because his family ran a carpet manufacturing business. Money, then as now, was no guarantee of anything but Sommer proved to be good, and quickly. By 1932, partnering Luigi Chinetti, he was winning Le Mans in an Alfa Romeo and a year later he was partnering Nuvolari to try and do it again.

That led to initial friction because Nuvolari had not driven Le Mans before and Sommer, knowing of Nuvolari's reputation for driving cars to and past their limits, wondered if a sports car could conceivably survive that over 24 hours. Reportedly the friction began in practice, presumably as Sommer saw what Nuvolari was doing with the car, an Alfa Romeo 8C. Sommer thought he had found a simple solution. He proposed that, during the race, Nuvolari's time in the car be limited. How Nuvolari took that is not reported but we can imagine it. Whatever, the two drivers agreed to share the driving more or less equally.

Mind you, one report wrote of 1933[1] 'And yes, Tazio "The Great" came! The night driving scarcely seemed to fire him with enthusiasm but the solid Sommer promised to take care of that.' Hmm – hadn't Nuvolari won the 1930 Mille Miglia tracking Varzi in the dark?

Le Mans was first run in 1923, and by 1933 the original circuit had

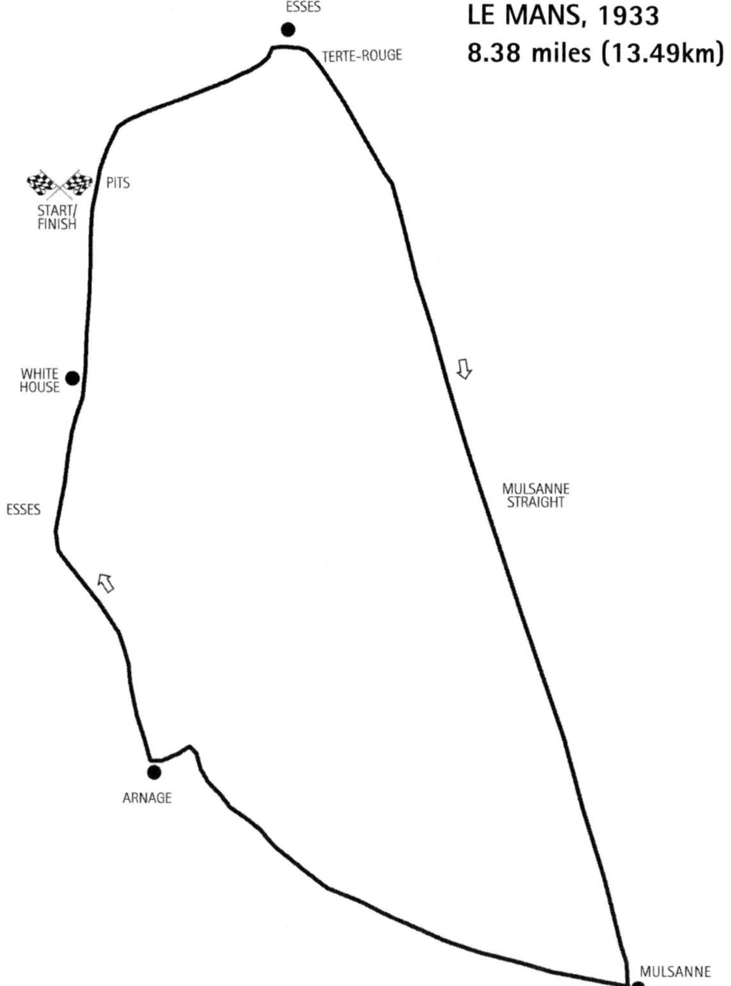

been altered for a third time. It was the matrix of the circuit used today: even the Dunlop bridge dates from 1932. By now it had a new and broad road 'protected by embankments and palisades leaving the Pontlieue road just after the grandstands and cutting across to the beginning of the Hippodrome straight. Halfway along, following a steepish descent, there is a tricky S-bend, and the corner at which the new road joins RN 158 is also unpleasant if taken fast, since the super-elevation of the corner is only carried halfway across. The surface of the circuit was on the whole very good, but near Arnage it had deteriorated and the dust made driving difficult.'[2]

This talk of the Hippodrome straight needs clarification because it will have a direct bearing on the race description. The Hippodrome was a café approximately a quarter of the way down the Mulsanne straight – hence calling that part of the Mulsanne after it. Just before it the road kinked slightly, and this may well be what the reporters called the 'Mulsanne kink'. The village of Mulsanne was at the end of the straight (see map) and the corner there V-shaped. It was a place of obvious danger, was sand-bagged and at least one runner came to grief there.

Something else needs clarification. Traditionally a team keeps its driver strategy fluid, which is a rather grand way of saying they can bring the car in and change drivers whenever they want during the race. What this means is that, often when you are trying to recreate the race, you can't know which driver was in the car. Sometimes contemporary reports say, sometimes they don't – and sometimes one report contradicts another. To circumvent this, I have called the 'cars' by using both driver's names (Sommer/Nuvolari, for example, or Chiron/Cortese) unless it is absolutely clear which driver *was* in.

One curiosity of the event was that the cars were refuelled from elevated tanks with gravity feed, and each tank supplied three pits. This meant the cars were grouped according to the fuel they used – for example, the MG of Norman Black and a couple of the Alfas (Sommer's included), all running on pure benzol, were together.

Sommer was 'a very wealthy Frenchman, as his brother was, and could afford to do motor sport without thinking of costs,' says Neil Eason Gibson. 'He did it entirely for pleasure, not for profit. He was just completely happy. He had lots of friends, people liked him and I don't think he was ever criticised for anything he did on a motor circuit. He was polite – he was like an English gentleman, that would be a good description. When I stayed at his house there was Goffredo Zehender [also a driver], Zehender's girlfriend, one other who I can't remember and the talk was basically motor sport all the time. That was just what he wanted. The house was a typical Ste Maxime summer residence, the pink colour they normally paint buildings. He was in a position to argue his case with Nuvolari, and Nuvolari behaved himself in that race because if you look at the lap times Nuvolari could have gone quicker than Sommer but he didn't overstretch the car.'

Chinetti, by trade a chief mechanic, won Le Mans three times (the first in 1932, the last in 1949) and was for decades a close friend and associate of Enzo Ferrari.

We've already met Chiron, a native of Monte Carlo (his father was maître d' at the Hôtel de Paris). He was handsome and employed by the hotel to dance with elderly ladies. An American woman sponsored him and his motor racing career was launched. Many years later he became the starter of the Monaco Grand Prix and he always stood in the middle of the track just in front of the cars with the flag. Many drivers thought '*we'll have him this year!*' when he let it drop to release them.

Practice was over a week and 'passed without any great surprises' among the 29 cars that would take part in the race.[3] The four leading Alfa Romeos (Sommer, Chinetti, Brian Lewis and Chiron) were all about the same speed. On the Thursday:

> *… towards 9pm a great storm broke over the circuit. However a large number of people were in the grandstands and the enclosures. Only a few drivers went out practising [Nuvolari not mentioned among them.] After the storm a thick fog settled on the Hunaudières straight.*[4]

There was no practice during the Friday daytime but in the evening Chiron beat the overall lap record – set in practice, not the race – held by Sommer with 5m 31.4s (146.3kph/ 90.9mph) the year before.

> *All was quiet at the garage Lenoir, where the Astons were kept, and the British competitors generally seemed content with their lot. Not so the crew of the somewhat decrepit Austin, who complained of clutch trouble. The supercharged Bentley driven by [Louis] Gas and [Jean] Trévoux also developed clutch trouble on the eve of the race, but by dint of superhuman effort of the crew, aided by Chassagne, the car was got ready in time.'*[5]

Always at Le Mans there is a curious sense of expectation and anticipation which is unlike any other race because the entry is so vast and housed in so many places, some surprisingly far away. The accumulating drama of a Grand Prix is centred around pit and paddock, and they become a stage with each person playing their part. Le Mans is a magnificent fragmentation – a panoramic view of countryside. *L'Equipe* caught that mood exactly.

> *The competitors only appeared on the circuit during the period of practice, that is to say between 10 in the evening and six in the morning. Outside this period they worked on their preparations or, in view of the tiredness to come, rested in the little villages round Le Mans. The whole Sarthois forest gave shelter to the competitors! They abandoned the town of Le Mans for an agreeable break in the countryside. It was made even better by magnificent weather, because we snapped our fingers at the heavy chance of thunderstorms we dread.*

A sombre beginning to the day of the race.[6] 'A minute's silence for local driver Guy Bouriat who, on 21 May, was killed at Peronne and all the British drivers knew also that their friend Birkin, the winner of Le Mans 1929–31, gravely burnt at Tunis at the beginning of May, had only a few days to live.'

That morning heavy rain fell, making the drivers check their visors and spare goggles. The rain stopped, however, and by midday the weather was altogether brighter. As 4 o'clock and the start approached, the sun shone.

Once the dues had been paid to Bouriat, and Birkin had been in everyone's thoughts:

> *Le Mans goes en fête for this festival, shops being closed during the proceedings. Hundreds of thousands of people line the circuit, and at night the lighting effects of the tribunes and pits, coupled with the dispensation of music, give a wondrous effect.*[7]

A traditional start: the cars lined up diagonally in front of the pits and the drivers on the far side of the track facing them, ready to sprint across.

> *Chiron had come to the starting line almost at the last minute in an excited and nervous condition* [but the reporter didn't

> say why], *while Sommer, who laughingly dismissed the sensational reports of a quarrel with his team-mate Nuvolari, was present early and had a remarkably well-organised pit.*[8]

The commentator counted down the final minutes then seconds and a Colonel Lindsay Lloyd dropped the French national flag – the *Tricolore*. Anticipating this, some drivers were already sprinting. *Motor Sport* noted, perhaps only partly joking, that Lewis in the Alfa got to his car and led the pack away despite not having 'cheated'. This Alfa was some way back down the diagonals but Lewis got it to mid-track pointing straight ahead and surged. Chinetti and Sommer weren't far behind. In fact the five supercharged Alfa Romeos set off more or less together.

By the Hippodrome straight Sommer led and was going so fast that at some stage he'd threaten the lap record. He completed the first lap from that standing start in 5 mins 55 secs (136.8kph/85.0mph). Chiron ran second but Sommer was in brilliant form and by lap six was shedding Chiron.

The gap was 1m 35s, moving out through 1m 45s to 1m 55s on lap 10.

Other times, other attitudes. On lap 8 Stanislas Czaikowski, a wealthy Polish count, pitted and emerged smoking a cigarette.

The first hour of the 24 was almost completed and only one car had dropped out, something of a record. Judging by the order and average speeds after an hour, Chiron seems to have struck back:

Sommer/Nuvolari	10 laps
Chiron/Cortese	10 laps
Lewis/Rose-Richards	9 laps
Chinetti/Varent	9 laps
Moll/Cloitre	9 laps
Bussiene/Mme Desprez	9 laps

Chiron's blue Alfa started to sound unhealthy while Sommer pushed his times up towards the lap record (144.3kph/89.7mph) set by Birkin in 1930. After 20 laps the gap was 2m 46s, Chiron still on his 19th lap. A couple of laps later Moll moved up to third, having overtaken Lewis, and a lap after that Chiron broke down at the Mulsanne kink. He returned slowly to the pits. On lap 25 *L'Equipe* claimed that Sommer beat the lap record *again* with 5m 38s: that was an average of 143kph, but it only translates to 88mph – slower than Birkin had done.

The rules said that refuelling could only begin when cars had covered 24 laps, and that now started. Evening was coming in, fine but chilly.

The lead car – Sommer/Nuvolari – had taken 2h 52m 28s to cover 30 laps and that gave them a lead of 4m 18s over Chinetti, still on his 29th. Lewis retook Moll and both had covered 28 laps. At the end of that 30th lap Sommer finally pitted and handed the car over to Nuvolari. The Chiron/Cortese car ran fifth.

Into the fourth hour Gas in the Bentley had a spectacular crash at the bend at Mulsanne. The Bentley 'shot into the sandbank at such a pace that for a few minutes the effect was that of a Sahara storm' *(The Autocar)*. The Bentley had 'charged the Mulsanne bunker head on. It smashed through the wooden palisading and hit a tree, bringing down a shower of branches' *(The Motor)*. Gas was 'slightly cut about the mouth' and although he got the car back to the pits it was retired.

Meanwhile Cortese, who had taken over from Chiron, forced the record up to 89.5mph (144.0kph).

At four hours:

Sommer/Nuvolari	40 laps	3h 54m 20s
Chinetti/Varent	39 laps	3h 56m 50s
Lewis/Rose-Richards	39 laps	3h 59m 50s
Moll/Cloitre	38 laps	3h 59m 25s
Chiron/Cortese	37 laps	3h 57m 20s
Prince Nicolas/Cattanco	37 laps	3h 59m 59s

Such times can be misleading because, by definition, a 24-hour race is about endurance and, ultimately, durability. For Chiron and the fleet Cortese to regain three laps was by no means impossible. Mechanical problems, bringing lengthy pit stops, could destroy even a big lead.

An announcement said that Sommer/Nuvolari had covered the first 500 kilometres (37 laps) at a faster average speed than Campari had done at Montlhéry in the French Grand Prix the previous week! That race had been over 500 kilometres and Campari covered it in 3h 48m 45.4s – an average of 81.4mph/131.1kph.

At the fifth hour the order of the first three was unchanged – Nuvolari had covered 50 laps, Chinetti/Varent a lap down, but

Chiron's car was now up to fourth because the Moll/Cloitre car had had a problem with the starter at a pit stop. The Chiron car was, however, three laps behind Nuvolari.

> *The commissioners reminded everyone that front and rear lights must be switched on at 21.30 [9.30pm] in conformity with the rules, and soon the cars were running with the aid of their headlights.*[9]

Le Mans changes tone at exactly this moment, and so markedly that it becomes almost a different event, softer, slightly mysterious because the beautiful cars are now no more than headlamps – luminous eyes – boring into the night.

> *As daylight faded, lights flickered on the tails of the competing cars, and suddenly the long line of pits and grandstands became ablaze with lights and gay with laughter and music ... hard-working mechanics wiped their hands on cotton waste and dissected cold chicken with a pocket knife.*[10]

At six hours:

Sommer/Nuvolari	60 laps	5h 54m 7s
Chinetti/Varent	58 laps	5h 55m 0s
Lewis/Rose-Richards	58 laps	5h 55m 18s
Chiron/Cortese	57 laps	5h 55m 18s

In the seventh hour the Lewis/Rose-Richards car moved up into second place and rain was falling, making the far side of the circuit difficult and potentially dangerous; but by the eighth hour Chiron was up to second and within 48 seconds of Sommer, who'd taken over from Nuvolari: Lewis/Rose-Richards had just had a four-minute pit stop.

Chiron, *Motor Sport* reported, 'was in just before midnight and had considerable difficulty in getting away. His starter jammed (a trouble which Sommer and Lewis also experienced) and he had to start the car by letting it run backwards in reverse. This lost him some time and he dropped back to third place.' He regained it by some 'brilliant driving'.

> *Chiron was troubled by a seized starter pinion, but overcame this difficulty in a wonderfully ingenious manner. Knowing that the starter would not work, he ordered the front end of the car to be jacked up high and the wheels to be changed. As the jack was pulled away with a jerk, he shouted 'Starter', placing his finger on the button, and, having reverse in engagement, brought his engine into life by a slight movement of the car as it dropped to the ground.*[11]

At eight hours (midnight):

Sommer/Nuvolari	79 laps	7h 55m 38s
Chiron/Cortese	77 laps	7h 56m 24s
Chinetti/Varent	77 laps	7h 56m 33s
Lewis/Rose-Richards	76 laps	7h 56m 22s

The order did not change to the ninth hour and *Motor Sport's* reporter 'ventured a walk along the new road to the Esses. The cars had two, three or four headlights and had no difficulty taking the corners as fast as by day. Crowds still lined the barricades, but many more were patronising the dancing floors and bars, which blazed with light amongst the pine trees. Others, weary with the day's excitement, had lain down on the bare ground and gone to sleep, and these and occasional tree-stumps made the going heavy.'

At nine hours the Sommer/Nuvolari car had covered 89 laps, Chiron/Cortese 87. This charge towards Nuvolari held the attention of thousands of spectators who might otherwise have been tempted to wander off and have a drink or a nap.

The order had not changed at the tenth hour. Sommer made a three-minute pit stop and that enabled Chiron to close up. At the tenth hour the Alfas were running in the first four positions. Sommer pitted for repairs to his wing. Seventeen minutes later Nuvolari set off, the car pushed rather than using the starting handle. At 12 hours (half distance):

Sommer/Nuvolari	118 laps	11h 54m 47s
Chiron/Cortese	116 laps	11h 58m 26s
Chinetti/Varent	116 laps	11h 58m 31s
Lewis/Rose-Richards	114 laps	11h 58m 7s

The Sommer/Nuvolari car had covered 1,592 kilometres, Chiron/

Cortese 1,565. Around 20 minutes after this, the commentary post at the Mulsanne kink reported that Nuvolari had 'an important fuel leak'.

Some five minutes later, he was into the pits with the off-side front wing adrift. *The Motor* says 'Sommer immediately jumped from the pit to the rescue. He and his mechanic worked feverishly but in the middle of the job there was a cry of "*essence*" [petrol] which was simply pouring on to the road. Driver and mechanic dived under the car, and before the two things were rectified 13 mins had elapsed. Further excitement ensued as the starter refused to get the engine going. Sommer, however, [got in], let the car roll back on the down grade, and, engaging reverse, the engine sprang into life.'

The petrol leak had been plugged using a bar of soap.

Chiron was now in the lead, followed by the Chinetti/Varent car – Sommer third. That was the 13th hour. Before the 14th hour, Chiron pitted and that gave the lead to Chinetti, 2 minutes 31 seconds ahead of Chiron, Sommer third. Mme Odette Siko was fifth in an Alfa Romeo.

At 6.40 in the morning 'Chinetti and Chiron came into view, bonnet to tail, the last named trying unsuccessfully to overtake on the hill past the grandstands. Past White House they roared together, but, between Arnage and Mulsanne, Chiron went to the front, and by the end of the 143rd lap he held a lead of about half a mile.'[12] At that stage Sommer/Nuvolari were more than a lap down.

Just before seven Mme Siko crashed. She skidded just before the Mulsanne kink and completely lost control of the car, which scythed down two pine trees and came to rest against another, hitting it so hard that the trunk actually broke in half.

> *Madame Siko was thrown clear as the first tree was hit, being shot through the air and falling at the feet of a gendarme with nothing more than bruises and a complete inability to understand what had happened to her. The car, on the other hand, literally burst, the pinions coming out of the gearbox, certain parts even being found fifty yards from the main wreckage. The chassis took fire on hitting the third tree and set fire to the brushwood and dry fir branches.*[13]

At 7.15am – into the 15th hour – Rose-Richards pitted and at 15 hours the order was Chiron, Chinetti, Nuvolari and Lewis, who'd taken over from Rose-Richards. Chiron pitted and that let Chinetti into the lead but Chiron, emerging fast, retook it. Nuvolari was at the wheel and he overtook Chinetti.

At the 16th hour:

Chiron/Cortese	155 laps	15h 54m 22s
Sommer/Nuvolari	155 laps	15h 57m 57s
Chinetti/Varent	154 laps	15h 54m 29s
Lewis/Rose-Richards	151 laps	15h 54m 29s

Just after this, Nuvolari, driving furiously, raised the lap record to 90.0mph (144.8kph). It was on the 152nd lap and he did it in 5m 35s. On lap 156 he beat the record again – 5m 33s – and raised it on lap 159 to 5m 30⅖s (an average of 90mph/146kph).

At 8.30am Nuvolari and Cortese, running side-by-side, flowed along the straight from the White House towards the pits and grandstands. Just beyond them, Nuvolari overtook and that got a reverberating cheer.

He forced the pace up so that when he completed the following lap he led by 11 seconds. He kept forcing it up until it reached 30 seconds. However at 9.25am – into the 17th hour – he pitted for fuel, adjusted the brakes and handed over to Sommer. This took some 40 seconds and inevitably gave the lead to Cortese. Sommer set about reducing that and eventually, somewhere out at the back of the circuit, overtook him because at precisely 10.00am he appeared alone and, passing the grandstands, waved a handkerchief. It meant '*I got him!*'

At 18 hours:

Sommer/Nuvolari	176 laps	17h 59m 6s
Chiron/Cortese	175 laps	17h 52m 27s
Chinetti/Varent	175 laps	17h 59m 29s
Lewis/Rose-Richards	170 laps	17h 56m 52s

Cortese got into a 'terrific broadside' on the Esses before White House, letting Chinetti up into second place and Lewis into third.

Cortese, who had taken over Chiron's car, was doing his utmost to catch No.11... and got into a series of skids, his hub cap on one occasion actually grazing the bank. Finally at the esses he overdid things... and crashed into the bank, knocking all the spokes out of his offside front wheel and damaging the steering. He drove back to the pits and retired.[14]

It was 10.30am. When Chiron, in the pits, understood what had happened to his car he was consumed by despair.

At 19 hours the order was Sommer, Chinetti three laps adrift then Lewis a further three laps back. Sommer and Nuvolari had beaten the lap record nine times. These positions remained unchanged to the 20th hour. Sommer came in for fuel at 12.10pm and further repairs were made to the front wing before Nuvolari took over.

The certainties of the race were about to be torn apart.

The Sommer/Nuvolari car had a fuel leak – a rivet had come loose in the tank – and at 1.15pm Nuvolari brought it in for repairs. Chinetti had gone past him. Soon after, Nuvolari had to stop a second time. Nuvolari retook Chinetti, and shortly before the end of the 21st hour Sommer/Nuvolari led the Chinetti/Varent car by 14 seconds.

Into the 22nd hour – 2.00 in the afternoon – it was anyone's race because the fuel tank was now leaking badly. Rose-Richards may even have had a remote chance but that seemed to have gone with a long pit stop and so, as it seemed, the race revolved around Chinetti. His car had no troubles at all. Or did it?

The field was reduced to 16 and the race had apparently settled down to a monotonous finish. The drivers of the fast cars found it far from monotonous, however. A puffy side wind on the straight past Hippodrome café made steering difficult. The leaders were doing over 120mph. Sommer's Alfa and the one driven by Rose-Richards were steady in spite of their speed but Chinetti seemed unhappy [he was having difficulty over the bumps].

The leading car was in trouble. A rivet in the petrol tank had come adrift and Chinetti, in spite of his slower speed, was gaining. Nuvolari took over but, not having any means of stopping the leak, could do nothing but come in often to replenish.

Suddenly one noticed that the entire staff of Arthur Fox's pit [Fox had entered the Lewis/Richards Alfa for the race] were chewing away for dear life. Their rival had not thought to include chewing gum amongst the spares carried on the car but somehow the Fox équipe conveyed their 'adhesive' to their rivals without being detected by the watching commissionaire. It was duly stuck in place to such effect that the Italian was able to increase his distance without filling up. Some sportsmanship![15]

The pit staff were kept chewing gum constantly in preparation for the next stop. Sommer said that[16] 'the more of this improvised solder that we gave our mechanic the more the tank leaked. The reason was a simple one. The lad had been treated to champagne by "hospitable" friends, and he was quite incapable of sticking the chewing gum on the right spot'.

One of the greatest finishes to Le Mans, or any race, was under way.

2.10pm: Nuvolari pitted, was told to go all out and 'roared away with a satanic grin.'[17]

2.47pm: Nuvolari pitted again. 'The camp was nervous because... fuel was flowing dangerously near the exhaust pipe.'[18] The stop cost 1m 36s and reduced the lead over the Chinetti/Varent car – Varent was in it – to 35 seconds. Next lap Varent cut that by seven seconds.

3.00pm: Nuvolari responded and forced the lead to a couple of minutes. He beat the world 24-hour record: it had been 3,017km and he'd now done 3,022.

3.15pm: Nuvolari pitted and feverishly threw seat cushions out apparently to try and get at his tools. While he was stationary the Chinetti/Varent car went by into the lead. Nuvolari abandoned any thought of the tools and went out after it.

3.21pm: Nuvolari and Varent pitted together. Chinetti took over the other Alfa – Nuvolari stayed in his.

3.30pm: Chinetti had forged a 21-second lead. Within a single lap Nuvolari reduced this to 7⅗s of a second.

3.45pm: Chinetti had to pit for fuel and Nuvolari led by 1m 15s – the race all over *but* Nuvolari's brakes were weakening. Chinetti was driving as fast as he could, so fast he ran against the sandbanks at

Mulsanne but kept on. The gap came down to 44 seconds – Chinetti had taken 23 seconds out of Nuvolari on a single lap.

3:52pm: Chinetti had caught Nuvolari.

3.54pm: Nuvolari had responded and now led by seven seconds.

They moved into the final lap, a lap of such intensity that Chinetti would swear he got past Nuvolari three times during it. Past the grandstands Chinetti overtook Nuvolari. Sommer watched in something approaching despair – even Nuvolari couldn't withstand this, not with a car which had failing brakes and a fuel problem which might halt it at any moment.

From Hunaudières the loudspeaker message bellowed 'Chinetti leading – Nuvolari right on his tail.'

But this was the Mulsanne straight and Nuvolari's power took him into the lead.

'With tears in my eyes and a raging heart,' Sommer would say,[19] 'I was leaving the pit so as not to have to witness our defeat, the defeat of the great Italian champion, when the loudspeakers began to bellow "Nuvolari has just passed Chinetti."'

At the Mulsanne right-hander – at the end of the straight – the brakes must have hampered Nuvolari because Chinetti got past him. Chinetti would remember 'I was laughing my head off at Nuvolari's signs as I passed him, trying to tell me that I was driving with my feet and not my head.' They were in woodland and the Esses – and Nuvolari forced his way into the lead again.

Chinetti responded to that by retaking him and at Arnage Chinetti, 'to try and increase my lead decided to use second gear, which I had not done since early in the race as it had not seemed quite right. It so happened I was unable to engage it and went off the road, brushing by a photographer who dropped his camera with fright.'[20]

Nuvolari was through, Chinetti chasing. They moved towards the White House and Chinetti thought he might even catch Nuvolari again and 'would probably have done so had not François Paco taken it into his head to cross the line in his little Alfa 1,750cc Alfa immediately behind the winner. When I saw him pull out of the line of cars waiting to cross the finishing line on the stroke of four' – so they wouldn't have to go round again – 'I had to jam the brakes on to miss him, which resulted in a series of gyrations.' Up the slight rise towards the grandstands Chinetti came back at Nuvolari for one final, supreme assault. It was too late.

Nuvolari won it by 9⅕ seconds. There was wild, wild excitement.

Only later did the story of the chewing gum emerge. Reflecting, *L'Equipe* wrote:

> *An English competitor, in the course of the race, had a small fuel leak. He took in his mouth 'le chewing gum' which he masticated continuously ... and blocked the leak. Do-it-yourself!*
>
> *A few hours later Sommer was also losing fuel. He blocked this with black soap which he had on board, but whenever he passed the pits it could be seen that the leak persisted.*
>
> *Sommer continued; Nuvolari took over and went out with the car in the same condition. Suddenly we could see that in a neighbouring pit everyone was masticating chewing gum. A commissioner said they should keep out of sight. They waited for Nuvolari's next pit stop, then suddenly emerged with a ball of chewing gum pâté to plug the leak – illegal, because the chewing gum was not on board.*
>
> *Fears were groundless, because no action was taken against Nuvolari.*

The details of all this are not as clear as they might be, but it seems that an amazing act of sportsmanship took place. The (unnamed) Englishman showed what chewing gum might do. Whether the Alfa team asked the pit next door if they had gum and would they all mind chewing it, or whether the pit next door saw what was happening and volunteered is unknown – but either way they did it, and everybody got away with it. Nor, as Charles Faroux wrote it in *L'Equipe*, is the reference to the commissioner – presumably monitoring the Alfa Romeo pit – clear: whether he didn't see the ploy, warned them to conceal their concerted chewing or looked the other way.

Somehow all this beautiful improbability makes one of the greatest Le Mans greater still.

The result:

Sommer/Nuvolari	1,953.6 miles (3,143.9km) (81.5mph/131.1kph)
Chinetti/Varent	1,953.36 miles
Lewis/Rose Richards	1,891.06 miles
Der Becke/Peacock	1,604.0 miles
Driscoll/Penn Hughes	1,583.67 miles
Ford/Bäumer	1, 481.96 miles

* * * * *

Intermezzo

High summer, 1933: after Le Mans, Nuvolari finished fifth in Barcelona and retired at Rheims, both times of course with the Alfa Romeo. The cars were no longer good enough to win – Nuvolari was hauling and hustling them to do that. He was now[21] 'determined to break with Ferrari, contract or no contract. A week prior to the Belgian Grand Prix at Spa, Nuvolari signed a secret pact with Ernesto Maserati. There was a colossal contretemps. Ferrari was apoplectic...' The Nuvolari/Ferrari relationship runs like a theme through our story – two men of enormous willpower – but mostly in the background. Just occasionally it explodes into the foreground, as it does here. It will be exploding again before the story is done.

Nuvolari won Spa in a Maserati and three weeks later won Livorno and, a week after that, won Nice in one too; was second at Pescara and retired at Marseilles. That was on 27 August.

He was now committed to go to somewhere entirely different. He had been there once before, in 1930, when he won driving an Alfa Romeo, although *The Motor* explained 'everyone knows that the finishing order – which saw only three minutes between Nuvolari in first place and Varzi in third – was due to team tactics, following a plan to share the load between all three drivers.' Campari was the third.

That might seem to have a bearing, however remote, on what had happened at Tripoli, but let's not get into all that again. Instead let's go to the lush meadows and twisting, leafy lanes round Newtownards, and a car Nuvolari had never driven before. The peculiarities of its gearbox would be explained to him using sign language, and that didn't bother him at all.

7

ROAD RUNNER

Ards 1933

ALMOST breathlessly, *Motor Sport* announced in their September 1933 edition, under a headline 'GETTING READY FOR THE T.T. RACE', that 'a last minute event of outstanding importance has been the nomination of the famous Italian driver, Tazio Nuvolari, to pilot the MG Magnette entered by Whitney Straight'. Nuvolari had been invited by George Eyston[1] and prepared to race a British car for the first time.

The TT was 34 laps of a 13.6-mile (21.9km) circuit, with five classes competing from 500cc up to 5,000cc. Nuvolari was in the 750-1,100cc class. It was therefore a handicap, and arranged in a way designed to baffle even the most attentive follower of it during the race.

> *The cars were handicapped by classes according to engine capacity and whether they were supercharged or not, the handicap being expressed in laps and time, one lap being equal to 13 and two thirds miles. A 750cc supercharged car was deemed to have covered three laps before it started...*

and so on (if I might abbreviate it in that way), although:

> *The time allowance was given at the start, certain classes*

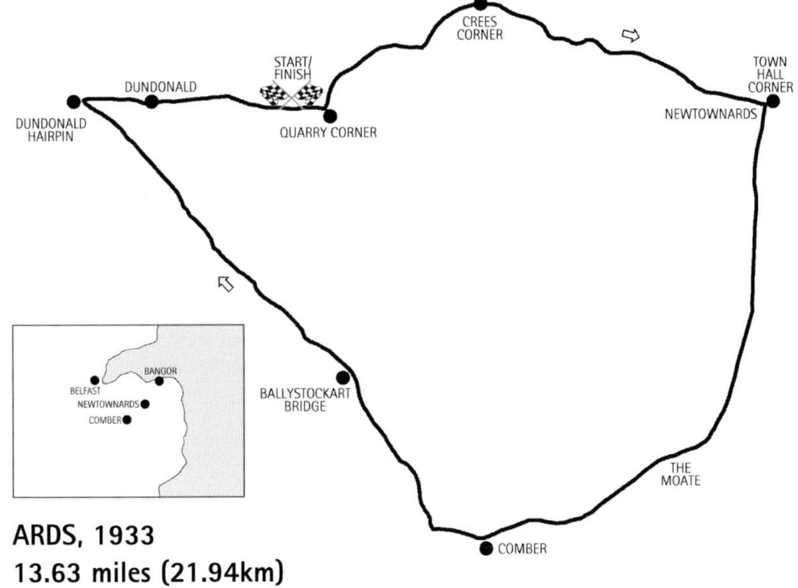

being sent away at definite intervals before the others, but all the machines had left the line before the first car completed one lap.[2]

If I tell you that during the race many, many spectators – perhaps most, perhaps all – did not have the remotest idea which car was really where or why, you'll understand. The local paper *Ireland's Saturday Night*[3] complained loudly that what the people in the grandstands wanted to know was who was leading on the road and not be offered a leaderboard governed by 'some abstruse mathematical calculation.' The newspaper gave an example of the confusion: at 4pm, local man Hugh Hamilton – from Omagh – was shown to be three seconds behind Nuvolari on handicap although he was physically leading him by 2m 4s.

Because this was one of Nuvolari's most masterful races – and as such demands inclusion in our story – I have recreated it in, I hope, enough detail to reflect that while, at the same time, preserving your sanity (and mine) by treating the evolving leaderboard in the simplest manner I can.

To compound the potential chaos, overall times do not seem to have been important either to the organisers or the reporters covering the race. Instead they gave average speeds, so that at 4pm, to follow the example we already have, Nuvolari had averaged 77.8mph (125.2kph) and Hamilton, three seconds behind, 73.0mph (117.4kph). I have left these speeds in, purely for interest.

The positions each half hour (which were officially announced) contain the gaps of drivers from the race leader, but even these are confusing. For example, *The Motor* gives its 11.00am, 11.30am and 12.00pm positions as 'on handicap' but thereafter does not use the phrase. Unless you know which is which, the gaps have no meaning – and even if you do know which is which, the gaps only have meaning if you know what each car's handicap was. I have therefore included those 'on handicap' and put the others in brackets so you can gaze at them or ignore them as you wish.

There were 31 entries, among them Earl Howe in an Alfa Romeo entered by Count Lurani, Eyston himself (Riley) and S.W.B. Hailwood (MG Midget) – father of Mike. Cars would run stripped of hood, screens, wings and headlamps in case they flew off and injured drivers, mechanics or spectators.

The *Belfast Telegraph* said as soon as the RAC announced the race would take place they found a 'welcoming and helpful spirit.'

> *The County Council of Down ... were equally ready in their assurance that – to put it very literally – no stone would be unturned to ensure that the road surface was in the best possible condition for racing. Corners were eased here, kerbstones, which in former years had constituted an element of danger, were removed there, and the entire circuit was specially treated to render it practically non-skid and as safe as the resources of human ingenuity could devise.*

I offer Lurani's words with the (by now) customary caveat that they are uncorroborated and describe events which may or may not have taken place. Lurani says that Nuvolari regarded this visit to Ireland as a holiday (he took his wife) and set off to it from Italy via London. 'After some complicated juggling with train timetables he arrived in London, where he was most warmly received.' He had a meeting with MG's directors and went on a tour of the city. This tour was no more than an 'excuse' because Nuvolari had forgotten to pack shirts.[4]

> *In a Piccadilly shirtmaker's he was surprised to be addressed in Italian; not wonderful Italian, but perfectly comprehensible. Ten minutes later the shop was crowded with people who somehow or other had heard the news, but these 'customers' were only interested in obtaining the little man's autograph.*

The Ards course formed a triangle.[5] The start–finish stood just outside the town of Dundonald on the road to Newtownards. Here were the pits under one long, narrow roof and, to either side of the road, grandstands. Some 200 yards down the road the cars reached Quarry Corner, a left-hander so sharp it was notorious for how many had come to grief there. In 1932, a driver called Freddy Dixon had gone through a hedge into a field of rhubarb.

Here the atmosphere of the race was established, because on a knoll inside the corner tightly-packed spectators leant over to watch the cars go by just in front of them. A pavement curved round beneath the knoll and occasionally people stood there within touching distance of the cars. From Quarry Corner the road rose, wriggling left and right as it went, with a hillside to the right where people gathered to watch. At one point tall trees overhung the road on both sides.

Then came Cree's Corner, a right with banking at either side, and Bradshaw's Brae, a two-mile descent into Newtownards: one of the two miles contained seven bends. The cars were moving at real speed as they came into a straight which passed under a railway bridge and took them into Newtownards. They were doing 100mph. Newtownards was, and is, a solid town.

The cars entered Conway Square by running close to the Town Hall. The drivers mounted the pavement and placed their cars within inches of the stone wall. Then they ran across the square, the buildings partially protected by sandbags and the crowd five or ten deep on the pavements.

Nuvolari would make this particular part his own stage, *racing* the MG at the crowd to gasps and great cheering; would slide the MG in perfect control to the delight and consternation of the unprotected spectators – no sandbags for them. One of the spectators, almost hypnotised by this theatre upon the stage, murmured helplessly 'what an ambulance driver he would make! What a fire engine driver he would make!'

The drivers then ran to Comber, the second leg of the triangle, and its square, reached by a narrow road. Another notorious corner here, a right-hander: a butcher's shop on it, sandbagged in case any cars ran wide. Many did.

They ran out of Comber towards a very dangerous S-bend – a left-right, once dangerously narrow but now broadened a bit – at a little place called Ballystockart midway between Comber and Dundonald. Then they were on a long straight to the hairpin bend at Dundonald, shaped like a wedge. It was a favourite vantage point because, as they twisted right, the cars slowed and they could be studied closely. Here the crowd would see Nuvolari working the wheel in a continuous series of delicate, tiny adjustments, *feeling* its adhesion, *feeling* its response as he went round, then adjusting-adjusting-adjusting again to make it point straight ahead.

The drivers now faced a mile-long sprint through Dundonald village to the start–finish.

The feel of the course was rural, and yet somehow intimate. This may have been because of the narrowness of the roads, or the sheer volume of spectators pressing to be as close to the cars as they could, or the amphitheatre of hillsides with so many watching from them. There was a sense of occasion with thousands sleeping in tents and others, rather splendidly, watching from deckchairs they'd carried into the fields.

The three towns the course passed through had the warm atmosphere of market-place communities, and then there was the bustle at the pits with so many people working here and there and giving the whole piece a sense of central drama.

Practice began on the Wednesday and Nuvolari saw the MG 'for the first time... soon after breakfast on Wednesday. The working principles of the Wilson [gear] box[6] were explained to him by a blend of sign language and odd Italian words: there was no interpreter and Nuvolari knew no English.'[7]

There is film of this. Nuvolari has obviously just sat in the car because his eyes rove across the dashboard noting the instruments while a man sporting a moustache leans in and makes dramatic gestures with his right hand while talking in an animated way.

> *In a very few minutes, he climbed in beside Alec Hounslow, who was to be his mechanic, and set off.*
>
> *Some wild things have been written about Nuvolari's practising at Ards, including a report that he executed three 360-degree turns in Newtownards Square on his first lap.*
>
> *Tazio was much too wise a bird to become involved in such extravagances. Determination and concentration made him the greatest champion of all, and he displayed these qualities in familiarising himself with this new and impressive car and intriguing gearbox. The main impression he gave was one of extreme enjoyment.*[8]

This is confirmed by the local paper, *The Chronicle*, who treated the build-up and race itself as a great event, and understandably so. Because the paper was in the long tradition of local weeklies, it gave a full picture and, unconsciously, caught the mood of the times.

> *Unfortunately… there was a serious accident, which resulted in the death of a young mechanic named W.E. Dunkley, of London, who was seated beside G.H.S. Balmain, an officer of the Royal Corps of Signals, the reserve driver in Lieut. J.G.C. Lowe's car.*
>
> *The car, an MG Magnette, was approaching Ballystockart, and when taking a right hand curve the car hit a kerb and overturned. Dunkley was thrown out.*
>
> *At Newtownards the greatest thrills were undoubtedly caused by … Nuvolari. He had the fastest time in his class for a lap of the course, the official figures being 10m 44s, which represented a speed of 76.3mph (122.7kph), and when it is remembered that the winner last year averaged 74.2mph (119.4kph), it will be noticed how fast Nuvolari's small car was travelling on Wednesday.*

Nuvolari seemed to be increasing in speed every time he came round and each time he rounded the corner into the Square he sent the grit scattering in all directions.

The weather was beautiful, and among the crowd gathered in Newtownards were Lord and Lady Castlereagh, who brought a party from Mount Stewart, including Colonel Hankey, Mr and Miss Humphries, Mr and Mrs Norman, Madame Paravacini and Master Murray-Smyth. They remained during the whole of the practice and evinced the keenest interest in the racing.

Practice continued the next day, and now Nuvolari increased his speed again. What we don't know, of course, is what the man's limit in such a car was, and how much he could increase his speed at will. Anyway…

The outstanding feature of Thursday's practice were the great speeds attained by some of the drivers, and the great skill displayed in their handling of the cars at the many dangerous corners and bends on the circuit. This was particularly noticeable in the case of Nuvolari, who apparently sent his small car flat out with the object of trying to find out what the vehicle was capable of doing. His MG certainly responded very gamely to his calls… the little car seemed to simply leap round the course, and in the hands of the famous Italian driver it appeared to treat the most dangerous of corners with disdain.[9]

Although Nuvolari wasn't fastest on Thursday (Rose-Richards in a Class 4 Alfa Romeo did 10m 5s) he lowered his best to 10m 26s, which was 78.5mph (126.3kph).

Brian Lewis, also in a Class 4 Alfa Romeo, had a 'narrow escape when a dog strayed on to the course, but Lewis braked violently' and missed it. In Newtownards another dog 'strayed through the crowds' but the crowd whistled and it responded by 'disappearing up Mill Street just before a car appeared'. Meanwhile on one of these two days 'two chaffinches were adhering to the front of one of the cars when it pulled up at the pits,' though whether the birds were hitching a ride or dead is not stated.[10]

Heavy rain fell in the afternoon.

It would seem that the Friday was a rest day although the weather improved – sun breaking through the clouds – and that gave hope of a dry race on the morrow.

At about 8.00am on the Saturday a misty drizzle began to fall and by 8.30am it had become steady. Visibility was not good although it might well improve by the start, at 11.00am.

> *Race fever, symptoms of which have been showing and growing for the past week, reached its climax this morning in Belfast. During the night motor cars wended their way from the furthest points of Ireland and ships forged their way across the Channel, all well laden with enthusiasts.*
>
> *All creeds, classes and conditions of men, and women, too, joined in the great pilgrimage. At eight o'clock, three hours before the race was due to begin, the centre of the city was crowded with people.*[11]

Nuvolari, accompanied by his wife and the Italian Consul, arrived at the pits early. His car, like several others, was protected from the drizzle by waterproof sheets. Nuvolari was described as the 'most picturesque figure in the whole kaleidoscopic picture' and 'dapper'. His wife said she'd watch from a seat in the stand.

The Motor relayed a rumour that 'Nuvolari, it was said, would not start owing to certain matters not unconnected with bonus.' There is no mention of when this happened – after practice, on the free Friday or now, as the crowd gathered. It remained, moreover, a rumour but, since we know that Nuvolari both liked and needed money to fund his lifestyle, might he not have been indulging in a little quasi-blackmail? Who, now, would dare refuse him whatever he was demanding in bonus? He'd have calculated that, too…

Earl Howe arrived early too, wearing blue overalls and holding a large golf umbrella – the same blue as his overalls. He strolled across to the stands to chat with friends.

By 9.45am, vantage points round the circuit were filling up while an immense crowd tramped along the straight from Dundonald. One estimate put the eventual crowd at half a million.

At 10.00am, the roads making up the course were closed and for the next 20 minutes the police and officials cleared the pits of non-essential personnel.

At 10.30am, the roads were clear and drivers warmed their engines.

It was regarded as something of an omen that when Earl Howe wandered back to the pits from chatting with his friends his umbrella was furled. The drizzle had eased, almost stopped.

> *The cars were drawn up in front of the pits and drivers and managers were discussing last minute plans. Lord Howe shrugs his shoulders at the mention of tyres, Whitcroft secures a sprig of white heather on his Riley, and Crabtree tries out the aeroplane speaking tube by which his passenger can communicate with him.*[12]

At 10.45am sharp there was a 'stir' as the viceregal party arrived: their Graces the Duke and Duchess of Abercorn accompanied by the Marquis and Marchioness of Hamilton and Sir William Morris, who had put up the prize money. The British Prime Minister, Ramsay MacDonald, was there, too, and chatted for a moment or two with several of the drivers, including Nuvolari.

By now, with four or five minutes to go, the VIPs took their seats in the boxes reserved for them in the stands.

> *Notables, among them Ramsay 'Mac', whose arrival by aeroplane was loudly cheered, took up positions in the decorated official box, hedged by seven-foot Ulster Constabulary, rigid, while the loudspeakers just got off the National Anthem in time.*[13]

The mists had melted, the road was drying. A hush fell over the great crowd.

At 10.58am a gust of wind caught the flags over the stand and scoreboard, and they fluttered 'gallantly' (as one report put it.)

At 11.00am, A.V. Ebblewhite – known as Ebby, a portly man famed for starting races – held an immense Union flag and let it fall. Three Rileys went away in quick succession then the rest at intervals: Nuvolari's group started a minute and 35 seconds after the leaders, Nuvolari 'tucked in awkwardly astern' *(The Autocar)* – I don't know what this means, either. The last Invictas left more than six minutes after the leaders. Nuvolari and Eyston were close together, but Nuvolari went past him on the first right-hander after Quarry Corner – he was in the mood.

As the 'stagger' began slowly to work itself out, Victor Gillow was in the lead with a first lap of 12m 26s followed by four MG Midgets. As Nuvolari passed the stand to complete the lap he overtook E.R. Hall in another Magnette. By the end of the second lap he'd passed six other cars so that, from 17th away, he was now running sixth – and fourth a lap after that although, of course, under the fiendish handicapping system, that did not mean he was actually fourth. Nuvolari, however, was genuinely magnificent in the corners. He was sliding dramatically and the thousands adored that. Sir William Morris was in the Square at Newtownards talking to a reporter and just then Nuvolari came through. Morris shook his head and smiled, which the reporter interpreted as *'I'm glad I'm not in that car with him...'*

At 11.30am, Hamilton led on handicap from S.A. Crabtree by 21s, then Gillow (37s), Dixon, Tommy Simister – a former bike rider – and Lewis.

On lap 5 Nuvolari averaged 77.6mph (124.8kph), a class record. He was making the Magnette drift in the Square at Newtownards before straightening it. Astonishingly this lap beat the existing class record, set by Dixon the year before, by seven full seconds.

On lap 6 he forced that up to 78.1mph (125.6kph) despite a frightening skid at the Square, which he caught instantly: he seemed to be headed directly for the sandbags at the corner of South Street but a 'deft twist of the wrist' sent the car in the direct of Comber. 'Still Hamilton, going like a scalded dog, kept away from his rival' *(The Autocar)*.

At Dundonald, Nuvolari was reported to be taking the corner so precisely each time he came through that the spectators estimated he was always within six inches of where he'd been the lap before. Nuvolari forced the pace so hard that by noon he was gaining on Hamilton.

At 12.00, on handicap:

Hamilton	74.0mph	(119kph)
Nuvolari	77.6mph	+ 53s
Dixon	74.9mph	+ 59s

On lap 9, Nuvolari broke the record again with 10m 25s, translating to 78.6mph (126.4kph), but by now the big Alfa Romeos of Lewis and Rose-Richards were into their stride, and so was the Riley of Gillow.

At 12.30pm:

Hamilton	74.0mph	(119kph)
Dixon	75.4mph	(+ 1m 5s)
Gillow	75.3mph	(+ 1m 15s)
Lewis	80.8mph	(+ 1m 33s)
Rose-Richards	80.6mph	(+ 1m 43s)
Nuvolari	77.0mph	(+ 2m 12s)

Ah, the fiendish handicap.

> *A handicap race is always difficult to follow even for those mathematical wizards who keep a chart of each car as it passes. It was made no simpler by the fact that the laps shown on the score board were actually those which the cars were beginning. For some obscure reason Nuvolari was shown at 12.30 to have dropped back to sixth place, though since he had at 12.22 accomplished a record lap of 10m 25s, and a few minutes later one of 10m 14s, it was difficult to account for.*[14]

That time of 10m 14s came after he received pit signals telling him to go even faster, presumably after they'd seen the scoreboard. It meant he bettered his own time by 10 seconds, and averaged 80mph (128.7kph). Lewis stopped at Comber with clutch trouble, abandoned his car, caught the train to Dundonald and walked back to the pits from there.

At 1.00pm:

Hamilton	74.1mph	(119.2kph)
Dixon	75.9mph	(+ 34s)
Rose-Richards	81.2mph	(+ 1m 28s)
Gillow	75.2mph	(+ 1m 37s)
Nuvolari	77.7mph	(+ 1m 51s)
Howe	78.6mph	(+ 5m 7s)

Gillow was gone soon after. He took Quarry Corner too fast – he'd been visibly wild there for some laps before this – and hit a telegraph pole hard but was uninjured. The pit stops began.

> *Rose-Richards and his mechanic took in [sic] oil, fuel, and water, adjusted shock absorbers, had a spot of bother changing one wheel of the four they replaced, and were away in four minutes. Nuvolari slid in and, with Hounslow, put in oil and water, changed four wheels, left a wheel against the counter, remembered it, nearly forgot a [fuel] churn... had light refreshment and got going after 3m 9s.*[15]

Nuvolari was still in the mood although Hamilton, driving superbly, still led. At 1.30pm:

Hamilton	74.2mph	(119.4kph)
Dixon	76.0mph	(+ 52s)
Nuvolari	78.1mph	(+ 1m 57s)

And now we come to a mystery because two sources (*The Motor* and *Ireland's Saturday Night)* give this position on handicap at 2.00pm, the third hour of the race:

Hamilton	74.6mph	(120.0kph)
Dixon	76.0mph	(+ 1m 47s)
Nuvolari	76.3mph	(+ 6m 23s)

The mystery is how Nuvolari lost some four minutes between 1.30pm and 2.00pm. Neither publication makes any mention of anything happening to him – like another pit stop – although *Ireland's Saturday Night* says the 2.00pm positions are on handicap but doesn't say that about the 1.30pm positions

Certainly, after 2.00pm Dixon pitted and was stationary for 4m 11s and then back out on the circuit he had trouble with his exhaust pipe, which was loose. That explains why between 1.30pm and 2.00pm he lost a great deal of time and went back to fourth.

Meanwhile Hailwood stopped in the Square with a carburettor problem and as Nuvolari went by Hounslow waved a greeting to him. Hamilton pitted and it went terribly wrong.

> *The mechanic seemed tired, and Hamilton, on fire to keep the*

lead, shouted at him, which made the man worse. A filler was left undone, fuel splashed everywhere, the rear axle jack worked but that for the front failed to lift the wheels clear, and another had to be obtained – little checks which nearly drove the driver to a frenzy.

Finally, the starter refused. The mechanic, using a spanner as a switch, set his glove and overalls alight with a spark from the terminal, but smothered the flames instantly, and then there was difficulty with the bonnet strap. Altogether a calamitous 7m 15s elapsed.[16]

This explains how Nuvolari got into the lead on lap 20 – Hamilton close behind – and explains the position at 2.30pm.

Nuvolari	77.0mph	(123.9kph)
Hamilton	72.0mph	(+ 47s)
Rose-Richards	79.5mph	(+ 1m 48s)
Dixon	72.2mph	(+ 6m 12s)

I suspect that, in the excitement of the race and the handicap (to any race reader) of the handicap itself, the people on the scoreboard had little idea what was happening – and neither did anybody else. *Ireland's Saturday Night* complained that 'the scoring board organisation right from the start left much to be desired. Not only was there considerable delay in the posting of the leaders and handicaps at the time at which they should have appeared, but a certain amount of the information disseminated was extremely misleading.'

It's easy to comprehend that Hamilton lost the time rather than Nuvolari gaining it, but that still doesn't explain how Nuvolari lost the four minutes in the first place. Never mind. Nuvolari did a lap of 80.2mph (129.0kph) – 10m 13s – a new class record. The 3.00pm positions were not announced until 3.20pm, which surely betrays the chaos.

Nuvolari	77.4mph	(124.5kph)
Hamilton	72.4mph	(+ 22s)
Rose-Richards	79.8mph	(+ 2m 12s)

The fact that Nuvolari had taken the lead on the 20th lap was not announced until the 26th...

Rose-Richards in the big Alfa Romeo now did fastest lap of the day with 9m 52s (83.0mph/133.56kph) but Nuvolari responded with another class record, 10m 11s (80.4mph/ 129.3kph). At 3.30pm:

Nuvolari	77.7mph	(125.0kph)
Hamilton	72.8mph	(+ 9s)
Rose-Richards	80.1mph	(+ 2m 41s)

Interest was renewed that Nuvolari would be coming into the pits. This caused pit manager Hugh McConnell to hoist a signal to the effect that Nuvolari had 10s in hand over Hamilton, and also to lay out the pit counter in meticulous order. The impending visit, however, did not materialise, everything, judging by the driver's signals, being all right with the Magnette. It seemed like it, at any rate, because the engine was showing 6500rpm on the Newtownards-Comber straight, which is equivalent to 112–115mph (180–185kph).[17]

Hamilton was now racing at or near his limit because he overshot the Dundonald hairpin. Nuvolari might have been in trouble, too, because at the Moate, Hall hit the bank and that pitched him across the road just as Nuvolari was pulling out to overtake him. Nuvolari's reflexes were fast enough to make the Magnette miss him, although both men showed they had their wits about them.

That this had no effect on the little Italian was shown when his next lap put the 1100cc record up to 80.8mph (130.0kph) and a little afterwards he reached 81.0, which challenge Hamilton answered with a lap of 77.2, which is wonderful for a 750cc.[18]

Nuvolari answered that with a lap of 81.4mph (130.9kph) – another record. Both pits were holding 'flat out' boards to their drivers. At 4.15pm the gap was the same, and at 4.30pm:

Nuvolari	78.2mph	(125.8kph)
Hamilton	73.2mph	(+ 39s)

This is a further mystery. As *The Motor* said, 'excitement was intense because on handicap Hamilton was 54s ahead.' How could Hamilton be 39 seconds behind Nuvolari and simultaneously 54 seconds ahead? The handicap does not explain this because Hamilton was in front of Nuvolari on the road. *Ireland's Saturday Night* weighed in with: 'unofficial timing showed Hamilton to be 56s ahead of Nuvolari, although the latter was shown as leading on handicap. The question everyone was asking now was – could the Italian wipe out the deficit in the course of [the final] two laps?' Presumably this means *could Nuvolari physically catch and overtake Hamilton, never mind the handicap?*

Picture, instead, the strip of road leading to the grandstands and pits. This road curves gently to the left and, fringed by trees and hedgerows, might almost be a country lane. The crowd craned and saw Hamilton's MG Midget with its number 25 coming towards them, intent on travelling fast into his final lap. As he approached the crowd could see his mechanic signalling that they were coming in to the pits. The car had virtually run out of fuel.

The crowd craned again and here was Nuvolari's MG with its number 17.

As Hamilton's Midget was being refuelled Nuvolari went past – and he'd just done 81.4mph (130.9kph). Hamilton set off after him and excited voices over the loudspeakers described the climax: at Bradshaw's Brae and Newtownards he was 27s behind, the Moate 25, Comber 24, Ballystockart 25 again, Dundonald 36 – the race decided.

Picture now the MG coming down that long left to where the man with the chequered flag stood. Nuvolari passed him and as he did, the mechanic's hand was out from the side of the car, a gesture of purest exhilaration. When the car drew level with the pits, slowing, Nuvolari raised his right arm to acknowledge the crowd. Then he stopped – he was completely out of fuel. He had to be refilled to do the lap of honour.

He'd won by 40 seconds.

When he got out of the car he looked fresh and, surrounded by well-wishers, spoke a few words in Italian. He said it had been an honour to take part in something so sporting. When a huge garland was draped over his head he smiled broadly and a great cheer went up. He acknowledged it with a polite wave of his right hand, and the smile broadened.

The prize giving was at a dance that Saturday night and an immense crowd went to try and get into it. There's a lovely story recounted[19] by Doreen Ferguson, who lives in a farm beside the circuit. She says that when the races began there was an advert in the paper for accommodation for the teams and drivers. Her aunt May was 'a very keen driver herself and she had Nuvolari staying with her. Blow me if she didn't take him to the prize-giving in her own car!'

One of the speeches contained these words: 'The race was won by Nuvolari by driving and sportsmanship such as has seldom been seen anywhere.' The Duke of Abercorn presented the prizes and Nuvolari made a speech of thanks, again in Italian of course.

The Chronicle discovered that during the race a 'flock of chickens' had got onto the course but were 'arrested' by a policeman. At the Square a little girl emerged from the crowd and wandered onto the course. When a policeman reached her she looked up at him and burst into tears.

Meanwhile, the *Belfast Telegraph* carried virtually a whole column (of small type, and this on a broadsheet size page) under the headline 'LADIES' VIEWPOINT'. It began:

> *The T.T. Race is the greatest popular social event in all Ireland. It is, in fact, one of the few popular social events because it affords amusement and thrills to all, rich and poor, young and old. It affords also amusement to both sexes, and the thrill for the ladies is not confined to the fact that they will see and be seen by everybody. They are really interested in the race itself.*
>
> *Her Grace the Duchess of Abercorn, whose arrival with the Governor was the occasion for an outburst of cheers, was accompanied by the Marchioness of Hamilton. The Duchess wore a long coat of navy in fine nap cloth over a dark gown. The scarf was of white and pale blue and her small hat of navy silk straw. Her daughter-in-law was wearing a neat costume of dark brown cloth.*

If you want to know how far the world has moved since 1933, that paragraph tells you. It also tells you much about the world Nuvolari inhabited and why people behaved as they did.

The man himself has left us an immortal postscript. Someone asked him what the brakes on the MG were like and he replied he had no idea, he'd hardly used them.

The result:

Nuvolari	5h 56m 34s (78.6mph/126.4kph)
Hamilton	5h 57m 14s
Rose-Richards	6h 10m 6s
Dixon	6h 11m 50s
Hall	6h 12m 14s
Earl Howe	6h 18m 1s

* * * * *

Intermezzo

A week after Ards, Nuvolari finished second in the Italian Grand Prix at Monza and completed the season at San Sebastian, Spain, with a nasty crash when he hit a wall.

He crashed again early in 1934, rolling his Maserati at Alessandria. He'd recount that 'a heavy rain was falling, and my car was hard to hold. On braking at the approach to a bridge, with a curve in front, my car skidded and overturned, crashing into a tree. I... was pretty well shaken up.' He'd fractured his left leg, and thereby hangs a tale.

A couple of years later, after he'd won the Coppa Ciano at Livorno, a journalist noticed him limping and in obvious pain. Nuvolari pointed to the Alessandria crash and explained that sometimes he had to have an automatic gearbox: his leg was still so damaged he couldn't work the clutch pedal – meaning, I assume, he couldn't exercise the sensitivity he needed. He said: 'I might be limping but I am anything but finished. In fact, I think I'm just at the start!'

In the background, he and Enzo Ferrari were moving together again and, as Brock Yates writes, they 'engaged in lengthy second-hand negotiations. Jano acted as emissary, delivering by letter, by phone and in person a series of demands and counter-demands to the two headstrong parties. Nuvolari remained at his villa near Mantua and Ferrari in Modena.'

By temperament, both men were accustomed to getting their own way, and because of what they were – in terms of what they had to offer – they invariably got it. Now they were in a situation where both needed something the other one had. The result was the answer to that age-old conundrum of what happens when an irresistible force hits an immovable object: compromise.

Finally, after a meeting on neutral ground in Piacenza, roughly midway between Modena and Milan, a deal was put in place. René Dreyfus, who was his teammate that year [1935], recalls that in addition to a generous salary, Nuvolari received 50 per cent of the winnings. Because he was the junior member, Dreyfus was given 45 per cent of the purse but was required to absorb all his personal expenses. Nuvolari would lead the Scuderia Ferrari – and Alfa Romeo – into battle in 1935.

And this would be a battle. Gone were the elegant amateurs of the early days. Now the Scuderia was a bare-boned, hard-muscled professional racing operation. This immediately became apparent to outsiders like Dreyfus.' (And, in a revealing phrase or two, Dreyfus would subsequently describe the contrast between driving for Ferrari and Bugatti as total. At Ferrari, Dreyfus discovered the 'business' of racing.)

In 1935, Nuvolari won the Grand Prix of Pau in Ferrari's Alfa Romeo, retired at Monaco (a brake problem) and was fourth at Tripoli. In July he took the car to the most fearsome circuit of all, the one which made Ards look like a Sunday afternoon run in the countryside. He went to the Nürburgring and only one thing seemed certain. Against the mighty Mercedes and Auto Unions, he'd get the mother and father of a beating. The Germans were so confident of their superiority that they'd had the winner's garland made for a big man – whichever Germans won the race – and for the victory ceremony had provided no national anthem other than their own.

8

Triumph of the Will

— *German Grand Prix 1935* —

SLOWLY it began, and in the most gentlemanly way. That stands in wonderful contrast to what would follow, and what would follow belongs almost exclusively – and forever – to Nuvolari, although it involved, as the saying goes, a cast of thousands.

Just the other day I was talking to Murray Walker about the structure of the book and, immediately and unprompted, he said 'You have got the Ring '35 in there, haven't you?' 'Yes,' I said, about 10,000 words on it.' 'Good!' he said.

But let's keep to the original pace and reach towards Nuvolari's role in this epic event slowly.

At Dieppe on Saturday 20 July some 19 starters took part in a 1500cc race. Dieppe was then one of those French coastal resorts where elderly British ladies went to take the air, and this race had a particularly British feel to it. Earl Howe was among the 19 and so were young Dick Seaman, Pat Fairfield, Raymond Mays, a Mrs G. Stewart (wife of the head of Automobiles Derby) and 'B. Bira', a Siamese prince based in Britain and competing here in an ERA he'd just been given for his 21st birthday. Fairfield covered 30 laps in two hours and won. Next

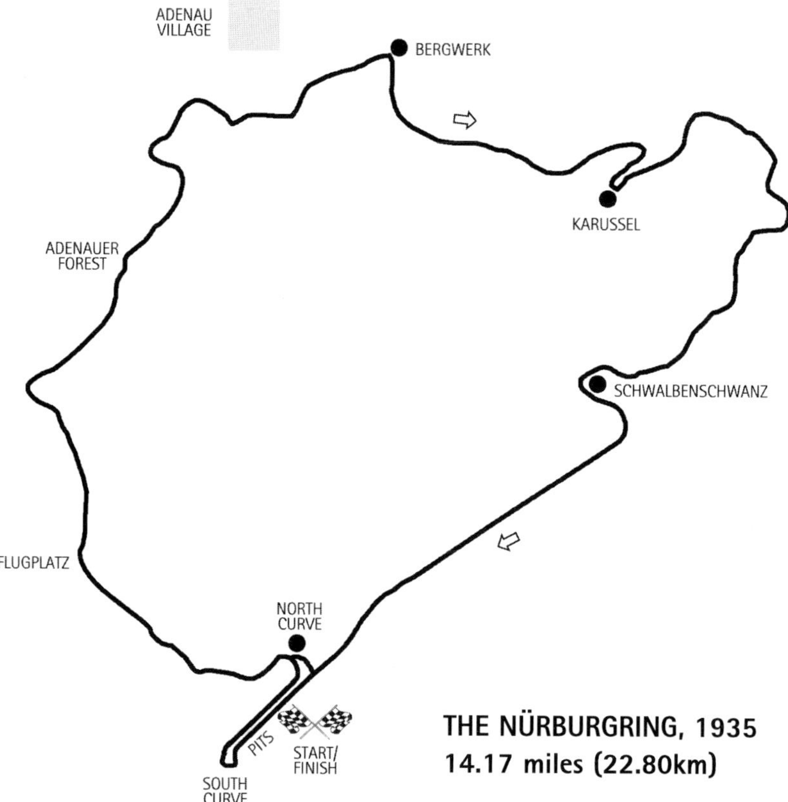

THE NÜRBURGRING, 1935
14.17 miles (22.80km)

day, Dreyfus driving an Alfa Romeo took the Formule Libre race, Hans Ruesch finishing sixth.

Mays, who also had an ERA, had travelled to Dieppe with a car designer and friend, Peter Berthon, and his description captures how gentlemanly it was. 'Followed my usual final tests down the fen road, last-minute adjustments, then the checking and packing of spares and cars, and so to Newhaven.'[1]

After the race Mays and Peter Berthon set off for home and 'once across the sea' the Bentley transported them to Bourne, the ERA factory in Lincolnshire, in 'an incredibly quick time'. There, work was being carried out on a new 2-litre car which Mays would race at the Nürburgring in the German Grand Prix. He cannot have known that it would be one of the most extraordinary races ever run: a single man pitted against a mighty nation.

The race represented a centre for something approaching an annual pilgrimage by an immense number of enthusiasts, and to represent that I propose to cite the memories of Günter Molter, subsequently journalist and author. Molter, then a 15-year-old motor racing fanatic, set off on his bicycle towards the Nürburgring, some 150 miles away. 'Lashed to my bike were a sleeping bag, a cooking stove and some food.'[2]

Because the 2-litre car was new, Mays decided to run it in on the journey to the race. Small wings were fitted, 'a hooter and a large fish tail, and drove her by road to Harwich'. Berthon drove behind in the Bentley. When they reached Harwich they were 'joined by the two Bedford vans, one containing the second 2-litre which the German driver von Delius was to drive.'

That was the Wednesday, which was also the first day of practice. The hours were as they would be on the Thursday and Friday (9am to 12pm and 3pm to 6pm) with a single session (9am to 2pm) on the Saturday. These sessions were truly practice: you went to the circuit when you wanted and did what you wanted.

Molter arrived but headed for a hotel near the town of Nürburg. He knew that the Mercedes team had its headquarters there. In a fenced area round the garages he saw Neubauer orchestrating everything. Molter's eyes feasted on the cars, the mechanics, the engineers, even the transporters. And they feasted, too, on Hermann Lang – like any youngster seeing one of the gods. The engines were started and to him they sounded like 'a kind of music.'

Ruesch, then only 22, can't remember which day he travelled – he must have arrived on the Tuesday – or whether he went with his girlfriend Marisa, who owned two road cars, one of them a Fiat. The travelling from race to race became a constant and a blur, each journey exhausting on narrow roads – 'there were no autobahns except in Germany. In the 1930s I lived mainly at my girlfriend's house in Milan and I'd get to the Nürburgring in her car. I was always in her car and I practically lived in it.' If the Nürburgring had been a new circuit to Ruesch he'd have driven round it to learn its secrets but, because he'd been there so often, he made his way straight to the Eifeler Hof Hotel in the nearby hamlet of Adenau.

So did Paul Pietsch, who'd be handling an Auto-Union. 'Once you'd been round the Nürburgring four or five times you had a pretty exact knowledge of it.' Whether Pietsch travelled there with his wife Ilse is unclear because she had, in his own words, fallen in love with Achille Varzi – also due to drive an Auto Union in Germany.

To reach Adenau you followed the narrow, contorting road across the middle of the circuit – some four kilometres – and went under a bridge at the far side, where Adenau began. The track went over the bridge and if anyone glanced up they could see it rearing away into the trees like a wild roller coaster.

The drivers always stayed at the Eifeler Hof and a ritual accompanied this: the manager, Paul Bergmann, knew which rooms they wanted: Nuvolari number 26 on the second floor, big double bed and bath, Rosemeyer 39, although Caracciola wanted a different room every race. Evidently this time Caracciola had 27 while Neubauer was next door at 28 and Fagioli next door to that at 29.[3]

Late one afternoon, Molter went there to try and get autographs, was successful, and still had them half a century later.

Even if Ruesch did take Marisa 'it was not so much of a problem booking in to an hotel [as an unmarried couple] in Germany, but in Italy it was not good.'

The Eifeler Hof is closed now, considered unsafe, and all we can do is imagine its solid decorum unchanging from year to year, the subtle interplay between the drivers meeting in the dining room or on the stairs, and conversations long forgotten.

Ruesch's Maserati was taken in a converted American Dodge which his mechanic drove. When that arrived at the circuit the Maserati was put in a lock-up garage overnight. 'We were assigned a one-car garage. There was all kinds of rivalry and, of course, we didn't trust people,' Ruesch says. 'My mechanic had orders to sleep in the garage. The mechanic was to sleep there to be sure that dear fellow competitors did not put sugar in the petrol…'

Neubauer, in *Speed was my Life,* describes the Varzi-Ilse Pietsch love affair discreetly by giving Pietsch and Ilse pseudonyms: Lil and Peter.

> *The 'friendship' between Varzi and Lil was now a general subject of conversation, even among the mechanics. The only one who did not seem to realise what was going on, who was completely wrapped up in racing cars, was Peter. But the day soon came when he had his eyes opened.*

Early on the Thursday morning (7.55am) a Herr Martin, working for the Mercedes Press Department, telephoned headquarters to report what had happened on the Wednesday: Geier and Lang had been present as well as reserve driver Gartner and Hartmann. In the afternoon von Brauchitsch did a few fast laps and towards the end Ruesch and Rosemeyer also went out. The crowd, reportedly, was already substantial, as it would be on each practice day. The pilgrims had journeyed not only from the Rhineland but from all over Germany, from Holland, France, Belgium and Britain, too.

Molter, watching practice from near the pits, could identify all the cars and drivers easily – although all the drivers tended to dress the same except Nuvolari, 'non-conformist as usual in yellow shirt, light blue cotton trousers and a brown leather jacket.'

On the Friday afternoon von Delius took the ERA out and, as Mays would remember, did some fast laps. He pitted for adjustments and they went out together. Mays felt his car was now properly run in and followed von Delius round the 'sinister' circuit – it is Mays's own word. The 'extra torque' of the 2-litre engines created a specific problem when he accelerated out of those corners which were both quick and uneven. Mays watched von Delius and saw he was going well, could even see his rear-axle 'juddering and jumping.'

In the climb after Adenau – approximately from where the road beneath led to the village – the circuit twists and turns. Von Delius naturally moved out of sight. Mays pressed on and took a fast left-hander at, he estimated, some 80mph. Emerging from it onto a straight he saw 'dust and earth flying and people rushing in all directions.' When he reached all this he looked over to the left and now he saw the 'radiator of a car through the shrubbery.' He braked and brought his car to a halt, and hurried there to help.[4]

The car seemed to have struck a tree very hard and come to rest up a bank at an acute angle. Within moments spectators had surrounded it, some touching it. Mays 'hardly dared approach' and for the most human of reasons: a glance had shown him the back of the car crumpled and a tree angled across the cockpit. However, amazingly, he found von Delius 'sitting down' – presumably beside what remained of the car – concussed but otherwise unhurt.

The incident does not have a direct bearing on Nuvolari, but it does have an indirect one because it demonstrates how difficult and dangerous the circuit was. Von Delius had, evidently, misjudged his speed in the fast corner and his car had spun several times before going off. Then – backwards – it struck the tree.

As Mays would remember, von Delius had enjoyed an escape which bordered on the miraculous because on that side of the circuit there was a ravine and a single tree – it had protected von Delius from the ravine.

Nor was von Delius alone in being fortunate near here because the engine of Taruffi's Bugatti blew up on the descent to Adenau, spreading a lot of oil on the track. Taruffi remembered:

> *... as soon as I realised what had happened I pulled on to the verge and ran back to warn other drivers. I was too late to warn the first car. Rosemeyer's Auto Union hit the oil and went into a terrifying slide – but Rosemeyer held it, leaving me amazed at the quickness of his reactions and the way he got the car under control.*[5]

Mays subsequently offered to share his car with von Delius but then it developed a crankshaft problem. For a time both ERAs were out of the race but then Berthon discovered that von Delius's engine was undamaged. The mechanics worked through Saturday night taking the Mays engine out and replacing it with the von Delius engine.

On the Saturday, according to Neubauer, Varzi crashed and through that the love affair between him and Ilse Pietsch became extremely public.

> *Among those in the Auto Union pit were Peter and Lil. Suddenly the telephone rang and the racing-manager [Willy] Walb lifted the receiver. There was a hush. A voice could be heard at the other end of the line:*
>
> *'Varzi's car has left the track and crashed.'*
>
> *A stop-watch dropped to the ground with a clatter, and Hans Stuck, who noticed Lil had gone pale, helped her to a chair. Then came the news that Varzi's car had been wrecked, but that he himself was unhurt. There was a general sigh of*

relief and the clamour of voices broke out again. Only young Peter stood staring, white-faced, at his wife. The truth had suddenly dawned on him.[6]

On the Saturday, too, the Mercedes operation to maximise hospitality and publicity began. Journalists from all over Bavaria, for example – including the *Stürmer* magazine (an anti-Semitic weekly) – would be transported to the Nürburgring in five cars, departing the Grand Hotel in Nuremburg at 9.00am sharp, lunching at 12.20pm at the Gasthaus Bavaria in the town of Aschaffenburg, departing at 1.30pm. They'd have a 'coffee pause' at Darmstadt, arriving at 2.30pm and leaving precisely one hour later; they'd stop for a glass of dry white wine not far from Frankfurt, then press on through Adenau to the Hotel Mayer-Hauser in Antweiler 30 kilometres away, arriving at 'approximately' 9.00pm. Of itself, this convoy is perhaps unimportant, but what it represents – the scale, scope and seriousness of the operation in the context of 1930s motor racing – is not. And the fact that they were in an hotel 30 kilometres away suggests no accommodation had been available any nearer for a long time before the race.

The German Grand Prix *was* an immensity just as the Nürburgring was mighty and somehow monstrous. Unconsciously the place and its scale were perfectly suited to Nazi pageantry and the Nazi rituals of Hitler salutes, swastikas and uniformed men patrolling the grid. A German driver would win in a German car, that was clear. The winner's floral garland had, as I've said, been made large to suit whichever of the big, strong German drivers won it.

The times drivers set on these practice days were irrelevant for grid position because that was decided by lots and, anyway, with a race over 22 laps – 501km/311 miles – on such a circuit, there was ample time and distance for grid positions to become irrelevant, too.

The organisers proposed a novel way of allocating grid positions – they would be decided by an 'acceleration test' of 1,400 metres from the starting line to the South Curve and then to a line on the straight after that – behind the pits. The idea was to make sure the quicker cars began the race at the front of the grid and didn't burst through the slower cars. The drivers didn't like the 'test' because the North Curve looked too close to the finishing line and if drivers were forcing their cars to maximum speed they risked going over the banking. The organisers gave way and it was back to drawing lots – but, however constituted and projected, the essence of what would happen was absolutely clear. The Germans were going to win a crushing victory.

There were five Mercedes with engines of just under four litres (von Brauchitsch, Caracciola, Fagioli, Hermann Lang and Hans Geier); four Auto Unions at 4.9 litres (Hans Stuck, Bernd Rosemeyer, Varzi and Pietsch). These were all immensely powerful, sophisticated machines.

Against them Nuvolari had an old Alfa Romeo. Thereby hangs a mystery and a mythology. How old was the old Alfa really? Nuvolari, evidently, was anxious that people didn't get a good look at its engine.

People asked him if he'd expected to win but he replied 'I was convinced that I would race an excellent race. After Montlhéry I said to Jano we needed to prepare an excellent car because the Nürburgring is a very difficult circuit with very high speeds and our car has to be manoeuvrable. That's why I arrived at the German Grand Prix with my old single-seater, but greatly improved and adapted for this race.'

Tyre wear would be relevant. At the end of the practising, the chief technician of Continental Tyres, Karl Dietrich, examined those on Caracciola's and von Brauchitsch's cars because both drivers had recorded fast times. Caracciola's showed normal wear, Dietrich concluded, although the left rear was slightly more worn than the right rear because that was the one taking the most load in the corners. Dietrich predicted Caracciola would need only one set for the race.

However, the wear on von Brauchitsch's tyres was much more pronounced, especially the left rear. Before Dietrich would allow this tyre to be removed he showed how it had been worn to the canvas inner-tubing. He spoke to von Brauchitsch and Neubauer, with two journalists listening in. Dietrich predicted that von Brauchitsch would need two stops and, even with those, von Brauchitsch's ruthless style of driving might bring danger.

Two races would be run simultaneously, intertwining only each time the mighty were lapping the meek. Everyone expected Nuvolari would make a brave but obviously futile attempt to stay with the Germans while the rest tried to stay out of their way. The rest were Chiron and Dreyfus (to be replaced by Marquis Antonio Brivio) in the other Alfas;

five privateer Maseratis (Ruesch, Zehender, Etancelin, Italian motorcycle rider Pietro Ghersi and Hartmann), Taruffi in the Bugatti and the Mays/von Delius ERA.

The grid (with race numbers):

11 Balestrero (Alfa Romeo)	12 Nuvolari (Alfa Romeo)	1 Stuck (Auto Union)
7 Von Brauchitsch (Mercedes)	16 Zehender (Maserati)	
14 Chiron (Alfa Romeo)	5 Caracciola (Mercedes)	17 Etancelin (Maserati)
10 Mays (ERA)	21 Ruesch (Maserati)	
6 Fagioli (Mercedes)	3 Rosemeyer (Auto Union)	2 Varzi (Auto Union)
4 Pietsch (Auto Union)	20 Hartmann (Maserati)	
23 Taruffi (Bugatti)	9 Lang (Mercedes)	22 Ghersi (Maserati)
15 Brivio (Alfa Romeo)	8 Geier (Mercedes)	

The full system of autobahns did not yet exist and the immense crowd, estimated at between 250,000 and 300,000, came mostly by motor vehicle along the tortuous road following the valley of the River Ahr after turning off the main road 40 kilometres away. In addition, the German railways (the Reichsbahn) laid on 20 special trains. If Count Lurani[7] is to be believed:

... all through the night... the road from Cologne to Adenau

was flooded with rivers of light pouring from the thousands of cars whose occupants wanted to find the best positions on the Eifel terraces. The German public took the occasion to camp out even when the weather was inclement. To the smell of the asphalt which had been almost entirely relaid around the curves... was added the sharp odours of fried sausages and beer.

The *Volkisher Beobachter* newspaper reported that 'as early as Saturday night the roads far beyond Adenau were jammed by long queues of cars, pedestrians, motorcycles and bicycles. Number plates from different European countries could be seen. Car parks mushroomed around the starting area.' Camp fires were burning and – this was years before portable radios, of course – people sang to harmonicas.

Molter had been staying in a hay barn at a farm near Adenau, paying the farmer a few pfennigs per night. On the night before the race, even the barn had filled.

A newspaper in Koblenz carried a headline which distilled what everybody felt about the race: 'MERCEDES-BENZ OR AUTO UNION?' That any driver or car other than these two might win was an absurdity.

Rain threatened – it had rained overnight – as the drivers woke and began their preparations. Pietsch, who must have had much on his mind, put on his overalls, 'the material better than those worn by mechanics,' and ordinary, everyday shoes. 'Special driving shoes did not exist.' He picked up his gloves, which had leather palms and leather strips down the back of the fingers, and his cotton cap. 'Helmets were worn a bit, but that was only around 1938–1939.' He knew that by the race's end his hands would be raw, despite the leather of the gloves. He went down to breakfast thinking, as he always did, about what he feared: 'living as a cripple or an invalid. Just one moment in the race might be enough for that.'

Manfred von Brauchitsch, a strong man with a handsome, almost imperious face, woke and gazed out of the window to see what the weather was like. He relaxed in a warm bath and found he was having 'sinister' thoughts about what might happen in the race. Then he reflected ruefully that the thousands who'd come overnight were looking forward to a nice day in the countryside whereas he'd be working hard and nobody seemed interested in how he felt.

He put powder on his feet, then pulled on his socks and shoes. He fixed the collar and zip of his overalls with safety pins to stop them flapping open as the headwind tore at them during the race. He stuck plasters on his hands because changing gear had chafed the skin during the practice days. He went down but didn't eat much breakfast. Leaving the hotel he realised he'd forgotten a chestnut given him by a 'charming girl' for luck after yesterday's final practice. He hastened back into the Eifeler Hof to get it.

Nuvolari said: 'The Alfa Romeos are better than is generally assumed but the two German constructors are much ahead of us – although now that our cars are fully developed, as it were, the situation has become a bit more favourable. However we will have a particularly hard time here, especially as it seems there is no doubt Mercedes or Auto Union will win under any circumstances. When there are long distances involved, prediction is difficult although Mercedes carries the main hopes. We'll get the most out of our cars and you can be sure of that.'[8]

At the Hotel Mayer-Hauser in Antweiler, the press group were at breakfast at 7.00am, departing for the circuit at 8.00am. They had printed instructions that, once at the track's parking area, they could disperse but had to meet there again 20 minutes after the race for the long journey home. They'd spend that night at the Dom-Hotel, Cologne, no doubt discussing the German victory.

The race was due to begin at 11.00am.

The drive from Adenau to the pits and paddock – back under the bridge, back across those four kilometres of the narrow road – 'wasn't a problem because,' as Pietsch says, 'most of the crowd were already in their places. One drove quite normally to the track.'

There, as Lurani attests, a panorama of movement had been organised. It was in the

> *... slightly vulgar manner typical of German stage management. A mass of swastika flags fluttered from the flagstaffs on the central stand overlooking the pits. The sound of an aircraft foreshadowed the grand parade. Like a falcon*

the slim shape was seen to dive steeply right over the spot where the various flags were being raised. It was the prototype of the Stuka, an aeroplane still unknown to the world.[9]

Ruesch wasn't impressed by this, by the swastikas and soldiers marching up and down, so many people seemingly in military uniforms. 'You see, we racers – and I'm sure it's true today – didn't see the rest of the world. I didn't see all this Nazi business going on because to me it made no difference. To me a race at the Nürburgring was a race at the Nürburgring whether there was Hitler or no Hitler. To me, the interest was in the race and what I could do, if I had a chance to win – or if I didn't. The result was the only thing we were interested in. I only learned from the newspapers the day after that there were hundreds of thousands of spectators. I couldn't have cared less how many spectators!'

This is contentious, and the more so in 1935. That March, Hitler took possession of the Saarland (occupied by France since World War One); that April, Germany repudiated the Versailles Treaty limiting the size of her armed forces; that May, Hitler broadcast that he would not make arms reductions; that June, the French expressed fury that the British had signed a naval treaty with Hitler; that July, Nazis were beating up Jews along Berlin's main shopping street, and an anti-Semite was made chief of Berlin police the week before the German Grand Prix. And whoever won the race would receive the Führer's Trophy – Hitler's Trophy. Political events formed the background to the race, as to everything else, but it was still possible to ignore – or at least accommodate – them.

Pietsch echoes Ruesch – 'I was a racing driver and the politics didn't interest me. Hitler? Goebbels? I didn't care' – but there remained the matter of accommodating the regime. 'In Italy I didn't give the Nazi salute but as a German when I came back to Germany I had to. I had no choice: if I hadn't done it, that would have meant trouble. Then in Italy Mussolini took over and it got difficult there, too.'

Von Brauchitsch seems to have found the accommodation because when he arrived at the circuit, feeling confident and looking forward to the race, he found an open-topped road car in the paddock and lay down in the back seat, covered by summer coats so curious passers-by wouldn't keep gawping at him. Although all around mechanics worked on the cars and engines were running, von Brauchitsch put earplugs in and dozed off. He had decided he wouldn't sign any autographs before the race.

The *Volkisher Beobachter* reported 'there was a grey sky and a western wind tugged at the huge flags so strongly that their poles bent. A fine country rain made the track wet' (and a mechanic woke von Brauchitsch up!). 'The great day of German motor racing was covered in gloomy light.'

Von Brauchitsch had with him his famous hatbox, where he kept goggles, sunglasses, a pair of old gloves he wore during practice and various odds and ends. He walked to the pits and, preparing for the start, decided not to use new gloves because the old ones were so comfortable.

Neubauer, who as manager of the Mercedes team had a profound professional interest in the opposition, describes the mood in the Auto Union pits as 'almost unbearable'.

> *Stuck was studiously avoiding his deadly rival Varzi, while Peter was also keeping out of his way. Walb, who knew something was wrong, was like a cat on a hot tin roof.*[10]

Adolf Hühnlein, the leading motorsport official (whom it was rumoured had access to Hitler), arrived to cheering from the crowd. Lurani recorded:

> *... the wailing of a siren split the still atmosphere and the loudspeakers announced the arrival of Herr Hühnlein. A burst of applause greeted the appearance of the various cars. Nuvolari... walked in front of his outdated monoposto. Round his neck Tazio wore a small tricoloured scarf, and had substituted a red leather helmet, surmounted with the tortoiseshell motif, for his usual linen helmet.*

In fact Nuvolari also wore an overcoat and, goggles over his forehead, chatted politely with Hühnlein who, of course, was wearing uniform. The *Volkischer Beobachter* carried this (astonishing) paragraph about the 'endless minutes' with the cars waiting on the grid. 'Some drivers prepare thermos flasks for the long drive. This way, they can peacefully have a mouthful of coffee on the way. Rosemeyer even takes a little box containing lemon slices with him.'

How many of them thought, or dreamed, of prize money we can never know (winner 20,000 Reichsmark, then 10,000, 6,000, 4,000, 2,000, 1,000).

Some 500 journalists watched and prepared to report the race. Apart from Germany, they came from France, Belgium, Luxembourg, Holland, England, Sweden, Norway, Denmark, Czechoslovakia, Austria, Switzerland, Hungary, Bulgaria and Italy. Mercedes had invited, as guests, leading motoring officials from Belgium, Barcelona, Norway, Hungary and Czechoslovakia. Yes, fascination with the German Grand Prix covered the continent.

On the grid Ruesch wasn't frightened. 'Why should I have been? The Nürburgring was dangerous but not more dangerous than other circuits. Let's take Alessandria [in northern Italy]. I had my accident there and Nuvolari broke his leg in a Maserati. That was a town: they took certain streets and made them into a circuit whereas the Nürburgring was built as a racing circuit.'

Pietsch wasn't frightened, either. 'Death? You believed that it would not happen to you and didn't think about it. When it did happen you were sorry but that still didn't make you think it would happen to you. If you had sat there in your car thinking today I am going to die you would have stopped racing.' He prepared, knowing the brakes would be an important factor: 'very hard and not very good.'

Lang, so new to Mercedes, would explain that Neubauer didn't expect him or Geier – the other newcomer – to win. 'To beat the "aces" was impossible, as yet. But I had to beat someone and it would have to be Geier.'[11]

Nuvolari was in a different position. As Motor Revue described it, on the 'front row, a small, wiry man, all of 1.55m high and 43 years old, leant against the red Alfa Romeo with starting number 12 – he was one of the eldest of those who were going to go on the dangerous trip. Many considered him the greatest driver of all time, nobody ever doubted that he was the most vivacious and boldest. His lean, angular face was dominated by its bent nose and distinctive chin. Two years ago, he had had himself carried into his car for several weeks because his left leg was in plaster after an accident, which could have happened to him again this season, when in the Grand Prix of Pau he had to jump out of his burning car at a speed of little less than 100kph to prevent himself from going up in flames. But his constitution was that of a bull. He slept 12 hours a day, he didn't drink, he hardly ate meat but lots of fruits, eggs and vegetables and he took long walks.'

> *He was driven by a will that was often stronger than the car he was driving. Sometimes you would see him passing the pits, angrily pounding his fists against the side of his car, as if he wanted to encourage it to give more. He was nobody to go easy on engines...*[12]

A strange and very personal mystery was being played out amid the might of the gathering anticipation. A blonde woman stood in the pits, stopwatch in hand, watching one of the drivers intently. The driver seemed serious and that worried her because normally he was funny and good-humoured. She wondered if, last night, she had asked him things she shouldn't have done. Before he fell asleep, she asked him about the blue and white striped scarf he always wore during races. The scarf was given to him by a woman long ago, but he never spoke about her.

With two minutes to go, the driver got out of his car, hurried to a hut and returned to the car. She wondered why.

Someone tapped Nuvolari on the shoulder and wished him good luck. 'I think the weather may improve today,' he said. Nuvolari's son Giorgio watched from the Alfa Romeo pit and his wife watched from the stands.

Raymond Mays, on the fourth row of the grid but with the Mercedes of von Brauchitsch and Caracciola virtually in line in front of him, would remember the engines being fired up, would remember the Mercedes's scream and the Auto Union's roar. Cumulatively he found them 'quite frightening.' Compounding that, the special fuel the Mercedes used had the pungent odour of boot polish and 'acted like tear gas.' Mays called out to his mechanic – '*handkerchief! handkerchief!*' – because the tear gas made his eyes stream.[13]

Still the fine rain fell and mist hung in the distant trees. The Nürburgring brooded. The start was controlled by lights, rather than an official dropping a flag, for the first time. A red light came on holding the grid immobile. A yellow light came on indicating 15 seconds to go. Stuck's Auto Union stuttered forward as he switched his engine on. Then a green light: go. At precisely that instant Stuck's engine stalled and his mechanics sprinted to help him even as the cars surged away. One of the mechanics – Friedrich – was struck by Varzi's rear wheel, fracturing the base of his skull. Varzi, a 'sensitive, introverted and highly strung man (after each race his mechanic had to bring him a lighted cigarette) was not able to get in form again.'[14]

Caracciola's Mercedes just shoots clear of the pack, and Nuvolari with his Alfa is so close to Fagioli's Mercedes that the scarlet and silver wheels almost touch. Spray is flung high, and car after car hurtles past, while the crowds in the stand leap to their feet amid cries of 'Hinsitzen!' ('Sit down!')[15]

Pietsch had stalled, too, so that of the four Auto Unions three were at the back of the field. Caracciola led from Nuvolari, Fagioli, von Brauchitsch and Mays. The more powerful cars behind Mays were surging past by the North Curve and, although the ERA had 'pretty formidable' power Mays's pit orders were to take it easy.

On the big electronic scoreboard by the pits the figure 5 lit up. Caracciola was number 5, of course, and it meant he was leading at Schwalbenschwanz, the horseshoe before the long, long run to the start–finish line. The vast crowd watched Caracciola come into view and cross the line into the second lap.

Caracciola	12m 07.2s	
Nuvolari	12m 19.4s	+ 12.2s
Fagioli	12m 21.0s	+ 13.8s
Rosemeyer	12m 23.0s	+ 15.8s
Von Brauchitsch	12m 24.2s	+17.0s
Chiron	12m 29.1s	+ 21.9s
Brivio	12m 37.1s	+ 29.9s

I've included Chiron and Brivio because they were both driving

Alfa Romeos and although the gap from them to Caracciola is not yet a chasm, compare it with Nuvolari: almost double. Mays pitted, briefly.

Deep into the second lap Rosemeyer 'devoured'[16] Fagioli and Nuvolari. Meanwhile Brivio's transmission failed, leaving only two Alfas – Balastrero had crashed on lap one. Already the race was assuming a shape: Rosemeyer, a driver of courage and consummate touch – some speak of him on a level with Nuvolari – forcing his Auto Union into the phalanx of Mercedes while Nuvolari, outpowered on the straights, danced his Alfa up the hills and down the dales, gained in the corners. This was brave fare from a born racer but ultimately would surely prove to be useless. Lap 2 seemed to show that because Nuvolari even let Chiron past him.

Caracciola	24m 04.1s	
Rosemeyer	24m 16.4s	+ 12.3s
Von Brauchitsch	24m 27.4s	+ 23.3s
Fagioli	24m 31.3s	+ 27.2s
Chiron	24m 35.4s	+ 31.3
Nuvolari	24m 46.4s	+ 42.3s

Why Nuvolari slowed his pace to this extent remains a mystery but it is fair to surmise that the crowd now regarded him as essentially out of the race. How could an ancient car hope to regain 42 seconds against all the brutish German power? Chiron was still in front of him as they came round again.

Caracciola	35m 52.2s	
Rosemeyer	35m 59.1s	+ 6.9s
Fagioli	36m 22.3s	+ 23.2s
Von Brauchitsch	36m 23.4s	+ 24.3s
Chiron	36m 32.3s	+ 33.2s
Nuvolari	36m 51.2s	+ 52.1s

Astonishingly, Chiron got past von Brauchitsch on lap 4.

Caracciola	47m 30.4s	
Rosemeyer	47m 34.4s	+ 04.0s
Fagioli	48m 01.2s	+ 30.8s
Chiron	48m 16.2s	+ 45.8s
Von Brauchitsch	48m 17.3s	+ 46.9s
Nuvolari	48m 40.0s	+ 1m 09.6s

Equally astonishingly, Chiron held von Brauchitsch at bay across lap

5 although by now it seemed that the race *had* assumed its shape, with Caracciola maintaining a steady lead.

Caracciola	59m 04.4s	
Rosemeyer	59m 10.0s	+ 5.6s
Fagioli	59m 49.1s	+ 44.7s
Chiron	59m 52.4s	+ 48.0s
Von Brauchitsch	1h 0m 2.4s	+ 58.0s
Nuvolari	1h 0m 16.1s	+ 1m 11.7s

Chiron's transmission failed. He travelled 'slowly past the back of the pits and the scarlet Alfa comes to a stop at the next corner. Chiron climbs sadly from his car and walks back to his pit, while the crowd cheer him. He is a popular favourite. He gesticulates excitedly as his mechanics question him, but the battle is over for another Italian car.'[17] Of the three Alfa Romeos, only Nuvolari's was still running. Lap 6:

Caracciola	1h 10m 42.3s	
Rosemeyer	1h 11m 10.1s	+ 27.8s
Fagioli	1h 11m 31.0s	+ 48.7s
Von Brauchitsch	1h 11m 49.2s	+ 1m 06.9s
Nuvolari	1h 11m 57.4s	+ 1m 05.1s

Rosemeyer, as it would seem, was over-driving his Auto Union because he hit a bank. Nuvolari went past him and Rosemeyer pulled into the pits. 'A wheel is not running true, and in an amazingly short space of time it is changed. Mechanics advance a green battery box to the rear of the car and engage a portable electric starter' – something so novel that *The Autocar* thought it worth mentioning.

The Motor saw it a different way. 'Rosemeyer went into the pits, having driven into a ditch and bent his back axle slightly, also driving dirt into the carburettor. He resumed after a long delay.'[18]

Rosemeyer dropped to fifth, and Nuvolari was past von Brauchitsch. The whole shape of the race was changing: Nuvolari accelerated and across the 14 miles would start cutting into Caracciola's lead. Lap 7:

Caracciola	1h 22m 37.4s	
Fagioli	1h 23m 10.1s	+ 32.7s
Nuvolari	1h 23m 25.4s	+ 48.0s
Von Brauchitsch	1h 23m 29.0s	+ 51.6s

Rosemeyer	1h 23m 37.2s	+ 59.8s
Varzi	1h 24m 21.0s	+ 1m 43.6s

Von Brauchitsch responded on the next lap, retaking Nuvolari, and the whole pace of the race was quickening. Caracciola's average times show that, 114.3kph (70.8mph) on lap one but now 116.3. Lap 8:

Caracciola	1h 34m 14.0s	
Fagioli	1h 34m 40.4s	+26.4s
Von Brauchitsch	1h 34m 45.3s	+ 31.3s
Nuvolari	1h 34m 49.0	+ 35.0s
Rosemeyer	1h 34m 54.0s	+ 40.0s
Stuck	1h 36m 12.2s	+ 1m 58.2s

Still the pace quickened and Nuvolari cut loose, taking von Brauchitsch while Fagioli dropped back. As they crossed the line to complete lap 9 the quickening had brought a tightening: not just Nuvolari on to Caracciola but von Brauchitsch onto Nuvolari. More than that, Nuvolari had averaged 124.9kph (77.6mph), the fastest of the race so far.

He'd remember that the race showed a very theatrical side to his own character. He likened himself to a matador entering a bullring. 'We started with a terrible battle between myself and the Germans. As I tried to distance myself from them they tried some amazing acrobatic feats, coming close to me on the grass and at the barriers. The track was strewn with earth and grass. Bits of gravel, thrown up by their rear wheels, were coming at me. Under a very dark sky I could hear the high pitched wail of their engines and see the flames coming out of the exhaust pipes. But I never gave up. My car was gaining ground downhill and on the bends. [At one point] four of us crossed the line almost abreast and next to each other. It was a very scary battle, I must confess.'

Caracciola	1h 45m 39.2s	
Nuvolari	1h 45m 46.4s	+ 7.2s
Von Brauchitsch	1h 45m 48.3s	+ 9.1s
Rosemeyer	1h 45m 56.3s	+ 17.1s
Fagioli	1h 46m 07.0s	+ 27.8s
Stuck	1h 47m 28.2s	+ 1m 49.0s

'As they come back behind the pits the Mercedes [of von Brauchitsch] gets by again but the announcer at the Karussell, almost incoherent with excitement, tell us that at that point the Italian has retaken second place and is close on Caracciola's heels. The excitement in the grandstands is indescribable. People stand up and none has time to cry "sit down!" Nuvolari leads!'[19] Lap 10:

Nuvolari	1h 56m 42.1s	
Caracciola	1h 56m 51.2s	+ 9.1s
Rosemeyer	1h 56m 51.4s	+ 9.3s
Von Brauchitsch	1h 56m 52.3	+ 10.2s
Fagioli	1h 57m 20.0s	+ 37.9s
Stuck	1h 58m 35.2s	+ 1m 53.1s

The tourniquet tightened as they moved into lap 11. Von Brauchitsch's elbow was bleeding from hitting the bodywork of the Mercedes again and again; the palm of his hand had opened up from working the gearstick because he was changing gear so often; the pedals were so hot they were burning his feet, but he was heartened because at certain corners friends had gathered and were urging him on by waving hats they'd put on walking sticks. At one corner he noticed someone holding up a banner to him: 'ATTENTION! DANGER! DRIVE FASTER!'

Von Brauchitsch wondered why he'd had no pit signal, his only contact with the outside world. He asked himself '*have they forgotten me?'* He felt a certain loneliness and then he felt angry. Next time he passed the pit he stuck his tongue out at them.

The loudspeaker bayed that Rosemeyer had passed Caracciola and was second. Caracciola stayed with him and von Brauchitsch lurked immediately behind them. Von Brauchitsch got past Caracciola and Rosemeyer was worrying Nuvolari for the lead itself. One report says that Rosemeyer was 'on Nuvolari's rear wheels.'

As the cars moved into lap 11 the mechanics of the first four cars began to prepare for the pit stops which would come at the end of the lap. When von Brauchitsch passed he saw a board signalling to come in next time. Nuvolari's mechanics were arranging spare wheels and jacks. The Mercedes pit, evidently, was a place of 'orderly activity.'[20]

That the four cars were stopping together provided high drama and might well decide the whole race.

'It is a sight for the gods as mechanics leap to the wheels, and others insert the gigantic funnels for the refills. The Germans are busy with their cars, like ants. Jacks go under, wheels are spun off, churns of fuel emptied in, while hubbub arises from the packed stands.' This *Autocar* report also says that Nuvolari leapt from the Alfa Romeo and walked up and down sucking a lemon. *The Motor's* correspondent saw it differently. 'Chiron helped his team-mate, Nuvolari, to a drink and washed his face.'

A German report, *Motor Revue,* says: 'Nuvolari jumps out of the car, runs to the pit, jumps into the car again, gets out again, puts a water bottle to his lips, shouts something to Chiron, goes to one of the mechanics, jumps into the car again. Under the excitement Chiron does knee-bends, with beseeching movements of his arms while Nuvolari urges the mechanics to hurry...'

When von Brauchitsch stopped, a large towel was thrown over his head and shoulders so that any spilt fuel wouldn't run down his back. Someone handed him new goggles and a wet sponge to clean his face. He knew his old tyres would be carefully examined so that a judgement could be made about whether he'd have to stop again. He also knew that, as a back-up to this, a mechanic with binoculars watched the state of his tyres each time he passed the pit.

His Mercedes was away in 47 seconds and, as he accelerated, he could hear applause above the noise of the engine. Caracciola was next (1m 7s at the pits) and then Rosemeyer (1m 15s) – but Nuvolari's car was stationary. The pressure pump

> *...used to force the fuel into the tank somehow got blocked ... and the operation had to be completed by hand with a funnel. Nuvolari was fuming and poured a whole bottle of mineral water down his throat, swearing and taking it out on the mechanics.*[21]

The refuelling took 2m 14s and as Nuvolari regained the track he was sixth. The race was gone from him, whatever hopes he had nursed before the pit stop. To hold these German cars was hard enough: to regain time from them must surely be impossible. Von Brauchitsch had driven this lap 12 in 10m 33.4s, an average speed of 129.6kph. Lap 12:

Fagioli	2h 19m 42.3s	
Von Brauchitsch	2h 19m 48.4s	+ 6.1s

Rosemeyer	2h 20m 27.1s	+ 44.8s
Caracciola	2h 20m 32.4s	+ 50.1s
Stuck	2h 20m 37.1s	+ 54.8s
Nuvolari	2h 20m 41.4s	+ 59.1s

Neither Fagioli nor Stuck had pitted, of course, but Fagioli would now. The stop lasted 51 seconds and he emerged fifth. Von Brauchitsch now did a 10m 32.0s (averaging 130kph/80.7mph). Behind him, the race was detonating. Nuvolari caught and passed Stuck and Caracciola – and Rosemeyer had a broken petrol pipe. He would have to pit. Nuvolari went past him like the wind and, with Fagioli in the pits, was suddenly second. These things happen in motor races and impossible is always a dangerous word *but*, in an activity measured in seconds and fractions of seconds, Nuvolari was still 1m 9s away – a lifetime. Lap 13:

Von Brauchitsch	2h 30m 22.3s	
Nuvolari	2h 31m 31.3s	+ 1m 9.0s
Rosemeyer	2h 31m 32.0s	+ 1m 9.7s

So Rosemeyer pitted, pressing him back to fifth. Caracciola inherited third place and ran there for the next six laps. He could not live with the pace von Brauchitsch and Nuvolari were setting and progressively fell back.

There is a suggestion that Caracciola had a problem with his brakes because, in the later stages, Stuck caught and passed him. One authority (Cyril Posthumous) describes Caracciola as 'somewhat brakeless'. Worse, he was not well.

Later, Caracciola would complain of 'sudden feelings of weakness' during the race which were so strong that everything went black and he couldn't see the track. He was examined by a doctor and was discovered to have a huge tapeworm (which was removed the day after the race).[22]

I have mentioned Caracciola to show that he was no longer a central part of the drama. That had devolved to von Brauchitsch and Nuvolari. Up to this point I have given the first six after each lap but now – to distill the drama further – I am going to give only the first two. As von Brauchitsch passed the pits, on this lap, Neubauer made a gesture as if he was closing a big suitcase: '*calm down*'. Reportedly Neubauer said 'the lad should not drive like a madman.' Lap 14:

Von Brauchitsch	2h 40m 54.3s	
Nuvolari	2h 42m 20.1s	+ 1m 25.8s

Lurani describes Nuvolari's driving as 'inspired, fearless, untouchable'. He had eight laps to catch von Brauchitsch. History beckoned. Nuvolari prepared to respond – but not quite yet, because von Brauchitsch was going even quicker. Lap 15:

Von Brauchitsch	2h 51m 36.2s	
Nuvolari	2h 53m 03.4s	+1m 27s

Paul Pietsch, running a distant tenth on this 15th lap, sets out the context of the Ring. 'You couldn't see the crowd because you were too busy and you couldn't hear them because the cars were so noisy. You had no idea where you were in the race except when you passed the pits and saw the board. Someone in front of you might have dropped out but you wouldn't know until you saw the board. You knew that, say, you were at least third because two cars were ahead and nobody had overtaken you. Similarly you knew you were in the lead… until Nuvolari came up and went past!' Such mental arithmetic was irrelevant now. Nuvolari knew only von Brauchitsch was ahead, and, in essence, von Brauchitsch knew that only Nuvolari was behind. Lap 16:

Von Brauchitsch	3h 02m 33.3s	
Nuvolari	3h 03m 50.2s	+ 1m 16.9s
	Gained on the lap: 10.1s	

As Nuvolari passed the pits, Decimo Compagnoni 'made a signal, which Tazio acknowledged and went by with his foot hard down'.[23] This signal – if it happened! – can have been little more than camaraderie or encouragement because Nuvolari was at the limit already. Lap 17:

Von Brauchitsch	3h 13m 32.1s	
Nuvolari	3h 14m 35.2s	+ 1m 3.1s
	Gained on the lap: 13.8s	

By now, Neubauer was visibly agitated in the Mercedes pits. At one point Lurani describes him as 'puffing like a pair of bellows'. Evidently Neubauer touched his hat – invariably he wore a homburg – as a form of superstition. Lap 18:

Von Brauchitsch	3h 24m 43.0s	
Nuvolari	3h 25m 20.0s	+ 37.0s
	Gained on the lap: 26.1s	

Von Brauchitsch responded, although he was working the Mercedes and its tyres very hard indeed. Nuvolari was forcing him to do that. Nuvolari, this tenacious little man who did not take part in motor races but *raced* in them regardless of consequences, was moving to a strategy he'd worked out during practice. More than that, Nuvolari must have known he was creating one of the great pursuits in motor sport history, although whether he cared about that is obscure. The ferocity and the urgency of the hunt held him, and he *raced.* And von Brauchitsch, himself so strong in mind and body, did respond by *racing,* too. Lap 19:

Von Brauchitsch	3h 35m 31.1s	
Nuvolari	3h 36m 14.2s	+ 43.1
	Lost on the lap: 6.1s	

Light drizzle had begun to fall. Three laps remained and, despite the gap being more or less stable – and still very considerable – Lurani says that 'Herr Hühnlein nervously twisted a typewritten sheet in his hands. It was the text of the speech, specially prepared for the triumph of Mercedes-Benz, which he was to deliver before 10 microphones and 50 journalists'.

Neubauer was looking at his stopwatch in an agitated manner. On this lap 20 Stuck, driving a dogged race, overtook Caracciola for third place.

Von Brauchitsch	3h 46m 29.1s	
Nuvolari	3h 47m 01.3s	+ 32.2s
	Gained on the lap: 10.9s	

Again von Brauchitsch responded although *The Autocar* noted that 'the Italian has speed in reserve', adding: 'It is the sign of a crisis when Neubauer begins to walk up and down in front of his pit.' The crisis was about von Brauchitsch's rear left tyre, and Nuvolari's strategy was about that, too. During the practice Nuvolari had watched von Brauchitsch carefully and noted how he drove and braked without taking care of his tyres properly, and how worn his tyres were.

Nuvolari had reasoned '*if I push him to go fast he will damage his tyres so much he will have to stop twice for new ones – and then I will win.*' This had not happened but a variation of it was happening. Neubauer, at the rim of the track, noticed that the left rear tyre was worn down to the 'breaker strip' and that meant the tyre might let go.

He consulted the tyre technicians and had a fine judgement to make: if he brought von Brauchitsch in at the end of the next lap – 21 of the 22 – it was almost certain to cost von Brauchitsch the race because Nuvolari was too close to him. Neubauer decided to risk that the tyre would safely hold to the end. Lap 21:

Von Brauchitsch	3h 57m 13.2s	
Nuvolari	3h 57m 48.3s	+ 35s
	Lost on the lap: 2.9s	

Lurani describes the final lap as a 'dance of death'. Nuvolari was catching the Mercedes – but not fast enough. At the Flugplatz, some five kilometres into the lap, Nuvolari had clawed back five seconds. At Adenauerforest, seven kilometres in, he'd clawed back another three. They ran on, across the road to Adenau and the Eifeler Hof Hotel so close by, ran through the right of Bergwerk, ran towards the 13km mark and the Karussell just after it; and as they ran to that the ferocity of the hunt had brought Nuvolari to within 200m of his prey.

The Karussell was a kink then a right-right-right horseshoe, then two semi-kinks, then a left-left-left horseshoe leading to a right-hand curve. Now you know why it was called the Karussell.

A voice from the commentary point at the Karussell shouted 'VON BRAUCHITSCH IS BEING CLOSELY FOLLOWED BY NUVOLARI!'

Von Brauchitsch would remember getting into a skid, would remember Nuvolari hesitating because a skidding car is like a wild animal: it might twist and turn anywhere.

Then the commentator shouted 'VON BRAUCHITSCH HAS BURST A TYRE!'

The left rear had given way and with each rotation was being torn to pieces. Günter Molter saw 'chunks of rubber flying everywhere'.

The commentator shouted 'NUVOLARI HAS PASSED HIM!'

The Mercedes 'tilted, swerved across the track and... Nuvolari barely had time to dodge him.'[24] At this instant Nuvolari saw 'something black fly into the air. It was von Brauchitsch's tyre. Inside I felt something very sweet that I had never felt before but the crowd were suffering and that made me feel sorry for them.' Nuvolari also felt a sense of regret that the tyre had beaten von Brauchitsch before he could. 'I had just about caught up with him and would have played him nicely on the last corner leading to the finishing straight. A real pity.'

The crowd in the grandstands on the start–finish line were all on their feet.

'VON BRAUCHITSCH IS TRYING TO CATCH HIM ON A FLAT TYRE!'

That can only have been a gesture although von Brauchitsch estimated his speed on three wheels at around 140kph (86.9mph). He'd glanced at the right rear and seen that it, too, might let go at any instant. Stuck was past him, Caracciola was past him and all von Brauchitsch could do was try to nurse and coax the Mercedes home, some seven miles away. And the right rear did give way.

'Now we turn our eyes to the changing numbers on the indicator board,' *The Autocar* wrote. 'Now the little Italian appears, and such a shout goes up as never before was heard.'

Stuck was next, but one minute 38.3 seconds after him.

The result:

Nuvolari	4h 08m 40.1s	(121.1kph/75.2mph)
Stuck	4h 10m 18.4s	
Caracciola	4h.11m 03.1s	
Rosemeyer	4h 12m 51.0s	
Von Brauchitsch	4h 14m 17.4s	
Fagioli	4h 15m 58.3s	

Fastest lap: von Brauchitsch 10m 32s (129.9kph/ 80.7mph)

The rest is mythology built upon fact – separating the two is not at all easy. When Nuvolari, sweating profusely, got out of the car he was 'overwhelmed' by his mechanics and son Giorgio.

Von Brauchitsch pulled up far beyond his pit because he did not want the people there to see him crying. When he got back to his pit he laid his head on a pile of new tyres and reflected bitterly that all he'd have needed was two of them. A photographer crept up from behind, von Brauchitsch noticed, threw a bottle of beer at him and only just missed.

Pietsch's hands were bleeding, but that wasn't from changing gear. The skin had been torn wrestling the steering wheel for four hours.

Canestrini, of *Gazzetta dello Sport,* had long preferred the classic racing style of Varzi compared to what Nuvolari did, but after the race he wrote a critique, firstly pointing out that 'von Brauchitsch paid very dearly for his foolish tactics' and then adding: 'It was one of the best victories of Nuvolari's career because he fought on his own against a great German coalition: their constructors' superiority, and at their own Grand Prix, and in front of an incredible German crowd.'

The loudspeakers had still not announced Nuvolari's victory and the Italian flag had still not been hoisted on to the tall pole – nobody could find one, and of course the organisers were so sure that a German driver would win that they had no copy of the Italian national anthem, the Marcia Reale, to play. Nuvolari instructed Compagnoni, his mechanic, to go the pit and look in his – Nuvolari's – case where he would find a gramophone record of it. Nuvolari took this everywhere for luck. According to Lurani, an Italian flag was eventually raised to 'polite applause'. There seems to be a slight dispute about this because some reports speak of hearty cheering and others of the 'hush of dead women'.

Hühnlein made an improvised speech saying that German sport would always recognise 'an honest and great performance' before placing the enormous garland over Nuvolari's head. It hung down, dwarfing him. Nuvolari made a sign with his right arm, drawn between the Nazi salute and simply raising the arm: an uneasy compromise. Then they played the Marcia Reale.

What happened after this is speculation, as it must be. Presumably at some point Hühnlein had to make a very awkward telephone call to Hitler, explaining that neither a German car nor German driver had won.

We do not know how Nuvolari celebrated, or even if he did. Great displays of emotion were rare, and might have been seen as unmanly – hence von Brauchitsch driving past his pit to conceal the tears. We do not know how Nuvolari evaluated this victory which, well over half a century later, remains a source of wonder. Indeed, you can argue that it was his greatest race. Perhaps he took it as it came, as his due, and then concentrated on the next event, the Coppa del Montenero at Livorno. To such people – and this holds true all the way to today – life is always about the next race, not the last one. That's what Michael Schumacher will tell you, every time.

We do know that when von Brauchitsch got back to the Eifeler Hof everyone tried to comfort him. Chiron gave him a massage (!) and

Nuvolari gave him flowers. Von Brauchitsch also spent time with his mechanics and that seemed to console him.

Perhaps the drivers all had dinner in the dining room, the conversation polite and barely audible from table to table. No doubt most of them had breakfast together the following morning before they went their separate ways, as quietly as they had come six long days before.

* * * * *

Intermezzo

From this moment on the superiority of the German cars could not be denied or withstood. Cholmondeley-Tapper[25] distills this:

> *The immense superiority of these German cars ... offered a great challenge to Italian and French racing-car manufacturers, who were bringing out quite new models in an effort to beat their German rivals. Enormous strides had been made in this field, and although my Maserati was only two years old, it was ill-equipped for competition with the new cars. When fitted with a very high rear-axle ratio, the all-out speed of my car on the Avus track was just about 170mph; on the same track the German cars were lapping at this speed, with a maximum of well over 200mph, and Alfa Romeo, Maserati and Bugatti were not far behind.*
>
> *But the Maserati's worst trait was certainly the appalling road-holding... even Nuvolari had found this Maserati a terrible handful and forcibly condemned its poor road-holding after crashing badly with one in... 1934.*

It is true that Nuvolari won at Livorno and at Pescara, but neither Auto Union nor Mercedes took part. They dominated the Swiss Grand Prix (Nuvolari fifth) and the Italian (Nuvolari fastest lap but retired, piston failure); they dominated the Spanish Grand Prix (Nuvolari retired, broken suspension) but at the Czech Nuvolari finished second (but six minutes behind Rosemeyer in the Auto Union – Mercedes hadn't gone).

Only Nuvolari's extraordinary skills stopped this theme continuing through 1936. In May, however, he crashed practising for the Tripoli Grand Prix. A tyre burst at some 120mph (193kph) in one of the corners and the Alfa Romeo snapped out of control. The car headed for a ditch and he 'just managed to get up from behind the wheel' before it struck. He was thrown, in his own estimation, some 75ft (22m) but landed on swampy ground. He was taken to hospital and they said he'd displaced bones in the small of his back. He was bandaged and forbidden from walking.

He explained that he didn't care for walking, anyway. He did care for travelling in his racing car and that was what he was going to do. He added that the Grand Prix would 'give my back an excellent massage'. He discharged himself and finished eighth having massaged his back for 2h 37m 55s, which translates into 39 laps.

Hans Ruesch says that across Nuvolari's career he 'broke practically every bone in his body. I saw him in Tripoli and he was still bandaged, he couldn't bend. The mechanics had to lift him into the car because he couldn't step into it himself. And then he raced.'

Ruesch remains proud that 'I was twice faster than Nuvolari,' as if that was the benchmark against which all was judged. It was no doubt the same with Fangio. It certainly was with Clark: teams used stop-watches on their own drivers in qualifying not to see if they'd got pole but to see how far behind Clark they were. Senna wasn't far from that standard and Schumacher, as I write these words, *is* that standard.

Anyway, Ruesch's life was 'total, complete frustration, you see, because as an independent I had to race with cars that the factory drivers threw away when the cars were finished. A passion made me race – so I tell you about one of the times I was faster than Nuvolari. People don't know about that. Enzo Ferrari knew about it.' Ruesch got a two-year-old 3.8 Alfa Romeo. 'They had a new car ready and that was the 12-cylinder 4.2, exactly the same chassis as the 3.8 but, of course, the more powerful engine. In the autumn they went to the circuit of Milan and for the Scuderia Ferrari it was the most important circuit of all. There was the entire Ferrari team, Nuvolari, Trossi, and I had just received this car because it was the end of the season.

'I'd gotten rid of my Maserati, a terribly dangerous car: very powerful but a miserable chassis – Nuvolari broke a leg in a Maserati of the same type.

'In the Alfa Romeo the circuit of Milan was practically a test for me because I was trying out a car new to me. We had practice for grid positions and Nuvolari was of course number one – pole. I went out later because I'd received the car late. I made my *rounds*, made my *rounds*, made my *rounds,* and what happened? *I* had pole! Nuvolari was already dressed and ready to go out for the evening. He had a suit and a tie on. They called him back and he had to put on his racing clothes: then he went out and retook the pole position.'

This is a delightful diversion. Returning to the main theme…

In early June 1936 Nuvolari won the Penya Rhin at Barcelona against both the German manufacturers. He defeated Caracciola after a great duel: he had to slow towards the end to conserve fuel but by then had built enough of a lead. A week later he competed in the Eifel race at the Nürburgring.

B. Bira[26] left an evocative description of what being at the Nürburgring that weekend was like. He was staying at the Eifeler Hof.

> *We came down at dinner time and I was very surprised find the… hall filled up to the brim. In fact it was with difficulty that we managed to make our way through to the dining-room.*
>
> *They were odd looking people wearing odd costumes, ranging from smart town suits to Tyrolian* lederhosen.
>
> *Out of this medley I saw a group standing by the bar, which was conveniently placed in the entrance hall. This group was busy surrounding something or somebody, and this made me very curious. I had to make a closer investigation by pretending to get a drink at the bar. When I got close to them, whom should I see being surrounded ? It was none other than that 'Golden Tortoise.' This was the nickname of Tazio Nuvolari! The Italian maestro was there in flesh and blood.*
>
> *Actually up to that moment I had not had the pleasure of speaking to him or being as close as six feet from him,* so you can *imagine my thrill on this occasion.*
>
> *It was rather difficult to see him very clearly, as that 'rugger scrum' which surrounded him was over-powering, especially as he was only five feet two or so in stature. I just caught a glimpse of his hair, which was well plastered down…*
>
> *He was not old to look at, yet he had a sprinkle of grey hair*

on the temples. His chin was very prominent and when one saw him in a racing car he looked like a determined demon. His satellites [hangers-on?!] were excelling themselves that evening. The maestro was truly pleased with them, and he joked and laughed with them freely. I on the other hand, was quite content in watching everyone enjoy themselves and I kept my eyes wide open like a small boy at his first Christmas party. I had always heard that Grand Prix drivers took racing pretty seriously, and some even gave up smoking and drinking, but here in Adenau all of them seemed to be holding a cocktail glass or a cigarette.

In late June Nuvolari won again, beating Rosemeyer in the Hungarian Grand Prix at Budapest and a week later beat Varzi (now in the Auto Union) at the Milan Grand Prix. He retired in the German Grand Prix when he was running second, won the Coppa Ciano at Livorno (Mercedes did not enter) and finished second to Rosemeyer in the Italian Grand Prix at Monza.

Then he prepared to show those extraordinary skills to a new continent altogether.

9

AN ITALIAN IN NEW YORK

Vanderbilt Cup 1936

IF THE German Grand Prix was run against a backdrop of aggressive right wing politics – *Deutschland über alles* – the Vanderbilt Cup on Long Island on 12 October 1936 was equally political but in subtly different ways.

I know, I know: sports people always complain that sport ought to be non-political and kept resolutely away from politics. Looking today at the 1930s in general, however, you can't make that separation and have any true understanding of the importance of what was happening. We could select any number of examples: not just the Nürburgring race but the Winter Olympic Games in Germany (which the Olympic president threatened to cancel unless vitriolic anti-Jewish propaganda was taken down), the 1936 Berlin Summer Games and the furore Jesse Owens, the black American athlete, had caused – only two months before the Vanderbilt; the Max Schmeling-Joe Louis heavyweight bouts, white Aryan against Negro; the England football team who played in Berlin and didn't know whether to give the stiff-arm Nazi salute; Hitler (let's say) financing the Mercedes and Auto Union racing teams because they

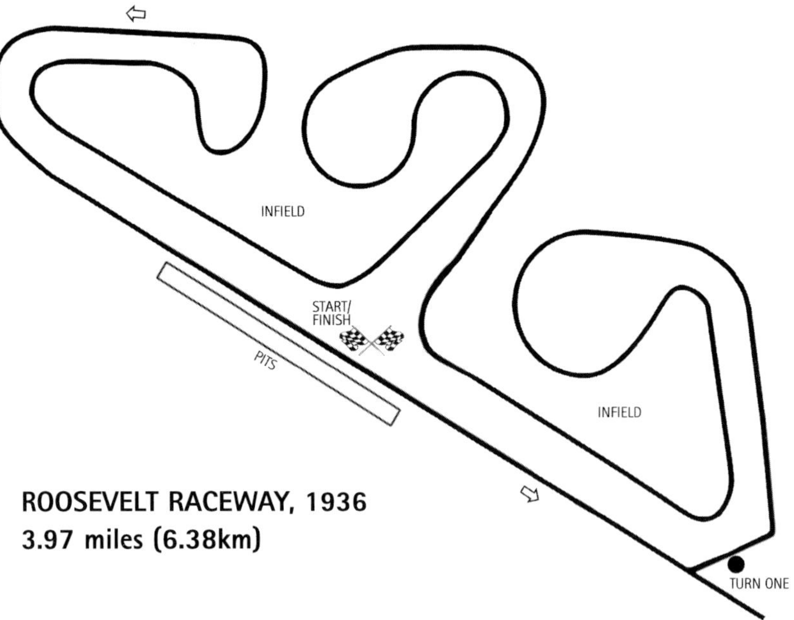

would bring prestige to the Fatherland (and frighten their opponents); and so on.

Where does the Vanderbilt Cup fit with all this?

There's a faint echo from *The New York Sun* newspaper which, on race morning, carried this: 'No love is lost between the French and Italian pilots in view of the present political unrest abroad, and Jean Wimille would give his eye teeth to clip Nuvolari's trig [trim] moustache today. Those boys are out for blood!'

There's a louder echo from David Owen.[1] 'Mussolini's first attempt at empire-building in East Africa' – defeating and colonising Abyssinia – 'had resulted in sanctions being imposed on Italy in reprisal. This meant that Italian teams were no longer able to compete in events like the French Grand Prix.'

The importance of the race was cast into another dimension, too.

When Nuvolari had won it, the *Corriere della Sera* wrote: 'Today Europe won and by Europe we mean Italy and Mussolini. The [American] dominators of Indianapolis have been dominated. The most famous 'acrobats' of the steering wheel [the Americans] have got to start again. A new world order is about to be born in terms of motor sport and old prejudices are about to be removed. From today,

European machinery in general and Italian in particular will be seen in a different light. Who better than Nuvolari, an authentic representative of a great nation on the march, to do this? Who better than Nuvolari to take this great honour on this anniversary of the discovery of America?'

We shall be seeing a much more pragmatic view of the triumph soon enough.

Amanda Gadeselli, who translated and distilled a vast amount of Italian material for this book, studied political science and she gives *this* backdrop:

> *The 1930s and 1940s were a period of mobilisation of the people in Italy. It was a very, very poor country that had always suffered a great exodus through immigration and this was the first period – under Fascism – that there was some form of political stability.*
>
> *It was the beginning of industrialisation – Italy was extremely slow to do that – and the area where it happened was mechanical engineering. Fiat were obviously part of that – you had the new Fiat 500, for example. You also had a world famous Italian, Nuvolari, winning motor races and often in an Italian car. It was that era – he was a great flag-bearer. Up until then Italy had always been laughed at by the big powers because what Italy had contributed was artists, music and singing and dancing and great lovers. Nuvolari represented a new Italy.*

The subtle differences extended beyond this.

Just before Nuvolari sailed from Genoa[2] for the Vanderbilt Cup,[3] an unnamed Italian who had lived in New York for over 30 years had a conversation with him. This immigrant had come back to watch the Berlin Olympics and was now visiting his homeland. He explained to Nuvolari: 'A victory for Italy in the race would be equal to winning a great battle in war. To American people all winning is important, especially in industry, sport and science. They are mightily impressed by it in these fields. We are very proud of Mussolini because he has given us prestige abroad but we Italians who have now become

American citizens need a national hero [beyond a political leader]. Before we "only" had Caruso, Toscannini, Valentino – musicians, singers, lovers [there it is again] – and spaghetti! Now, if you win, America will admire Italy for something else.'

Simply put, the teeming Italian immigrants in New York, whether first or second generation – and many, no doubt, doing menial jobs – would be given respect and self-respect.

The Vanderbilt Cup, which would also involve American domestic politics, was much more than just a motor race.

William K. Vanderbilt had sponsored races at Long Island from 1904 to 1910 and they would be resurrected by the building of the Roosevelt Raceway in the 1930s. As Joel E. Finn, a historian of US road-racing in the 1930s, whose father Barney was a leading force in developing the Long Island circuit, explains, the new races were named after George Vanderbilt although 'he had nothing to do with the races, organisation, finance and so on. He was just the titular head, chosen because he was the only Vanderbilt they could come up with to name the event after.'

The Raceway was a major construction work with grandstands and a four-mile circuit. The 1936 race – 75 laps giving a distance of 479 kilometres – was the first there. I'll be giving you a detailed breakdown of the track's shape in a moment.

The Scuderia Ferrari sent Nuvolari, Brivio and Giuseppe Farina and a full complement of mechanics. They left Genoa in late September on a ship called the *Rex,* which held the Blue Riband for the fastest Atlantic crossing, set three years before.

The night before departure Nuvolari dined in Milan with Varzi, whose life was now breaking apart. As we have seen, he had fallen in love with Ilse Pietsch. She had introduced him to morphine. He was now an addict.

When the *Rex* arrived in New York, Nuvolari dutifully posed with the ship's captain, the other drivers and Canestrini, the skyscrapers of Manhattan framed in the background. Half of Broadway was on the quayside to welcome Nuvolari. Police stopped the traffic on Fifth Avenue and Nuvolari, as it seemed, toured like visiting royalty in an open-top vehicle. President Roosevelt faced re-election on 3 November and the Italian-American votes were important.

Finn, who kindly read this chapter and made many corrections to the background, said I was 'confusing race hype on the part of the organisers and sports press with reality. They tried every angle to stir up PR for the event, including playing the ethnic nationality card. This was especially true as race day approached and it became certain that the Americans were not competitive.'

We are back, too, in our familiar territory of mythology.

Nuvolari described his arrival and a sinister development. 'Straight away we were surrounded with great enthusiasm, almost to the point of suffocation. Thousands of people were gesticulating and pushing. The welcome didn't really surprise us – Hollywood films had already prepared us for this, and more.'

The sinister development 'came in the form of two individuals who, after having welcomed us with over-enthusiastic Italian-American jargon, took me to one side and in low voices said "you are a great racing driver, Mr Nuvolari, and it's really a pity that you won't be able to win the Vanderbilt Cup." Very politely I replied "it will be very difficult for me to win but it is not altogether impossible." The two said "No, Mr Tazio, it's definitely impossible because we have bet $50,000 dollars against you. Do you understand?" Now I replied "I'm not concerned with your affairs. Please excuse me. I've got to leave."'

As Moretti writes in *When Nuvolari Raced*, disentangling the mythology that surrounds Nuvolari's visit to Manhattan is not at all easy. The tales that are told embrace 'multi-millionaire ladies in love with him who beseiged him in his hotel room; gangsters who tried everything – from threats to beautiful blondes – to persuade him to let himself be overtaken by a local driver, even for a single lap, in order to win a bet.'

Finn points out that all this – 'mob threats, rich women proposing marriage blah blah' – is actually 'Nonsense. Nuvolari and his group pretty much kept themselves to themselves the whole time they were in New York. Their night-time activities were managed by the staff of the Vanderbilt Cup Commission and the Italian Consulate with security provided by the New York Police. The police kept everyone away from Nuvolari.'

The Roosevelt Raceway – someone likened it to a 'huge, flat, prehistoric reptile sprawled over the land'[4] – had opened for practice in early September and immediately an 'awful truth'[5] was revealed. The circuit was much slower than original estimates. It comprised '16 unbanked turns of varying lengths and radii up to 330 degrees ... and featured a 3,775-foot-long main straightaway that ran the full length of the grandstands.' The American drivers were unhappy, not least because they were accustomed to powering round ovals but here 'the turns were not of a constant radius or exited directly to another turn in the opposite direction. The Americans could slide through the first turn in fine style and then find themselves on the wrong side of the track for the next turn with transmissions inadequate to keep engine rpms in the optimum operating range.'

The Motor, acerbically, described how 'the much-vaunted circuit which was to put all European courses into the shade proved a sort of glorified dirt track' – elsewhere it is described as a very loose dirt track surface – 'with corners bounded by armoured walls. The Europeans decided that as a road race it was a farce, but as a circus it was tremendous. Nuvolari took a careful look at the course and quietly said "it is necessary to make the acrobatics, therefore I will employ them."'

This race might have appeared as something of a cultural clash. The American drivers had, inevitably, exotic names[6] as well as a different approach to driving: Babe Stapp, known as the Texas Tornado and/or the California Cyclone; Wild Bill Cummings, a former Indianapolis grocery boy; Billy Winn, the Detroit demon; Louis Meyer, with a 'comfortable fortune' from racing; Tony Gulotta, who'd escaped with his life after crashing at Indianapolis; Ted Horn, blond, broad-shouldered; Dave Evans, colourful Texan and iron man; George Connor, known for his youth, good looks and daring; William 'Shorty' Cantlon, who'd invaded the East Coast from his native Detroit; Lou Moore, 'probably Hollywood's favourite automobile racer'; Wilbur Shaw, an overnight speed sensation; Frank Brisko and Chester L. Gardner, the veterans; Russ Snowberger, a former Delaware blacksmith; A.B. 'Deacon' Litz, a 'jovial heavyweight'; Joel Thorne, son and heir of a New York banker; and Milt Marion, fearless on the eastern dirt tracks.

However, Finn says you have to remember that 'the Americans ran only on ovals with cars specially adapted to that use. Further, they were all privateers financed by their winnings and just scraping by. There was very little outside sponsorship in the United States and no backing from any of the auto manufacturers. The cars had almost nothing in the way of brakes and the transmissions were often single speed. There was no way they could be competitive on such a course as the Vanderbilt.'

Incidentally, the Americans had official practice, which the Europeans termed training.

The track had in fact opened for unofficial practice on Sunday 27 September and, as Finn tells me, 'various entries practiced all that week.' Official qualifying began on Tuesday 6 October and continued until Sunday. The race was on the Monday. Incidentally, where I have quoted American sources verbatim I have let them have their spelling.

Nuvolari's car was scrutineered at 9.00am that Tuesday. The official sheet had categories to be filled in, covering such items as engine displacement, bore and stroke and fuel capacity (45 gals). Some have a modern ring.

ENTRANT	Ferrari
CARBURETOR	Weber
IGNITION	Bosch
SPARK PLUGS	Champion

The tyres were by Pirelli.

The qualifying system worked as it did at Indianapolis for the 500-mile race there, with times on the first day taking precedence for grid positions over *faster* cars on subsequent days. Nuvolari ventured out on this Tuesday and said the track was 'completely different' from anything in European circuits. He prophesied it 'will be a hard test of the drivers. The first five laps were the most difficult for me.' He aborted his 5-lap run with gearbox problems, which meant, of course, that those who set times this day would qualify further up the grid whatever he did subsequently. Swanson reached 106.7kph (66.3mph) and Etancelin (60.4mph) but Brivio took pole with 67.03mph. He had lapped the circuit in 3m 34.829s.

Nuvolari qualified on the Wednesday and here is his run:

3m 26.52s	69.727mph
3m 25.92s	70.100mph
3m 26.09s	69.872mph
3m 25.99s	69.906mph
3m 25.60s	70.039mph
	Average 69.929mph

This caused some excitement because it was almost three miles an hour quicker than Brivio had gone. *Corriere della Sera* reported that the Americans were mighty smitten by the little guy. 'His first qualifying round [sic] yesterday really impressed them. They declared that they had never seen such excellent racing and such ability at the driving wheel with a car that did over 233kph. They were electrified by the reckless way he took the continuous series of bends flat out. The American drivers, who between them had seen hundreds and hundreds of race victories, made the following comment: it was like watching a wolf at a hundred miles an hour.'

The Motor reported that Nuvolari 'out-daredevilled the American dare-devils with a practice lap of over 70mph and cornering in wonderful broadsides like you see on the films. Amazing man.'

Rain washed out the Thursday but on the Friday *Corriere* reported that 'on his second test [run] Nuvolari faced a series of 16 bends without easing off the accelerator at all and no one was surprised when the loudspeakers announced that he had broken the lap record.'

One American, witnessing this, said that frankly the other racers looked like they were driving boats – rowing boats.

I cannot resist quoting Finn who captures the atmosphere beautifully. 'The Alfa Romeo team would appear in the pits promptly at 10am each morning with the "hack" 8C-35[7] ready for practice.'

This hack was for all three of the Alfa Romeo drivers. Their race cars were used sparingly, and mainly to verify the effectiveness of various modifications.

'They would immediately begin lapping,' Finn continues, 'Nuvolari going first with his special seat installed, followed by Brivio and then Farina. At exactly 12 noon they would... adjourn for lunch behind their pits, prepared by a team cook and laid out with china and silver on linen-covered tables. At 1pm sharp the team would recommence practice, continuing until 3pm when the drivers would discuss the lessons learned and make set-up decisions for the following day.'

> *All day the circuit had been very lively with high speed tests because there was a lot of competition among the drivers to ensure they got one of the 45 places in the race. Some of the drivers who qualified today are American Wild Bill*

Cummings, Mauri Rose and Ted Horn. These three drivers drive a specially designed and constructed race car and although they have this they haven't been able to beat Nuvolari's time. Cummings, who won the Indy 500 in 1934 and who was second last year, is considered the most competent and brave racing driver in the United States. Rose recently won the 100 miles at Syracuse and was fourth at the Indianapolis 500 this year. Amongst the other drivers who qualified today were the Englishmen Lord Howe, Brian Lewis and Major Gardner. The French contingent of Wimille, Sommer and Raph, and the Australian Freddie McEvoy, also qualified.[8]

There was a curious footnote to this report. 'Following the drivers' protest, the race organisers have decided to abolish the compulsory use of crash helmets during the race.' They were not compulsory in Europe, and we've already had Ruesch ruminating on that – and his wartime French helmet! – while explaining that Nuvolari wouldn't countenance wearing one.

Babe Stapp removed his white enamelled crash helmet and said: 'They tell me the foreigners have kicked up a fuss about wearing helmets. Well, they can have their ordinary caps but give me this contraption every time! See this dent? A rock hit me there at Indianapolis. It was kicked up by the tire of a car ahead of me. I wouldn't be here talking to you now if I hadn't been wearing this headguard. It's made of a composition of sawdust, airplane linen and cork, but the layers are compressed.'[9]

'Meanwhile [the Italians] are continuing their preparation on the car. Brivio established the best time after five laps and will take his position on the front line. Farina will start on the second row and Nuvolari will be among the starters on the third row. Taking into account those three positions, the Italian racing superiority is obvious because of overall power and high speed.

'Tomorrow testing continues for places and in the meantime the press continues to talk very highly of Nuvolari. His name has become very popular and he is now considered a great favourite but the critics don't hide the fact that they hope the American drivers will produce something from out of the bag.'[10]

Tomorrow was the Friday and now *The New York Sun* carried

RACEWAY KINKS BAFFLE PILOTS

'It's worse than any Turkish bath I've ever sweated in.' Dapper little Wilbur Shaw of the butterfly wing moustache and the sharply etched features came to the door of his garage yesterday and blurted out his opinion of the pretzel-shaped racing strip.

'For the spectator,' Shaw continued, 'this should be the greatest show since Nero fed the Christians to the lions in Rome's Coliseum, but as far as we drivers are concerned this twisting grapevine of a course is just a pain in the neck! That bunk the magazine writers have been spilling about averages of eighty to one hundred miles an hour gives us drivers a laugh. It can't be done without roller skates or wings. Aside from Nuvolari, none of the Europeans fantails around the curves like our American boys.'

Nuvolari's Alfa Romeo has a six-speed transmission and a super-charged twelve-cylinder motor. We timed Nuvolari at 17 seconds for the straightaway, which measures 3,775 feet. He was hitting 140mph. 'We Indianapolis drivers can't make that peak speed because our cars have to be geared way down in order to negotiate the turns. We Indianapolis boys will have to make up that lost time by skidding the corners. I've got a hunch that these foreigners won't look so hot on the curves when we begin fish-tailing around 'em.'

Was it on the Saturday that Swanson cut inside Nuvolari in one of the loops? 'He didn't think I would stick her through that rat-hole opening,' Swanson said. 'If the Italian had spun at that moment it would have been just too bad for me.' That seems to have caught the mood of the Americans: brash, brave and slightly bemused.

The Sunday was the final practice day.

When the checkered flag fell on the last of the entrants to qualify ... there were sixteen members of the Roosevelt Raceway Spinners Club. This exclusive society was made up of those who went into spins on the sharp, flat, hairpin turns of this twisting, winding nightmare of a course – the most difficult in the world, according to the field of international racing stars [here].

Three of the members are entitled to wear something special on their membership badges to indicate a more serious spin than their brethren in the club. They are Meyer, Rex Mays and Bill McGurk, all of whom definitely put their cars out of the contest, although without injury to themselves.

When the Americans tried skidding around this road race course, spins were inevitable. The lone exception was that of Lord Howe ... who caught a cinder in the eye as he swung around the broad curve into the main straightaway... he lost his goggles and control of the car, spinning several times.[11]

The front of the grid:

Count Brivio (Alfa Romeo)	Billy Winn (Miller Special)	Wilbur Shaw (Gilmore-Offy Special)
George Connor (Miller Special)	A.B. Litz (Miller Special)	Albert Putnam (Studebaker Special)
Phillip Shafer (Shafer-Buick)	Nuvolari (Alfa Romeo)	Farina (Alfa Romeo)

Finn recounts how (presumably after final practice) his father Barney, who'd helped develop the circuit, and Nuvolari went to a nearby midget dirt track – midgets were, as their name implies, small racing cars – but Nuvolari told Barney afterwards 'it was the only race car he couldn't seem to work out how to master.'

Finn writes of race day: 'As the event neared on Columbus Day, 12 October, the New York area newspaper sportswriters worked themselves into a fine froth of hyperbole describing the coming race, the dangers and accidents expected and the personalities of the competitors. Nuvolari was described as the "Mad Man of Modena" who had a "Contract with the Devil" while Billy Winn was touted by another writer with "Winn Will Win".'

The prediction was for a big accident into or in turn one with '45 raging, sliding speed demons all fighting for the same patch of track.' To try and avoid such a crash the grid had been arranged with a hundred feet (33 yards/30 metres) between each row in the hope that the gap would prevent the cars bunching.

The Italians woke in their Garden City hotel and found there was a strong, biting wind from the north bringing so much cloud that it covered the sky – and from one moment to the next threatened rain. The morning was fresh but, Canestrini thought, beautiful.

He noticed how the sky was also full of 'silver' aeroplanes, both civilian and military. Air travel was clearly much more common in the United States than Europe, and this struck Canestrini hard enough that he mentioned it.

The Italians, after a 'happy' breakfast, said cheerio to a group of friends and departed the hotel in road cars preceded by three policemen on motorbikes who would clear a path through the traffic to get them to the circuit. To warn the traffic they were coming the policemen used their sirens. Cars, buses and hundreds of people were already gathering at the circuit entrance.

Gazzetta dello Sport did not hesitate to point out that it was a national holiday to mark the 'impressive discovery of our great navigator' – Columbus.

The policemen 'rapidly' cleared a path and a few moments later the Italian drivers were in the circuit. The three were met in their garage by some fans whom mechanics were trying to keep at bay. People were shouting to them 'good luck' in English and *'in bocca allo lupo'* – an Italian expression meaning good luck – as the drivers began their preparations for the race.

The day before, you could have had odds of 5 to 1 on Nuvolari but now nobody was taking bets on him any more.

Race Director Arthur 'Art' Pillsbury summoned all the drivers to his office and told them that they should be scrupulous observers of the rules. No doubt this had two purposes: the general one applying to any race, and the specific fear of a tremendous crash at turn one on the opening lap.

Of more pressing concern to the organisers was the small crowd as the 11.00am start approached. An estimated 30,000 were there, although this rose to some 60,000 by 1.00pm.[12] The race itself would last until just after four in the afternoon so the late-comers still saw plenty of action. The circuit could accommodate 175,000 and, the grandstands virtually empty, it must have been almost eerie. However, *The Motor* noted that 'the day was clear and brisk' and the crowd included 'all the rank and fashion, and a few pages of the Social Register.' They would have 'their fill of thrills, although many were disappointed at the speed – never having seen a road race on a circuit rather like Monte Carlo. Indeed, the crowd never grew very excited.'

The 1936 Indianapolis 500, run on 30 May, had been won by Louis Meyer at an average speed of 109mph. Pole had been set at 119mph. Small wonder that the crowd, born and raised on speeds like that, would find even Nuvolari's 69mph tame – if they were reading about it in the newspapers. Being there might have been quite different.

The driver parade presented the crowd with a multi-coloured spectacle, because although the European cars were painted in their usual national liveries (red for Italy, green for Britain, blue for France) the Americans had been painted in the 'most bizarre and fantastic fashion' (Canestrini).

After the parade they settled on the grid. The last notes of the American national anthem were melting into the wind, the same wind which caught the *Stars and Stripes* as it was being raised and unfurled on the central flagpole.

The engines were revving hard now, the sound was 'deafening'.

The green flag fell at 11.08am.

One car hesitated on the grid and the others surged round it, some not missing it by much. Brivio was in the lead.

The first turn was a long left-hander. Brivio got there first, Winn perhaps 20 yards behind him and Nuvolari – already – 30 yards behind that. As they came out Nuvolari was in the lead. Absolute domination of the race was already in place. Raph spun early but caught it and continued although he'd had a push and would be excluded.

Completing the lap, Nuvolari led Brivio by about a hundred metres, Winn was running third, then came Farina and Wimille.

On lap 2, Shaw hit the barrier on the east loop and had to be towed back to the pits. On lap 3 Ted Chamberlain had trouble with the fuel line and pitted for repairs; next lap three of the Americans pitted for adjustments to their cars.

Nuvolari averaged 68mph for the first 20 miles – lap 5 – and held it at around that speed (almost as fast as he did in qualifying, as one reporter noted) until lap 15, when his speed fell to 67mph. In fact, by the fifth lap Nuvolari was in among the back-markers.

Finn writes: 'The competitors quickly spread out... and it became impossible for spectators to follow all the action on the 16 turns and 4 miles of track, even with the aid of a huge scoreboard manned by 140 operators. The announcing system was, by all accounts, loud enough to be heard by the dead, and though the commentary was continuous, it was boring and uninformative. There was always the possibility of an incident or crash somewhere on the circuit but attempting to gaze everywhere at once was a practical impossibility.'[13]

The notion of the crowd having their 'fill of thrills' turned out to be something less, with the odd spin and the odd bumping into the barriers.

Nuvolari moved away – on the long straight he was reaching 150mph – Brivio holding second while Farina and Winn scrapped over third, the power of Farina's Alfa Romeo enabling him to overtake on the straight, Winn getting it back in the corners. This struggle ended on lap 17 when Farina struck a barrier. It happened at such a slow speed that he was completely unhurt. So Winn ran third.

The American crowd was seeing exactly what the Irish crowd had seen at Ards three years before: Nuvolari adjust-adjust-adjusting in the corners, *feeling* for the adhesion. In a right-hander, his outstretched arms working not like two pistons but like a conductor's baton, he *felt* for the inside line while Albert 'Al' Putnam in a Studebaker Special found his car's impetus carrying him wide. As it drifted, Nuvolari adjust-adjust-adjusted the Alfa Romeo inside him, caught a wobble with an instant correction – and was gone through.

Around one third distance – lap 24 or 25, perhaps – 'astute spectators began to notice that Nuvolari's Alfa was emitting an odd whine and trailing a fine, clear mist each time he passed.'[14] Nuvolari pitted on lap 26 for repairs to a fuel line, the six spark plugs were changed and he set off again. Brivio, however, had gone by into the lead. Nuvolari regained it within a lap and would win the special prize money for the leader on each lap for 74 out of the 75.

'Nuvolari,' *The Motor* reported, 'drove with tremendous vim, passing others just as easily on the bends as he did on the straight, where the Alfas were exceeding 140mph. It is said he lost 13lbs in weight during the exhausting race, but refused a relief driver.'[15] As one American writer phrased it, he 'passed cars in every direction but overhead.'

The pit stops for fuel were between laps 40 and 60 and this time Nuvolari did not lose the lead.

Inside the final 12 laps Winn had a puncture far from the pits and eventually retired. Count Brivio held second place comfortably but three laps from the end a petrol pipe broke. By then he and Nuvolari had slowed: no need to hurry now. Brivio pitted on lap 72 for water (the car was overheating) and a new set of plugs but that took eight minutes, and although he remained second the right side of the bonnet hadn't been properly secured. At speed it came up like a flap almost obscuring the driver behind it. Brivio had to pit again, and that let Wimille through.

Nuvolari continued imperiously to the end.

As he crossed the line – the man with the flag was high up on something like a dais – he seemed unhurried. He took both hands off the wheel to lift his goggles from his eyes, the car continuing straight ahead. Then he rested both hands lightly on the wheel as if, now, a caress was sufficient to hold the beast under perfect control. When he'd brought the car to a halt it was surrounded by well-wishers while he rose from the seat and drank from a bottle – a proper swig, using both hands.

Nuvolari was mildly mobbed, smiled, and was presented with a cup which seemed bigger than he was.

The result was calculated, incidentally, by when the leading cars had covered the 75 laps. This went down to a driver called Richard Decker (Duesenberg-Miller Special), 16th – who took 36 minutes longer than Nuvolari to do it. The finishers after that were flagged off.

The result:

Nuvolari	4h 32m 44.05 (65.998mph)
Wimille	4h 40m 55.94s
Brivio	4h 45m 44.40s
Sommer	4h 46m 59.51s
Fairfield	4h 56m 48.53s
McEvoy	4h 57m 25.82s

George Vanderbilt presented Nuvolari with a cheque for $20,000 in an envelope. Nuvolari accepted it without emotion – or opening the envelope. This provoked much comment. (The cheque, of course, was for Enzo Ferrari).

The comment was based securely around this: in 1936 the $20,000 was the equivalent of 240,000 lire, and an Italian earning 1,000 lire a month was doing very well. As a reference point, a Fiat 500 – launched that July – cost 8,900 lire.

Anyway, the cheque in his pocket Nuvolari departed immediately – before Fairfield had completed his 75 laps.

Next day all the New York papers carried a front page a picture of Nuvolari embracing the huge cup and shaking hands with Vanderbilt. The journalists described him as a 'Man Without Nerves', the 'Motor Racing Cowboy', the 'Italian Speed Devil', the 'Human Arrow'. The race reports are all written in a tone of surprise that Nuvolari was of such small physical stature.

We have already seen what play the Italian papers would make of the victory, although Finn points out that 'they played it up in a big way because they weren't capable of winning European races [against Mercedes and Auto Union]. At least they got something to brag about. The Americans thought the whole deal stacked in favor of the Europeans, and therefore couldn't get very excited about what happened. They knew they couldn't win and ran only because they were paid to.'

To emphasise the point of what the Italian press did make of it, here is *Gazzetta della Sport*. Their front page was built around a picture of Nuvolari, arm raised in triumph, and a headline 'TAZIO NUVOLARI CONQUERS WITH ARROGANCE'[16], with a sub-heading which said he had beaten all his adversaries in the old world and new, and he had confirmed the absolute superiority of the Italian automobile industry. Under a Garden City dateline, Canestrini wrote:

> *After thirty years of not being able to compete, today Alfa Romeo realised a magnificent and prestigious win with Nuvolari. He was able to have absolute dominance over all 43 competitors who started the race.*
>
> *The conquest of the Vanderbilt Cup signalled an Italian triumph that could have been even more complete if a black cloud of misfortune hadn't cast its shadow over our magnificent Brivio in the last three laps, causing him to lose 9 minutes and 15 seconds.*

Next day, too, when Nuvolari asked the cashier in his hotel for the envelope – it had been put in a safe – the cashier couldn't find it and something approaching a panic followed until it was found. Nuvolari didn't panic, though. It was Enzo's loss, not his.[17]

In many ways the little, taciturn man from Mantua was a gentleman. After the Vanderbilt he had many offers to advertise American products (one source said that his signature would have been enough: no further effort required) but he said no. Evidently friends chastised him for turning away such easy money but he said 'I know. But there are so many Italians in this city who sweep the streets, work on the roads and sell ice cream. We have to show these Americans that we, too, have our dignity.'

Now if it was start or appearance money they'd been offering and he'd been negotiating, his response would have been different.

When he got back to Genoa Varzi stood on the quayside to greet him and so did Enzo Ferrari (to get his cheque as fast as possible?). Thousands of ordinary people had gathered, too, and they chanted 'Niv-ola! Niv-ola! Niv-ola!'

Mussolini had just opened the Milan motor show and, to prove that Italian industry was on the move, Pirelli launched a major advertising campaign, themed 'in the fourteenth year of Fascism'. Pirelli were showing not just their own superiority but were 'serving glorious aims and collaborating with the building up of industry'.

In November, Louis Chiron wrote from his home in Paris to

Nuvolari. There is a lovely period feel to the letter (and, incidentally, Chiron uses *tu*, the form of address only for family and close friends).

> *My dear Nuvolari,*
>
> *Excuse me for not having written to you since your return from America but, as you must be yourself, we are all a little negligent. You understand that well.*
>
> *I was very content and with a few friends we rejoiced in your victory in America, and I think that it will have permitted you to win some handsome dollars.*
>
> *My dear Nuvolari, I write to you today first of all to congratulate you, as I have just said, and then to ask you a favour which you cannot escape and equally cannot refuse me. It's that I really want to complete my collection of photographs, which you saw at my house, and of which only yours is missing.*
>
> *I would be infinitely grateful if you could send me one as soon as possible, with a dedication recalling the years spent side by side.*
>
> *I thank you in advance and ask you to accept my sincere friendship while at the same time asking you to give my salutations to your wife as well as all your family.*
>
> *In friendship,*
>
> *Louis Chiron.*

* * * * *

Intermezzo

The Vanderbilt Cup was the last race of 1936. Nuvolari was only able to relax when the seasons were over. During them he competed too many times for anything else, and the time that travel took must be factored in. What today would be a brief aeroplane flight or a saunter along motorways effortlessly averaging 100kph was then a slow and tortuous struggle. Any old route map will tell you that. Many of the journeys must have been done by train but how long did that take from Mantua to, say Spa or the Nürburgring or Barcelona?

When the season was over, Nuvolari liked to go off into the mountains and shoot. He described as a 'great joy'[18] having a gun under his arm and a pair of good gun-dogs at his heels. He found the mountain air rejuvenating and skiing invigorated him. He was further invigorated because skiing was then a young person's activity and it made him feel young. It would be interesting to know how quickly Nuvolari learnt to ski and whether his natural balance enabled him to pick it up quite naturally – like driving. It would be even more interesting to know if he favoured downhill rather than cross-country: downhill with its speed and danger.

The close season, as he once explained, gave him time to do his admin work and no doubt catch up on correspondence. It also enabled him to spend time with his family.

The 1937 season was to be relatively quiet, although it began at Turin in April with a thump. He crashed so heavily in practice that he missed the race. He'd remember the road surface lacked grip – it had only been laid recently, so presumably it was too smooth – and he skidded in a tight corner, hit the kerb. The car 'reared up, threw me, and then turned over.'

Dick Seaman wrote to Monkhouse: 'I have come to the conclusion that one is always apt to get caught out at the beginning of the season, because one tries to drive in the same way as one had been doing at the end of the previous season without realising that one is very lacking in practice.' By implication, even Nuvolari was liable to make the same mistake.

He returned to Tripoli (the Lottery rules had been changed) but retired after five laps; he returned to America in July for the Vanderbilt Cup but retired after 16 laps.

Neubauer noted[19] that when their ship docked in New York and the cars were being unloaded 'there were whistles from the crowd on the quayside and shouts of "Nazi". Rotten cabbages were flung at the cars.'

In racing terms, something significant did happen in August during the Swiss Grand Prix at Bremgarten: Nuvolari drove an Auto Union. He'd been approached early in the season because Varzi was gone from the team and Rosemeyer, a friend – they socialised together – wanted him. Rosemeyer was loyal enough to want Auto Union to be strong and good enough to fear competition with no man, even Nuvolari. Moreover the new Alfa Romeo, which he raced at Pescara – the race before Bremgarten – proved a 'terrible disappointment'.[20] He'd have the Auto Union although initially he found its mid-engine layout hard to master. Many other drivers did, too.

If there was a period feel to Chiron's letter after the Vanderbilt Cup, here is more. On 12 November, Rosemeyer's wife Elly gave birth to their son Bernd Junior. Next month she wrote to Nuvolari from Berlin – in French, which in those days was the nearest anyone had to a common second language. It is typed but the final paragraph, beneath her signature, is hand-written in flowing, confident characters.

Dear Mr Nuvolari!

We will be enchanted to see Madame Nuvolari and you at the baptism of little Bernd. It will take place on the 30th of December at 3 o'clock.

I ask you to let us know as soon as possible when and how you are coming to Berlin.

Best regards from Bernd and myself.

Elly Rosemeyer.

Do you want me to make some hotel arrangements? Unfortunately I can't put you up at our house because of little Bernd and the nurse.

In January 1938 Rosemeyer was killed making a land speed record attempt. Auto Union urgently needed a leading driver. They signed Nuvolari.

Because this book is about Nuvolari's greatest races, I am running lightly and quickly across the 1937, 1938 and 1939 seasons to reach the next one. I mention in passing the nationalistic pressure which Nuvolari found himself under to remain with Alfa Romeo while Mercedes and Auto Union were, in the modern parlance, the only cars to have. He was a racing driver whose currency in life was winning, and in one sense at least that made him extremely modern because he'd go where the winning car was. He'd had no qualms about leaving Maserati when the Alfa Romeos were better, even if that meant learning to love Enzo Ferrari all over again – something not to be undertaken lightly. If, now, going where the winning car was meant Germany, he'd go there. Fangio would have understood. In his time he'd do that whenever it suited him – even if that meant, late in his career, learning to love Enzo Ferrari as well. Clark never did because he never left Lotus. But Senna left his spiritual home at McLaren for what he thought would be a winning Williams, and Schumacher left Benetton so Ferrari (the car, not the man) would learn to love *him*. Everything changes and nothing changes.

In 1938 Nuvolari won the Italian Grand Prix at Monza and the Donington Grand Prix in October. It's tempting, if you're a Brit like me, to put Donington in among the great races – but, having recreated the race in great detail in another book (*Hitler's Grands Prix in England,* Haynes, 1999) I don't feel I can present the same material again. The Donington race was a very, very good one, involving a tremendous Nuvolari recovery after losing time at a pit stop, and if you want that, you know where you can find it.

In precis, certain parts of Donington were heavily wooded then and during practice a stag ran in front of Nuvolari's Auto Union. Not even his reactions were able to avoid hitting and killing it. (The head was subsequently stuffed, mounted and presented to him.) This incident does not seem to have perturbed Nuvolari or the people running the race in terms of trying to prevent it happening again. Later a deer got up as von Brauchitsch approached. He missed it and waved at it as he went by.

In the race, Nuvolari led but at one-third distance his engine seemed to be misfiring. He pitted. Repairs cost him time and he emerged fourth, almost a minute behind the leader, Müller. Remorselessly Nuvolari increased his pace – a generation of people who were there still remember the controlled ferocity of this, remember how he beat his fist against the side of the Auto Union in frustration if any slower car held him up – and won it from Lang by a minute and a half. That seems a big margin (and in truth it was) but the race had lasted more than three hours.

The late John Dugdale, who worked for *The Autocar,* took the unusual step (in 1938) of going to Nuvolari's hotel to interview him afterwards. I spoke to Dugdale about this but the mists of time had drifted over it and he couldn't recall much with clarity. 'You'd better look up what I wrote!' he said.

This is what he did write. 'Nuvolari these days is positively dapper, with his short athletic figure, his carefully brushed iron-grey hair, and neat clothes. In racing kit he is a most picturesque person.' Christian Kautz of the Auto Union team acted as interpreter and it may be that the interview lacked depth because of that. To be spontaneous, broadening from question and answer to a in-depth conversation, is difficult when everything has to be translated. More likely Nuvolari was polite and reticent, as people were in those times. Dugdale asked him about various aspects of Donington and he answered pleasantly enough without giving much away. One driver had laid oil and the others, coming up, spun in all directions. Nuvolari explained how rather than fight the Auto Union, and risk slewing, he let it go free and when it was past the oil (the car on the grass!) he regained control of it quite normally, and continued on his way.

It was an astonishing piece of driving but he described it in a matter-of-fact sort of way, keeping Dugdale at arm's length. This is another reason why he comes to us, still, as a stranger.

By now the long shadows of war were falling and I intend to step quickly across them because there are libraries heaving with books covering every minute and every aspect of the conflict. I am just setting a context for the next great race.

In March 1938, Hitler had brought Austria into the Reich. In April Franco's Fascists were winning a series of victories. In September, Czechoslovakia was sacrificed to the Nazis and dismembered. In March 1939 Hitler marched into Prague, completing the operation. In May he and Mussolini signed the Pact of Steel. In August, Hitler and Stalin signed a non-aggression pact. At that moment Hitler had protected his back so he could destroy Poland and then turn on Britain and France. That motor racing continued, as life itself continued, in a passable imitation of normality, is no surprise. There was nothing else anybody could do.

An air of inevitability hangs over 1939 although that is only in retrospect. After the immense slaughter between 1914 and 1918, with young soldiers rising from trenches and trotting towards machine guns, a primitive, deep feeling existed that *somehow* this could never happen – or ever be allowed to happen – again. Many clung to that right up to the point of no return, and some clung to it even after that.

Nuvolari began the season in May at the Nürburgring, where he finished the Eifel race second in the Auto Union.

Lang would remember that the race:

> *... gave us the chance to meet the new Auto Union cars, which had been in preparation for a long time. Lap times got quicker and quicker, and record lap after record lap put in. Obviously all wanted to be in the first row of the starting grid. Just before the end*

of practice, I put in a lap in 9m 55s, the fastest yet, and thus No.1 position on the grid. Next to me was Nuvolari in an Auto Union, and then Caracciola. Behind me, Brauchitsch and Seaman.[21]

The race presented a 'mathematical problem' because it was of only 10 laps – 228 kilometres – and Mercedes carried sufficient fuel to go that distance but the tyres would only last a maximum of eight laps.

We particularly noticed that Nuvolari always did a series of laps, but never at record speeds, keeping to about 10 minutes per lap. He was given his lap times from the pits and we naturally also kept our watches on him. 'They are trying to make their tyres last for 10 laps and are training Nuvolari to keep to these times,' said the wily Neubauer.

Caracciola took the lead, Nuvolari second. Lang reasoned that he had to get in front of Nuvolari because both he and Caracciola would have to stop to change tyres. Because Lang's account is so graphic about what it was like to take Nuvolari on, I quote it in detail. Nuvolari

... was a tough and tenacious fighter. The little 50-year-old Italian with his slim yet sinewy body could show us younger ones a trick or two yet ! As I caught up with him, he seemed to forget his tactics and took up the fight. Intelligent driver that he was, he knew that if I passed I could win, having new tyres which were bound to last. Keep him off at all costs, he must have thought, and wear out his engine.

A wheel-to-wheel tussle started, and I did not give an inch. On the other hand, I could not find a place where, with a supreme effort, I could have got by.

Lang set fastest lap and hung on in what was now a 'wild chase'. Nuvolari held him but at the right-hander before the long straight to the start–finish line, Döttinger-Höhe

... it happened. Again we entered the bend wheel-to-wheel, so close that I nearly touched his car.

On the exit, the impetus carried Lang's car to the outside rim of the track and

> *I could almost reach over to touch him. It was quite nerve wracking: an eye for an eye, a tooth for a tooth! Longer than ever I hung on to fourth gear. Long past maximum revs, beyond the red line. Silently I prayed : once, just once put up with this my dear engine!*

Lang changed into fifth and 'yard by yard I gained'.

> *A glance in the mirror showed Nuvolari's distorted face, chin pushed forward, then – a bang, the engine cut out. I dropped back and Tazio came to attack, I had to pull over to give him room. I felt as if I had been stabbed in the heart.*

Lang, thinking fast, worked out that the problem must be overheating plugs and realised that if he cut the engine that would cool them. He did and as he accelerated

> *... the engine gave forth with its clear song again and pulled joyfully as before. All this only took a few seconds at a speed of about 165mph. I stood on the throttle fit to bend it, and Nuvolari dropped back again.*

The race was decided.

The day after, Hitler and Mussolini signed the Pact of Steel binding Germany and Italy to common action in attack or defence.

The Belgian Grand Prix, at Spa in late June, was run in heavy rain. Yes, everything changes and nothing changes.

Dick Seaman crashed his Mercedes and later died of his injuries; Nuvolari crashed his Auto Union – it struck a tree – but was unhurt. It seems callous to treat Seaman's death in an abrupt paragraph, as I have just done, and I mean no disrespect to his memory. It's just that he has played a minor role in our story and an elaborate account of that night at Spa (complete with more Neubauer fiction) has no place here. Nuvolari was very closely involved that night as Seaman lay dying but of his thoughts we know nothing.

In the French Grand Prix Nuvolari led at what Lang describes as a 'fairly murderous speed' and Lang needed four laps to get past him.

> *The situation resembled the one at the last Eifel race: to start with, I had occasion to watch his superb driving style. How easily he handled the car on the bends, almost caressing the wheel! On a hairpin I got my car next to him and side-by-side we entered the straight, without either being able to gain an inch on the other. Occasionally I glanced over to him: again the white teeth, leathery face and jutting chin.*

He retired with an engine failure and he retired again in the German Grand Prix on 23 July. The race was led by Paul Pietsch in a Maserati until Nuvolari got past him on lap 3.

Pietsch 'lived in Italy in the late 1930s and raced 1500cc cars against people like Nuvolari. It was 1500cc racing so that the Germans – Mercedes and Auto Union – couldn't enter [with their more powerful cars]. They were so powerful there was no point in trying to compete with them: Alfa Romeo and Maserati simply didn't have the money to do that. Neubauer invited me to drive for Mercedes in *1940*. He was a very good team manager.

'He liked to be surrounded by people, he liked to have a drink – and eat! Hühnlein[22] was a very important man. He could ring Hitler and talk to him directly. He said "how is it possible that a German in an Italian car can lead the German Grand Prix? Why are you not in a German car? You must drive a German car."'

In *1940*...

By now Hitler was increasing the pressure on the Baltic port of Danzig, deep in Poland but claimed by Germany.

Nuvolari finished fourth in the Swiss Grand Prix on 20 August.

Three days after that Germany and the Soviet Union signed the non-aggression pact and agreed to dismember Poland, then share it. Everything was in place for Hitler's war. As events quickened towards that, day by day, there was a motor race to be run.

10

War and Peace

Belgrade 1939

THERE'S a strange, haunted feel to the Yugoslavian Grand Prix round the streets of Belgrade on 3 September 1939. It's almost impossible to see the five cars – two Mercedes, two Auto Unions and a Bugatti – with any clarity now because such an immense darkness was moving across them and everything else. This was the day World War Two was declared. In the Balkans that was more haunting still because World War One had started just up the road with an assassination in Sarajevo.

Even motor racing, an enclosed community with an in-built capacity to ignore everything beyond it, was both touched and trapped by all this. And yet, and yet... in the midst of events which were shaking the whole planet, Mercedes contrived to launch an attack on Auto Union for what they claimed were illegal pit stops. They were saying Nuvolari ought not to have won this symbolically important but obscure race.

For all the understandable reasons, scant details of the race itself survive. For example the British magazine *The Motor* made no mention of it in the issue dated 5 September, where ordinarily the race report – however brief – would have gone. Their minds were elsewhere. They carried a four-page feature headlined:

Motoring in Germany

Careering Round the Crisis on the Continent.

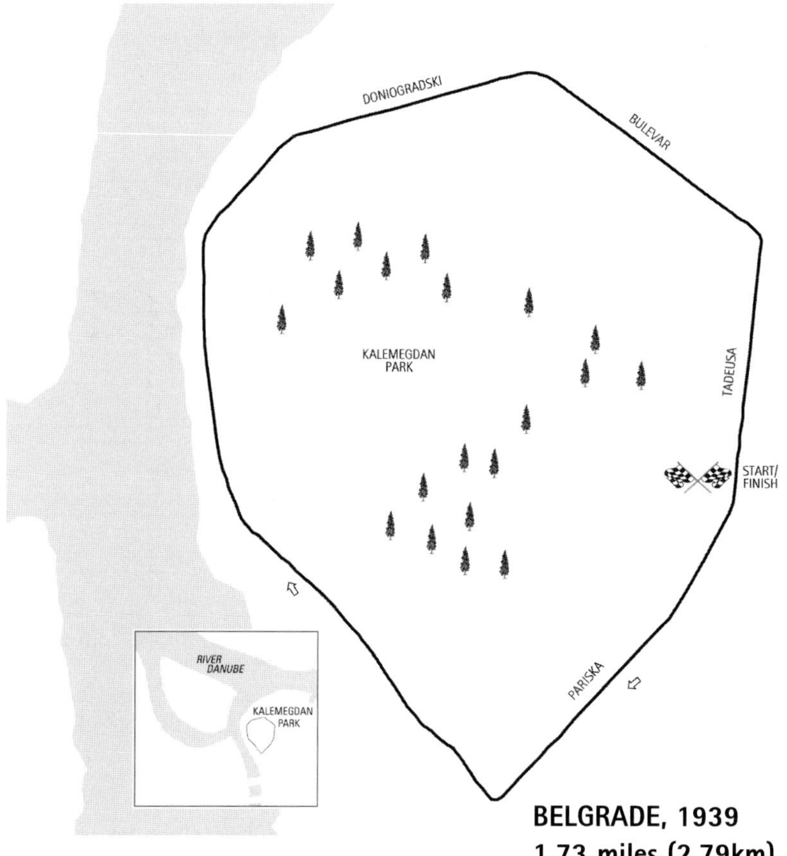

BELGRADE, 1939
1.73 miles (2.79km)

Another example, as Chris Nixon writes[1]: 'communications problems gave rise to a story that Hermann Lang had crashed, receiving injuries from which he later died in Vienna. Happily this proved to be quite untrue.'

Belgrade's race is frozen forever at the very end of an era and, perhaps, frozen as the very end of innocence – the darkness had arrived. That Nuvolari won seems to me entirely apt because he was clearly the best driver of the 1930s and therefore the appropriate man to add the final punctuation mark.

What remains very difficult is to time-travel back to the week before when, as so many people hoped, there would be peace and there would also be a Grand Prix to watch, quite normally. The darkness came closer day by day and, again for all the understandable reasons, many of the details about Belgrade are fragments, some openly contradictory.

Certainly Mercedes approached it in their meticulous way as if everything was quite normal. On 31 July, Neubauer sent a memorandum to 34 Mercedes personnel, including the nine directors. It said:

> *Regarding the second Belgrade street race on 3. 9. 39*
> *Today we have officially entered two cars for this race.*
> *The drivers are Herrs Lang and v. Brauchitsch.*[2] *The reserve driver will be nominated later on.*

The fact that only two drivers were going suggests Mercedes didn't regard Belgrade as a Grand Prix worth the full assault, the political situation argued for prudence or the drivers in general couldn't – or didn't want – to go.

Paul Pietsch, for example, had returned to Germany from his home in Italy and been called up. Neubauer claimed that Caracciola, who was living in Switzerland with his wife Baby, didn't go because of problems with his leg. In his book Caracciola makes no mention of that but wrote[3] that Neubauer had 'ordered' von Brauchitsch to go.

In late July and early August days, the crisis over Danzig had deepened and might easily escalate to war with Poland, which in turn would bring Britain and France into the conflict.

On 2 August 1939, Neubauer (or possibly someone else: the squiggled signature is not clear) filled out the details in another memorandum, this one of more restricted access. It was headed 'Short extract regarding the entry for the second Belgrade street race'. And, in a neat and precise way beloved of all office documents, it had sub-headings underlined. These included:

> Racetrack: *The actual race is in the area of Belgrade. The length is 2,794 metres. The cars have to do fifty laps, which is in total 139.7 kilometres.*
> Entry: *Category racing cars – Dinar 1,000.*

Start numbers: *These must be in four places (radiator, both sides and the back.)*

Starting places: *These depend on the times set in practice. The fastest drivers go onto the front row.*[4]

Practice: *The times are still to be announced.*

Scrutineering: *Takes place on 2.9 at 7 hours at the start.*

Start of the race: *For racing cars on 3.9 at 15 hours.*

Reserve driver: *There are no regulations regarding this and we have had to go back to the organisers.*

Prize money:	*First prize*	*Dinar 15,000*
	Second prize	*Dinar 10,000*
	Third prize	*Dinar 5,000*

A day later, Neubauer set out the travel arrangements.

Since the practice starts on 31 August, we have to drive 1400 kilometres and the roads from Budapest are probably in very bad condition, it is necessary that the two racing cars are ready on the evening of 24.8.

The convoy of vehicles has to start early on the 25th towards Vienna.

Friday 25 and Saturday 26, Stuttgart–Vienna = 650km

Sunday 27, Vienna–Pressburg, where the border is, and continue to Budapest = 300 km.

Monday 28, Budapest–Yugoslav border = 250 km. The border crossing is Mohacs [due south of Budapest].

Tuesday 28, Customs and continuation to Belgrade = 200km.

Wednesday 30, preparations.

Thursday 31, practice.

Due to the many Customs, it is necessary to have someone who knows Slavic languages and this is Herr Wychodil.[5] *Fuel: 1200 litres and the necessary tyres have been ordered and will be carried on the trailer. The convoy consists of two transporters with the cars, one transporter for materials and spare parts for two cars, one heavy lorry with fuel. It is not necessary to buy fuel along the way because we have it with us.* [This was Neubauer's precaution in case war did break out: the convoy could get home under its own steam].

The return: the trailer can probably remain in Vienna for the race on 17.9 and for which the practice begins on 14.9.[6]

These arrangements were set out in much more detail in a subsequent memorandum – four pages – which, curiously, is undated. The convoy was to be the two racing cars, the two transporters, two lorries carrying parts, a workshop and a 2.9-litre saloon car. The practice would be on the Thursday, Friday and Saturday from 4.00 in the afternoon to 6.00pm. Throughout the journey the convoy had to remain strictly in formation. In Belgrade, the racing cars would be housed at the Mercedes agency.

The arrangements for return journey are particularly haunting.

On Sunday 3 September everything is to be packed and ready so that the journey to Szeged,[7] *including the Yugoslav-Hungarian border crossing, can be made on Monday 4.9. Tuesday 5.9, to Budapest. Wychodil is organising the hotels in Szeged and Budapest. Wednesday 6.9, to Vienna. Thursday 7.9 and Friday 8.9, to Stuttgart.*

On 14 August, the start numbers came through: Lang 2 and von Brauchitsch 6. The Royal Yugoslav Automobile Club informed them that the race would be run in the opposite direction to the one previously indicated, and said a reserve driver would be permitted. The hand-over had to be done in front of the pits. Three mechanics were allowed per car for changing wheels and refuelling.

Auto Union also entered only two cars, for Müller and Nuvolari. Their convoy, starting of course from Zwickau, would make its way to Prague via Vienna.

On 25 August, the day the Mercedes convoy left, Louis Chiron was enjoying his fortieth birthday. He was at his villa near Como in northern Italy and, according to Caracciola, 'asked us to come down with Brauchitsch to celebrate. We remained together for quite a while. It seemed as if war might break out any day and we had so many things to tell each other. Before we parted we promised Chiron that we would phone him at once if we learned of such a catastrophe.'[8] Von Brauchitsch 'left us with a heavy heart and gave us his luggage for safe-keeping'.

The convoy's arrival in Belgrade was filmed: a camera pointed forward on the saloon car. It begins on a straight road in the city centre, three and four-storey buildings to either side. Heavy cars, mostly black, are parked nose-to-tail on the right and the sun stretches wedges of shadow across the road towards them. A man in white uniform – made brighter in contrast to the shadows and the parked cars – walks quickly across from one pavement to the other without even looking round at the convoy.

It reaches an intersection where a traffic policeman – dark trousers, white tunic and hat – directs it to the left and it overtakes what appears to be a horse-drawn cart, heavily laden. A crowd stand further back, clearly gathered for a purpose other than to watch. They are too far away. As the convoy turns, a man standing near a kiosk waves. Others nearby walk on, seemingly unaware of what is passing them.

The film cuts to a broader road with tramlines to the left and what may well be parkland to the right. This, surely, is part of the course. Two people are poised to cross but one restrains the other with a gentle gesture, and the convoy goes by.[9]

I don't want to read too much into this film but it does capture the normality of life, people going about their business and no signs of preparation for war – or indeed anything military at all.

On Thursday 31 August, von Brauchitsch[10] flew from Munich on a 'beautiful late summer's day' to Belgrade. He says that the Mercedes apprentice driver Heinz Brendel, along with Lang, completed the Mercedes team (but it wasn't Brendel, as we shall see). When von Brauchitsch landed he was met by a member of the organising committee and they travelled into the city. They had a coffee and then von Brauchitsch set off to inspect the course. What he saw was not encouraging.

The circuit, in the city centre, was 'roughly triangular in shape'[11] on roads round the Kalemegdan Park. It moved past the old city ramparts built by the Turks – this was the fortress, but the park also had a zoo – and one leg of the triangle ran near the banks of the Danube. The circuit comprised cobbles and tramlines. Lang described it like this: 'of similar character to the "round the houses" event in Monte Carlo or the town race at Pau. The circuit led past the old gate through which once Prince Eugen' – an Austrian who had waged war against the Turks in the 1680s – 'entered Belgrade, and circled the old castle hill.'

Von Brauchitsch found it short and 'rather round' with a very uneven surface, criss-crossed by the tramlines and a sequence of corners partly fringed by trees which were very close and unprotected.

'Fifty laps,' Neubauer said to him. 'Your circuit – like in Monte Carlo!' Von Brauchitsch had won there in 1937.

Von Brauchitsch spent the next two hours making an intensive examination of the circuit. He had the team's saloon and every now and then stopped it, got out and examined difficult places. The circuit was not flat at all but undulating with parts which had to be *climbed*. It was narrow, often twisting in a way which, somehow, maps don't show. The examination completed, von Brauchitsch prepared for the first practice session that afternoon.

We don't know how Nuvolari got there, although he probably took the train from Milan. It was a relatively straightforward journey through Zagreb. He is given no times for the first two days' practice and so probably only arrived on the Friday evening, qualifying on the Saturday – the third and final day.

Lang, however, would remember[12] that the cold he'd had was better 'and I was ready to race again but thunderclouds began to gather on the European horizon. Our participation in a race in the town of Belgrade was doubtful. Finally the decision came to depart for Belgrade. The organisers had taken a lot of trouble to run this event, we couldn't let them down and nothing had happened yet to cause serious anxiety. Our only special precaution consisted in Neubauer taking a fuel tanker lorry with us. After a wonderful trip through Hungary we were met by representatives of the Yugoslav Club at the frontier and were quickly given the impression of having arrived in the land of milk and honey.'

Auto Union arrived on this same Thursday, in time to have a brief practice. They could all feel an atmosphere of tension in Belgrade – wild rumours were making the people volatile – and they decided to stay near their hotel for the duration.

The fifth car scheduled to take part was an elderly Bugatti to be driven by a local, Milenkowitsch. It seems nothing is known of him and, because he is given no time,[13] the assumption must be that he did not take part in any of the three days' practice.

In fact, Mercedes had taken Walter Bäumer as their reserve driver although, curiously, he is not given any practice times, which suggests he arrived just before the race and didn't practice at all. He is scarcely mentioned, although in the race he would take over Lang's car and infuriate von Brauchitsch.

Lang was quickest on the Thursday. Von Brauchitsch knew that Lang and Nuvolari were to be his main opponents, and thought he wouldn't make life easy for Lang because '*this course suits me*'. He said that even though the circuit was so uneven that at points – especially in front of the grandstands – the cars were launched six metres through the air at 180kph (110mph) and catching them when they landed was no easy matter with corners rearing at you.

Lang	1m 17.0s	(129.2kph/80.2mph)
Von Brauchitsch	1m 17.4s	(127.8kph/79.4mph)
Müller	1m 18.3s	(126.6kph/78.6mph)

Typically, perhaps, von Brauchitsch would subsequently write that *he* had had the fastest lap and 'I was the hero of the day.'

If the Auto Union people stayed near their hotel, the Mercedes people took an evening stroll and they could feel the political tension in the air. However within the Mercedes racing family, the possibility of war was only mentioned occasionally.

At 5.45 next morning German troops invaded Poland.

Lang claims that the news had become more and more excited and 'daily we drove out to a nearby hill to hear the wireless news from home.[14] On the second practice day the news came: "War with Poland". A thousand conflicting emotions beset us: should we race or return home at once? The organisers begged us to stay. A cancellation would have caused them a considerable financial loss.'

They stayed.

Although a war was imminent, Hühnlein had 'ordered the Germans to stay on and race. Hühnlein wanted the race to be a frightening demonstration of German expertise.'[15]

While one and a half million German soldiers poured into Poland

and a new word – *blitzkrieg* – was added to the global vocabulary, Lang was quickest again. Von Brauchitsch, who would remember that a great crowd had come to watch the German cars – creating a festive atmosphere – was determined to go faster, and each time Lang did a quick lap he said 'Herr Neubauer, I am going to go out again!'

Lang	1m 15.2s	(131.8kph/81.8mph)
Von Brauchitsch	1m 16.4s	(129.6kph/80.5mph)
Müller	1m 17.0s	(129.2kph/80.2mph)

Typically again, perhaps, von Brauchitsch claimed that this second practice was 'very successful for me, though Lang and Nuvolari came very close to my time' – Nuvolari, of course, wasn't even there.

The *Stuttgarter Neues Tageblatt* newspaper gave the practice full coverage but added this intriguing little cameo in their piece, which had a Belgrade dateline: 'Meanwhile, we have received the news that Nuvolari is coming and also that Hans Stuck has been ordered to come to Belgrade. They are on their way.' This seems symptomatic of the confusion, that until then nobody knew whether Nuvolari was going or not. It is also the only mention of Stuck who, it is almost certain, did not go.

The *Berliner Volks-Zeitung* carried a brief telegrammed dispatch. It began: 'Yugoslavia is also interested in the tense political events. On Friday, the second day of practice, the German drivers thought they would abandon the whole thing but they were told to stay where they are.' This must have been the Hühnlein order.

Finally Von Brauchitsch took pole on the Saturday when Nuvolari had arrived and inevitably was at a slight disadvantage to the three others who now had two days' experience of the circuit. However, the *Berliner Volks-Zeitung* had a correspondent in Belgrade and he wrote: 'Since we didn't know if Nuvolari was coming this afternoon, the pleasure was tremendous when he suddenly appeared on the circuit. He drove some laps in his race car and very quickly mastered the course, coming closer to the times of the other drivers.'

Von Brauchitsch	1m 14.0s	(133.7kph/83.0mph)
Lang	1m 15.0s	(132.6kph/82.3mph)
Müller	1m 15.2s	(131.8kph/81.8mph)
Nuvolari	1m 16.3s	(129.8kph/80.6mph)

Lang would reflect[16] that 'the nervous tension told in practice.

Brauchitsch and I battled for fastest lap. For two days I was the faster, then on the third day he lowered my time. I immediately wanted to run again but Neubauer stopped me, saying that we were both crazy – as if it mattered whether we were on the left or the right of the starting grid! I agreed, but all of us were in a very nervous frame of mind.'

Accounts of events on the morning of the race, which was warm and sunny, are confused. Neubauer's recollections, in particular, are so misleading that the truth is even more difficult to penetrate than it might otherwise have been.

For example, 'I could see that both Lang and Brauchitsch were oppressed by the worsening international situation and in no condition to drive their best. The evening before the race we were sitting in our hotel when the news came through that German troops had invaded Poland. We looked at one another in horrified silence.'

Of course it can't have been the evening before the race because that was the Saturday and, as we have seen, Germany invaded on the Friday. Nor is it conceivable that it would have taken until evening for news to reach them that the attack had begun at dawn. The whole world knew within hours.

Lang might be more accurate when he says that the news of Britain declaring war came 'at breakfast' that morning: Britain declared war at 11.00am. 'All of us lost every inclination to race but Neubauer returned from our Embassy with the news that we must keep calm and start. We owed this to our hosts.'

That Neubauer would have gone to the Embassy to seek guidance is entirely feasible because it was a necessary and sensible thing to do.

Now we have reached one of the most celebrated, infamous and dubious stories in motor racing.

Neubauer would claim that he was having breakfast when Lang came in. Lang said to him that von Brauchitsch 'asked me to say goodbye to you for him' because he was flying home.

'"What?" I shouted. "Flying home? And the race?"'

'He said, "when the Fatherland calls, a von Brauchitsch must be there."'

'"Damned nonsense!" I roared. "The only call he's going to answer today is Neubauer's."'

Neubauer claims he set off for the airport, 'bluffed' his way onto a

Lufthansa plane and found von Brauchitsch there. He said he'd given him a lesson on behaviour and only after they both got off the plane did Neubauer realise it was bound for Switzerland.

Other reports suggest Neubauer rang the airport, had the plane – a JU 52 – stopped, and sent someone to haul von Brauchitsch off.

Von Brauchitsch's version[17] offers some confirmation of Neubauer's – but is shrouded in its own mists. Von Brauchitsch wrote that on *Sunday 1 September* he appeared, as usual, on the terrace of the hotel at about ten in the morning. Next door was an electrical shop and from a radio there they heard music for a special announcement. The German army had entered Poland in the early hours of the morning. 'We just said "that's the end of the race".'

Von Brauchitsch quickly made a decision. From his room he phoned a travel agency and asked for a seat on a plane – it was going to Vienna in half an hour. He packed, paid his bill and took a taxi to the airport. Nobody knew what he was up to and he didn't say goodbye to anybody. He thought his conduct unusual but in these circumstances 'appropriate.' On the plane he felt relief.

The plane stood for 10 minutes, motor turning, and von Brauchitsch began to think about the consequences of his departure for the team. Neubauer arrived – his hat at an angle on his head which, evidently, it always was when he was angry – with two people escorting him. Neubauer came onto the plane, stopped where von Brauchitsch was sitting and said 'Manfred, are you mad? You can't just disappear like this. We have to race.'

One report suggests von Brauchitsch, in fact, had a ticket to Zurich and would then go to Lugano where the Caracciolas lived – perhaps to collect the things he had left with them.

The truth of all this, I am convinced, will never be known. Neubauer and Lang both claim von Brauchitsch fled on race morning, whereas he claims it was on the morning of the Polish invasion, three days before. It appears highly instructive to me that neither Neubauer nor von Brauchitsch had done even the most elementary fact checking before writing what they did – Neubauer getting the date of the Polish invasion wrong (making nonsense of what he wrote) and von Brauchitsch saying that 1 September was a Sunday. The Sunday was 3 September, of course, one of the most striking dates in human history.

It means von Brauchitsch managed to get the start of World War Two wrong.

Maybe a measure of confusion was inevitable in the circumstances and memory is a most unreliable tool, anyway: Von Brauchitsch was writing in 1955 and Neubauer in 1958, more than enough time for memories to distort themselves – especially to people who clearly didn't check to refresh those memories.

I have recounted their versions because they seem to reflect the true mood of that confusion, whatever their veracity or lack of it. Into this situation came Nuvolari, who was to create the final masterpiece of movement of the decade, arguably one of the most fascinating in terms of motor racing.

What did he think of it all? It does seem that the Auto Union team conducted their affairs in a more restrained manner which, unfortunately for our purposes, means we hear less about them. Did he sleep well that night? Did he wake and, hearing the news of war at mid-morning or shortly after, isolate it from his mind? How did he think? All we do know is that some Auto Union personnel saw special war editions of the local papers on sale, felt the fevered emotion everywhere, wondered about the point of going on with the race and, after consulting headquarters, did go on with it.

The race was due to begin at 3.00pm and a crowd estimated at 50,000 had gathered to watch it.

As it started, the French ambassador to Yugoslavia, surveying the four German cars on the grid and their three German drivers, ostentatiously rose from his seat in the grandstand and departed.

On the grid, Lang had a feeling that this was to be his last race for a long time – possibly ever – and determined to win it. Von Brauchitsch felt exactly the same. The grid lined up on the cobbled road, temporary wooden grandstands on both sides. In the one on the right, behind straw bales, a group of what looked like sailors among the crowd watched, hands resting on the bales. They appeared more curious than excited. Above them, nailed to the wood, was a swastika.

The grid itself was a strange thing with only the five cars on it: the two Mercedes at the front, the two Auto Unions and the Bugatti spread across the road behind.

Von Brauchitsch seized the lead instantly. In his anxiety to get away fast, Lang had made a mess of the start. He'd given his car too much throttle. Within perhaps 20 yards of the line von Brauchitsch was clear by the length of his car. They went up a slight incline and over the brow, out of sight. 'Furiously' Lang set off.

> *... but there was no straight long enough to overtake and Brauchitsch cut all the bends. I could not see a way to overtake and kept glued to his rear. Neubauer, realising the dangerous situation, waved the house-flag, but Brauchitsch swept on and I had to follow.*[18]

Neubauer would describe how 'from the start' von Brauchitsch drove like a 'madman' and refused to let Lang pass him. In fact the race reports suggest von Brauchitsch was driving with so much venom that Lang, tracking him doggedly and managing to stay one car length behind, was never in a position to overtake, particularly in view of the circuit's rough surface and awkward corners.

Was Nuvolari biding his time? Was the old master happy to let the Mercedes race each other while he monitored, watched, waited as he adjusted-adjusted-adjusted, the Auto Union juddering across the cobbles? Or was he running as hard as he could? The darkness has engulfed it completely. All we have is fragments of film: of him following Müller into a sharp, uphill left-hander, his arms outstretched as he wrestles the Auto Union round, the arms whipping down to straighten the steering wheel and – tantalisingly – in the little straight that they are on Nuvolari adopts a completely different line to Müller. He might have been trying to overtake. Then they are gone from sight.

At this corner, one of the Mercedes came up to lap the hapless Bugatti which was so anxious to get out of the way that it went straight on as the Mercedes hugged the rim of the corner, going round. The Bugatti described a wide arc and set off panting up the incline, the Mercedes already far away. *This* would have been precisely what Hühnlein had wanted to demonstrate to the crowd which craned from windows, gazed down from rooftops, and stood many deep at every vantage point around the circuit.

The von Brauchitsch-Lang struggle went on for six laps. Deep into the seventh lap, Neubauer claimed von Brauchitsch took a corner so badly that he put a wheel off and it threw back sand and stones, although one report suggests the track was slippery there. Lang would remember

> *... suddenly something hit me and everything went dark before my eyes; with a tremendous effort, I tried to see again. Brauchitsch's car had thrown up a stone, which not only shattered my aeroscreen but also both glasses in my goggles. My eyes were full of splinters and when Dr Gläser took out the last bits the short and furious race was over.*

Neubauer says that when Lang pitted 'blood was streaming from his right eye.' Bäumer took over but he was a lap down.

Müller now ran second and Nuvolari third. Von Brauchitsch did not reduce his speed – Müller 13.8 seconds behind, Nuvolari 14.2. On lap 15 Nuvolari set fastest lap of the race, 1m 14s.

Müller had to stop at the pits and Nuvolari set about von Brauchitsch, who would remember having to 'race like mad' to keep him at bay. Neubauer, surveying this, saw how 'desperate' Nuvolari's driving was and thought a crash inevitable.

Von Brauchitsch came upon Bäumer [repeating, he'd remember him as Heinz Brendel, an apprentice driver]. Bäumer was clearly struggling and twice baulked von Brauchitsch who eventually overtook him so violently that he forced him into the straw bales at the side of the track.

On lap 16 von Brauchitsch spun, describing two revolutions, outside the French Embassy on a corner in an uphill section of the track. 'My engine died and I had to let the car run backwards so that it would start again. With the engine running again, when I wanted to turn the car round Nuvolari came like a shadow round the corner. Thanks to his extreme driving skills an accident was avoided.'

Neubauer commented dryly that 'had it been anyone else but Tazio Nuvolari, that would probably have been the end of both of them. With incredible coolness, Nuvolari gauged the distance between Brauchitsch's Mercedes and the stone wall at the side of the track. It was just wide enough!' Von Brauchitsch didn't give up and equalled Nuvolari's fastest lap (1m 14.0s, 135.1kph/83.9mph).

Nuvolari was not to be caught although during the race something suspicious happened and that produced a sting in the tail – the pit stops. We shall see.

The result:

Nuvolari	1h 4m 3.8s (130.7kph/81.2mph)
Von Brauchitsch	1h 4m 11.4s
Müller	1h 4m 34.4s
Milenkowitsch	+ 19 laps

After the race the Mercedes team heard that France had declared war on Germany – there had been some confusion between Paris and their Berlin embassy evidently, and it is entirely possible that the French ambassador in Belgrade left his seat in the grandstand and departed because *he* had just heard of the French declaration of war.

Auto Union began packing everything immediately and bought enough fuel to get them, they hoped, back to Zwickau. They left the following day. Mercedes, of course, didn't have the fuel problem. The normally meticulous Mercedes archival records are silent about the return journey, the predetermined plans of memorandums with their hotels and calculated kilometres per day now abandoned.

Lang says that their thoughts were entirely on getting home. 'In Hungary, they said, all fuel would be confiscated and Neubauer therefore decided to drive alongside the Drina towards the east and to Marburg, to get to Graz and Vienna.'

Marburg was the German name for Maribor, in Yugoslavia but close to the Austrian border: Austria was fully integrated into the German Reich and therefore home. This route cut out Hungary altogether but, as Lang remembered, the strict convoy formation had been dispersed for reasons of safety.

> *What awful, potholed, dusty roads! They led through endless maize fields and went on and on. We had to keep miles away from the main convoy and could recognise it by the enormous dust clouds in the distance. After passing the black, white and yellow frontier posts we felt at home again.*[19]

Auto Union took four days to get back. Their choice of route is not, so far as I am aware, recorded, nor that of Nuvolari.

Lang remembered reaching Vienna and encountering a black-out for the first time. He'd remember, too, the melancholy of realising that this wonderful era of motor racing had ended and would not be coming back. Neubauer 'distributed the remainder of the petrol in the tanker to us' so they could get back to Germany.

The sting in the tail? On 19 September Mercedes managing director Dr Wilhelm Kissel and director Max Sailer wrote to the head of the national sports authority for motor vehicles in Berlin.

> *We know there are more important things at the moment – the beginning of the war, where Germany's honour and future is at stake – but, nevertheless, we would like to inform you about what actually happened at Belgrade.*
>
> *Our driver von Brauchitsch had to change wheels in the 35th lap of the 50-lap race. After that had been done the racing car had to be started using the starter according to the rules and regulations but for this a time of 6 to 8 seconds is required – and that is probably public knowledge.*
>
> *At the end of the 38th lap the Auto Union of Nuvolari also had to change his wheels and contrary to the rules the car was pushed forward. Our team leader warned that this is forbidden but the crew of Auto Union completely ignored it and continued to push the car.*
>
> *We objected after the race. The lap chart shows that to the 48th lap von Brauchitsch was within 3–4 seconds of Nuvolari. If Auto Union had acted correctly when the wheels had to be changed, it would not have been possible that Nuvolari would have gained the advantage he did – 6–8 seconds. It would have been possible for von Brauchitsch to win the race.*
>
> *From the 48th lap von Brauchitsch gave up trying to overtake Nuvolari and finished at a distance of 7.6 seconds.*
>
> *According to the rules, Nuvolari's car should have been disqualified.*
>
> *In view of our own national rules that protests by German participants, particularly abroad, are not to be made, and in view of the political position, we did not do anything to lodge a protest. On the other hand, the head of our team went to*

von Eberan and showed him the rules of the race, which literally say

> *'Point Number 6, repairs:*
> *During the race, after a stop at a pit it is forbidden to push. The starter must be used.'*

Herr von Eberan declared that he had not received these rules. After further investigation at the Belgrade offices of the organisers we learned that these rules were actually given to Auto Union and it was shown in the presence of Herr Sebastian that this was the case. He had understood the rules and signed them himself. They are in a folder at the Belgrade Automobile Club.

Herr von Eberan made the excuse for how his crew handled the pit stop that the actual team leader, Feuereissen, wasn't present. He had been called up.

Equally, we noted that the racing car of the driver Müller was also pushed and it should also have been disqualified.

Thus Auto Union were in danger of having both cars disqualified, which probably would have happened if teams from other countries had been taking part in this race.

After the race a senior Mercedes employee got in touch with Auto Union to point out that in future these rules should be observed.

It goes without saying, nevertheless, that in their advertising Auto Union point to a victory against very difficult German and international opponents.

In addition, the Sport Report of Auto Union No.15, which we send you herewith, shows that they even made a remark regarding our driver Bäumer which was not called for.

However we can ignore all this, thinking of the times we are living in. We want this to be seen as just letting you know, because we felt we should inform you about it.

Heil Hitler!

With von Brauchitsch back in Germany, Caracciola and his wife 'set about taking care of his possessions. Baby wrapped the woollens in newspapers, put in camphor[20] balls, stuffed the shoes with tissue paper, bundled up the fragrant love letters[21] and then I helped her carry the bags up to the attic.'

It seems to me that World War Two can be portrayed, like all other major wars, in remote geo-political language – the strategies of advances and retreats – but each person of the millions involved had a human story to tell, and human stories are always about touching little details: woollen clothing wrapped in newspaper in an attic.

Did von Brauchitsch ever go back and reclaim it?

The darkness covers that as completely as it covers the advances and retreats which made the earth shudder.

* * * * *

Intermezzo

The war which Hitler began ended in the spring of 1945 with continental Europe exhausted, ravaged, choked with refugees, bankrupt and facing an Iron Curtain.

After Belgrade, Nuvolari had retreated to Mantua. It's easy to forget that Italy did not enter the war until 10 June 1940 and up to that moment any Italian could, at least superficially, believe that life was normal and going to remain normal. Nuvolari could therefore think about motor racing and, after Belgrade, examine his options for the 1940 season. He had an immediate problem in that Auto Union were in debt and owed him money. This was resolved after Christmas 1939 but 'other complications arose'. Clearly, with a major war going on, no German company would be racing in 1940.

He sounded out Alfa Romeo but they said no, thanks. Maserati offered him a drive in the 1940 Tripoli Grand Prix. He tried their car out on the autostrada and took it to Tripoli where he practised in it but did not race. Nobody seems sure why, although Moretti hints it might have been contractual problems with Auto Union.

While these were being resolved, Porsche invited him to go to Germany and see their new racing car, which eventually would be known as the Cisitalia, and he did so. (Much later, Ferry Porsche designed a mid-engined Formula 1 Cisitalia). Racing was of course out of the question, but

Nuvolari and Auto Union eventually settled all outstanding matters (with the caveat that if Grand Prix racing resumed he would drive for them.)

Essentially Nuvolari sat out the war, alternating between Mantua and Rome (where he had an apartment), dealing in cars and, towards the end, being evacuated with his family to Val d'Intelvi, scenic countryside between Como and Lugano.

He was in his late 40s and all he knew was racing cars. In this long silence – autumn 1939 to spring 1945 – we hear his voice only once. On 8 September 1943 he wrote to the board of Auto Union at their hometown of Chemnitz, Germany:

> *Thank you very much for the letter which was sent to me on the occasion of my fiftieth birthday.*
>
> *I was touched by your expressions of friendship and respect for my championship victories when I raced on your behalf. All the above has made me relive the hours I spent in co-operation and camaraderie with you, when my life was on the line.*
>
> *I thank you for the superiority of your machines.*
>
> *Your letter was like a very precious prize to me which I am putting with other notes of a similar nature which have come to me in the course of my life and in the course of my career as a racing driver, and which have meant a lot to me.*
>
> *On my twentieth anniversary of racing, I was lucky to have won in one of your superb machines after a very difficult race in Belgrade in 1939.*
>
> *In the same spirit of camaraderie I send my best wishes to you and your company.*[22]

In 1945 and 1946, daily life was beginning to return to something approaching normality. Sport, including motor racing – a problematical activity, requiring cars, circuits and fuel – would be *proof* that normality was coming back. A cricket commentator, John Arlott, has described this role of sport perfectly: men could now occupy themselves taking seriously things – like a cricket match – which were not important. Nuvolari had a bad war: not that it touched him physically but that he hated what had created it and what impelled it, what it meant.

The man and his moods. Happy, surrounded by friends in England. *(Neil Eason Gibson)*

Towards the end of his career he looked more and more sombre, especially after the family tragedies. *(Neil Eason Gibson)*

Spectating at the Mille Miglia, and smoking his customary cigarette.

The most famous victory of all, at the Nürburgring, 1935. The mood was militaristic. *(Mercedes Benz)*

Nuvolari after he'd won it. Adolf Hühnlein (just out of picture) is composing a new speech! *(Neil Eason Gibson)*

Almost all the drivers stayed here, and had done for years. It's in the main street of the village of Adenau. *(Author)*

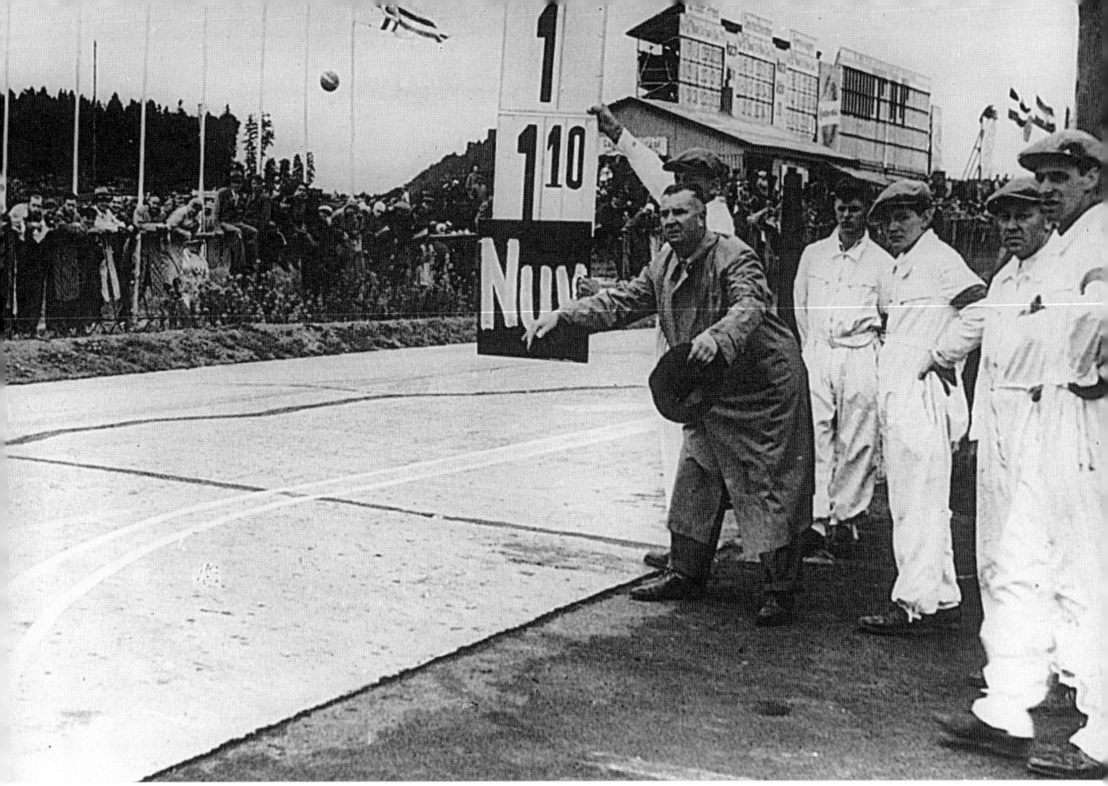

Towards the end of the race, Alfred Neubauer began to give von Brauchitsch desperate – and theatrical – signals. *(Merecedes Benz)*

The hunt is on. Here von Brauchitsch leads, Nuvolari not yet within sight. *(Mercedes Benz)*

The moments after von Brauchitsch's tyre exploded, shedding bits back along the road. *(Mercedes Benz)*

The tyre which settled the 1935 Grand Prix. *(Mercedes Benz)*

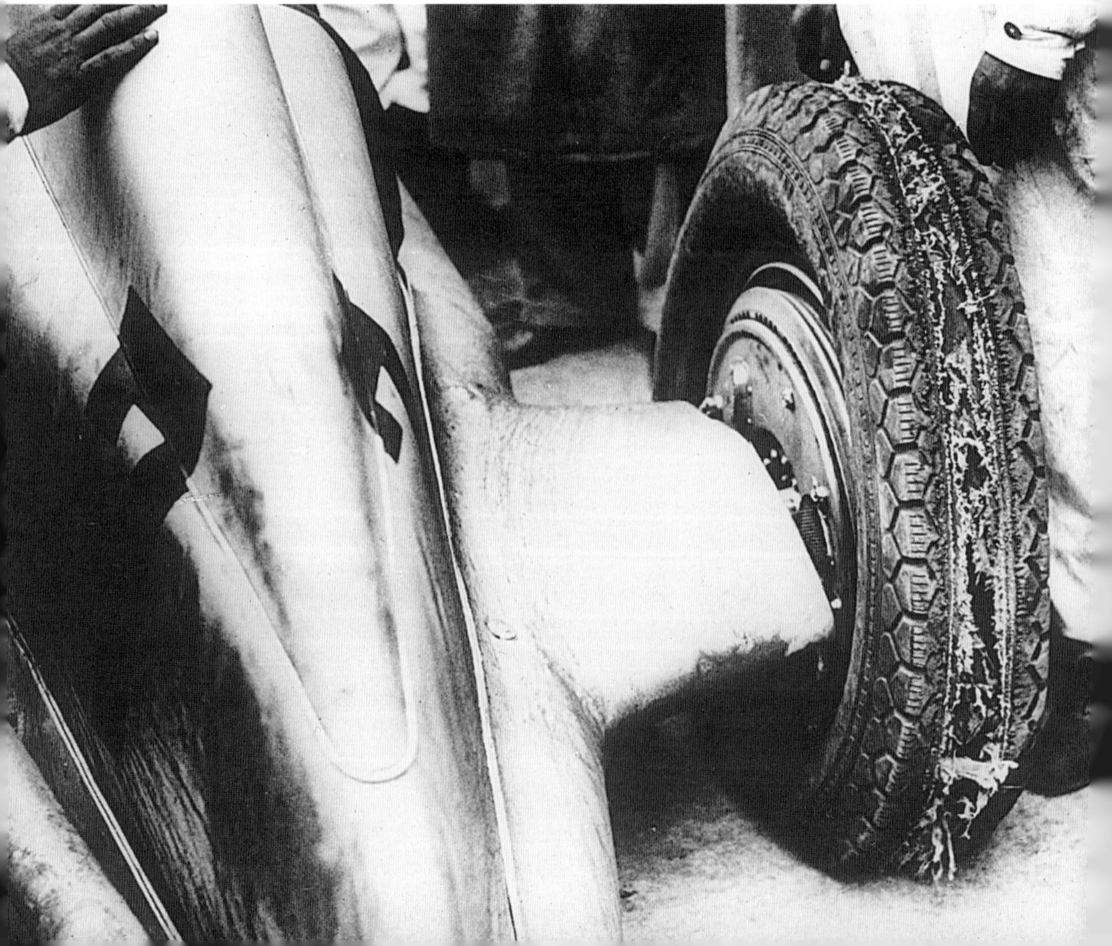

La Gazzetta dello Sport

SECONDA EDIZIONE

MARTEDÌ 13 Ottobre

LA COPPA VANDERBILT A ROOSEVELT FIELD

TAZIO NUVOLARI VINCE DI PREPOTENZA in terra d'America

sbaragliando tutti gli avversari del vecchio e del nuovo mondo e riaffermando la supremázia assoluta dell'automobilismo italiano

Brivio termina al terzo posto dietro Wimille, dopo aver marciato di conserva col vincitore sino a 3 giri dalla fine

(Dal nostro inviato speciale Giovanni Canestrini)

LA CLASSIFICA

L'ubbriacante carosello di 75 giri

Trionfo italiano nell'anniversario l'imperitura gloria di Cristoforo Colombo

I 43 concorrenti

BERTONI

SERTUM

DAILY MIRROR

FINAL 6 A.M.

New York, Tuesday, October 13, 1936

'LEG' CLUES IN SUITOR'S HOME

Story for this headline on Page

Italian Wins $85,000 Race

Time for Champagne

Sitting on top of the auto racing world, with his legs wrapped around the huge Vanderbilt Cup, Tazio Nuvolari, Italian winner of the Columbus Day 300-mile race on the Roosevelt Raceway, drinks a toast. Note "milkee" set to catch the champagne gurgle.

(Story on Page 20; Other photos on Pages 19, 20, and Back Page.)

Headline news as Nuvolari wins the Vanderbilt Cup.

The awkwardness of the Nazi era. This is Donington and Nuvolari has just won. His salute seems a careful compromise – but the ones to the left aren't. *(Neal Eason Gibson)*

The twilight years and, in close up, you can see how big the cars were – and how unprotected the driver was. *(Neil Eason Gibson)*

On a starting grid after the war. *(Neil Eason Gibson)*

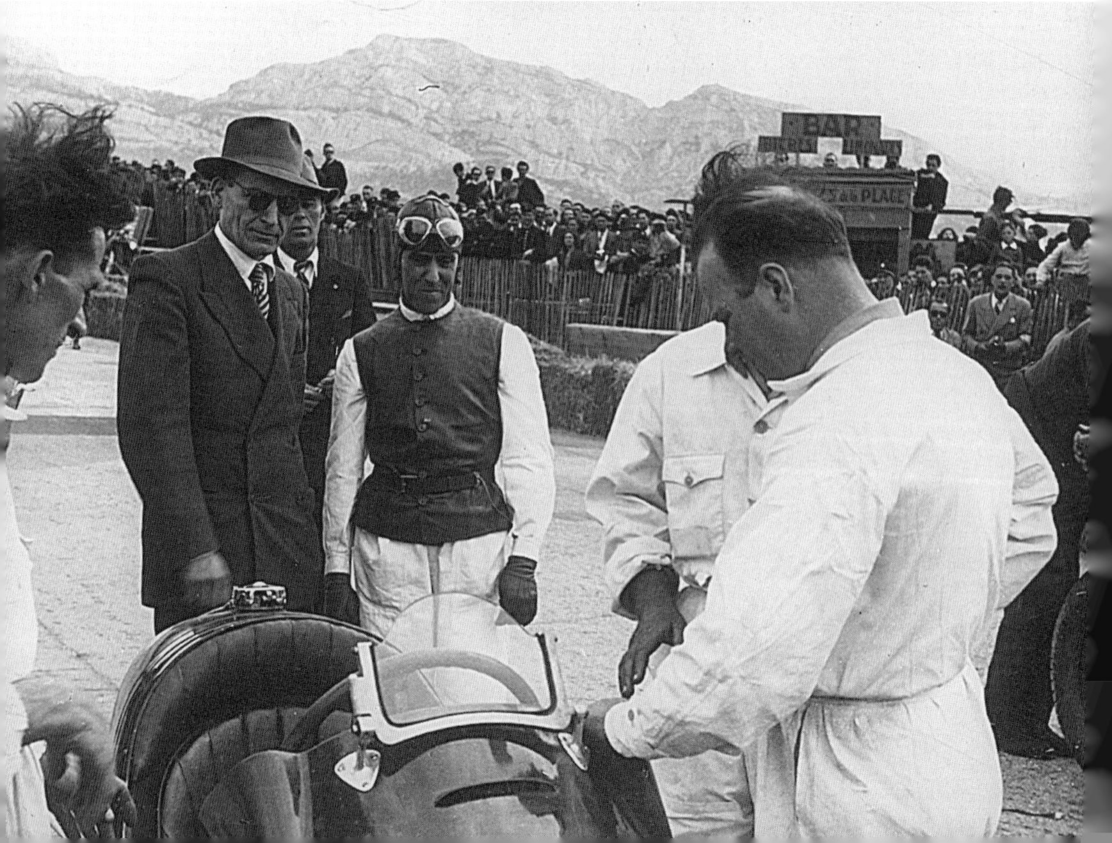

An amazing photograph of the 1946 Marseilles race: Nuvolari steers, Sommer works the pedals! *(Neil Eason Gibson)*

Nuvolari at Silverstone with Sir William Lyons. *(Neil Eason Gibson)*

The corner of Mantua where Nuvolari still lives – the museum. *(Author)*

Nuvolari lives! This is Neil Eason Gibson with part of his astonishing Nuvolari collection.

11

Final Gesture

Mille Miglia 1948

THE resumption of motor racing after the war was more difficult than virtually all other sporting activities. This has given a slightly sad, slightly unreal, slightly sporadic feeling to the end of Nuvolari's career.

The war in Europe ended on 7 May 1945 and in the Far East on 14 August. To write about the difficulties of restarting motor sport in the same paragraph as the liberation of Belsen or the nuclear bombs dropped on two Japanese cities is an obscenity; but if war achieves anything, it is that peace – and thus normality – is the reward for the destruction of tyranny.

The first post-war race meeting[1] was held on 9 September round the Bois de Boulogne in Paris. It comprised three races 'for vehicles which had survived the war.' Jabby Crombac, later to become a noted motor-racing journalist, went along to watch. 'There was great enthusiasm because life was starting again. What really struck me was the amount of smoke from the engines – they were all pre-war cars hastily prepared, so you had a cloud of smoke behind most of them.'

Nuvolari's second son, Alberto, died at Mantua on 11 April 1946, evidently of nephritis (inflammation of the kidneys). We do not know with any precision the impact this had on Nuvolari, but it seemed to

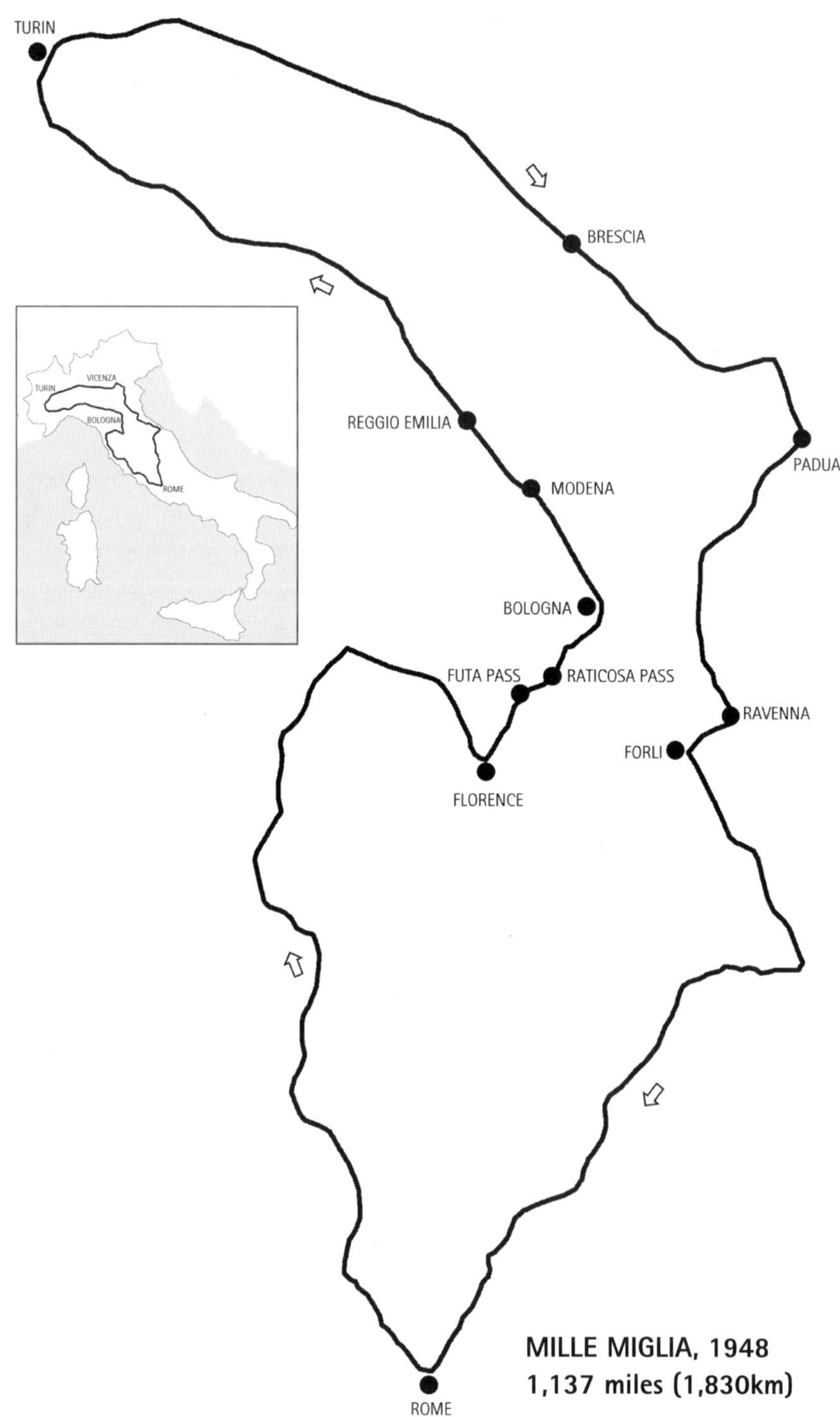

MILLE MIGLIA, 1948
1,137 miles (1,830km)

tear the heart out of him. It must have seemed to him a monstrous injustice that both his sons had died of natural causes, if I may phrase it like that, while he who had risked his life a thousand times remained alive.

He did not compete until 12 May 1946 in Marseilles (in a Maserati Tipo), then himself went to the Bois de Boulogne for the hauntingly named Resistance Cup. Crombac attended this, too.

Via a race at St Cloud, again in Paris, he went on to Como and Modena: he did not finish any of these races, but it seemed that entering five meetings in six weeks meant he was running as hard as he could against lost time. He was been 47 when the war began, and he was now 54.

In July he went to Albi in southern France for the Grand Prix there.

Rodney Walkerley of *The Motor* wrote two beautifully evocative pieces and I intend to quote extensively from both (firstly the one written a decade later, secondly the one written there and then) because they capture so much, not least the time which could no longer be recaptured.

> *The racing at Albi was like that at Dieppe in the early thirties and at Peronne, a typical French provincial meeting run with a happy informality and an unobtrusive efficiency which made the whole affair a pleasure.*
>
> *And there was little Nuvolari with a 1,500cc Maserati, a little grey at the temples, his eyes dark and deep-set, a little sadder than before because he had suffered the loss of his son, but his long, serious face with the enormous deep chin creased in a smile as I shouldered my way to his pit.*
>
> *He admired my 1.5 litre Riley saloon. He thought it elegant, clean-lined. He knew the Riley racing reputation. Could he take it round the circuit?*
>
> *And he drove it, at a speed which seemed excessive and yet effortless, with the merest touch of the brakes, for the first time.*
>
> *We took a corner at a remarkable speed. Then he said: 'It is the same for all racing. It is a question of equilibrium, not only the equilibrium of the car transversely as it corners, or*

from front to back, but during the passing from braking to acceleration. The two must flow together. The machine must never for one second hang inert between slowing down and picking up. It is another equilibrium. You find it with practice.'

From Albi (for *The Motor's* issue of 7 August 1946) Walkerley interviewed Nuvolari on the second day of practice. Nuvolari said

Things have not gone well for me. The war... that was a terrible mistake from the start. But what could I do? There were those of us in Italy who always regard England as a friend. It was terrible for us. But we could do nothing.

In my private life, too, things go very badly. All my life as I seemed to gain fame and glory on the circuits, my private fortunes grew worse and worse. Now I have lost my son, who was a fine boy – as tall as you – six feet, yes? Not like me. But he is dead. Now my wife goes to have an operation. She is very ill for a long time. I have no pleasure in life any more. Not even in racing. I continue to race because what else is there for me to do? Besides, it makes me forget. So I must go on and I am no longer young.

Later in the interview Nuvolari said:

I have never been to Albi before. My car is on the train so perhaps I will make a few late laps ['turns' was Nuvolari's word] *this evening or early in the morning. Always I arrive too late.*

Walkerley added:

Then they called the little man away to speak at the microphone where in his very correct French he had the crowd roaring with laughter at his diffident remarks that he thought the circuit offered many opportunities to the driver and that, perhaps, they would think it reasonable if he hoped to do well.

He won Albi and competed a further seven times in 1946, including the Grand Prix of Nations at Geneva. Clearly he had not lost his competitive edge, if I can put it that way, because Piero Taruffi[2] would remember him duelling with Wimille. 'As they went into a corner Nuvolari rammed the Frenchman's tail and put his car into a spin. When Wimille, naturally, complained after the race Nuvolari naively replied that he had left his braking too late and could not avoid the collision. This may have convinced the bystanders but it certainly did not satisfy Wimille, who looked very put out and incredulous.'

Crombac, a native of Geneva, attended here, too. 'He made a fantastic impression on me. The circuit was round the League of Nations building – a huge palace. Geneva is a fairly cold place during the winter and the streets, so soon after the war, were in a very poor state [attacked by frost and so on]. It was very bumpy. The Maserati had a live rear axle and that's what he had. The car was preceding him by [literally] leaps and bounds! If you see a modern Grand Prix car it goes straight as an arrow. This Maserati was bouncing from one side of the road to the other, and he was fighting it. He was small and bony. He was already very sick and I remember he was spitting as he went past: he had lung problems. He was very sun tanned. There were no crash helmets. He wore a red leather helmet, no protection in case of an accident, just something against the wind. He had a yellow tee-shirt with a turtle embroidered on it. There he was bouncing along in his cockpit, hanging on to his steering wheel. I don't know if he was deliberately overdoing it but he was certainly the most spectacular: not the quickest, because the Alfa Romeos were streets ahead. I was *caught* by the way Nuvolari acted in the car.'

Nuvolari did not begin the next season until April in San Remo. Then in June he went to the Mille Miglia. He had not competed in it since 1934, and intended to drive a Cisitalia. He did and damn nearly won in it, despite the fact that his health was no longer good. The car was an 'open version of a new 1100cc sports Cisitalia.'[3]

The course, now, went from Brescia through Padua to Ravenna and down the Adriatic coast, turning inland and wending a path to Rome, north up the Mediterranean coast, turning inland to Florence, up through Bologna and Alessandria to Turin, down through to Milan and Brescia again. The Minister of Commerce had to be persuaded to allocate 20,000 gallons of fuel – the scarcity of everything lingered well into 1947, and beyond.

The race began at 8pm on Saturday 21 June, the cars being dispatched at intervals of a minute, but the entry was so enormous that the last of them did not go until 3.00 the following morning. Clemente Biondetti, who'd won in 1938, was favourite in a 2.9-litre Alfa Romeo – he started an hour after Nuvolari. At Pesaro, Nuvolari was six minutes behind the early leader but on the run across the Appenines to Rome he accelerated – and so did Biondetti. At Rome, amid wild scenes – fuelled by a loud-speaker system which was linked to controls round the course and gave a running commentary – Nuvolari led Biondetti on the stagger by seven minutes. Between Rome and Florence, Biondetti clawed back five minutes. At Florence Nuvolari had covered 721 miles in 10h 13m 13s (averaging 69.9mph/112.4kph) and[4] 'handed the wheel over to his co-driver Carena for a spell.'

Nuvolari counter-attacked and by Bologna was nine minutes ahead. It was 'an inflamed duel' *(L'Automobile)*. He drove with a 'furious rhythm' *(Auto Italiana)*.

It seemed possible that the little car might actually win.

At Asti, up towards Turin, Biondetti had clawed the lead back to six minutes. On the run from Turin to Milan, Nuvolari went into a rainstorm and it soaked the open top Cisitalia. Lurani claims that Nuvolari then went through a dip in the road which had filled with water, and the engine cut. He lost many precious minutes and that gave the lead to Biondetti.

Even Nuvolari could not regain that, especially because the storm lasted all the way to Brescia. At one point it was so bad on the autostrada that Balestrero had to shelter himself and his car under a bridge.

> *The vast crowds lining the route did not know who was leading, because the electrical storms had put the telephone lines between controls out of order, but the magic name of Nuvolari thrilled across Italy.*
>
> *Nuvolari finished in second place at about 4.30pm on Sunday and was so exhausted by more than sixteen hours of driving that he had almost to be lifted out of the Cisitalia and*

carried into an hotel to receive medical attention. The winner, big, burly, modest Biondetti was in better shape.

Nuvolari said that the mountains were the most difficult part of the course, and rain seemed to fall all the time. He lost about fifteen minutes at the Ticino Bridge diversion on the Turin-Milan autostrada, where water swamped the engine and made a magneto change necessary.[5]

The result:

Biondetti	16h 16m 39s	(69.6mph/112.0kph)
Nuvolari	16h 32m 35s	
Bernabei	16h 38m 17s	
Ninetti	17h 0m 40s	
Capelli	No time	

Nuvolari raced only four more times in 1947 and began 1948 with the Mille Miglia again, having spent the winter mostly in bed. The circumstances of how he came to take part are not absolutely clear.

Some say Ferrari heard that Alfa Romeo intended to sign the little man for one last drive to defend their Mille Miglia... record. He then drove to Nuvolari's home ... and persuaded him to race. Others claim that Nuvolari came to Maranello and, after being shown the cars in the shop, decided to race on the spur of the moment. Both stories are probably apocryphal.[6]

One report suggests Nuvolari already had a contract with Cisitalia again, but his car was wrecked in an accident a week before the Mille Miglia. Another report suggests that he arrived in Brescia, where the race would – as usual – start and finish, looking 'a bit moody'. Some reporters interviewed him to discover why and he took a telegram from his pocket. It was from Cisitalia and informed him that it had not been possible to prepare his car in time, as promised, because of an incident to the engine during testing. Nuvolari still wanted to race and was looking for a car but obviously he'd have difficulty finding one at this late hour.

He contacted Enzo Ferrari. It was time to learn to love him one last time.

He had a choice between a coupé or open top and chose the open top because he 'reasoned the closed car would be restrictive for his damaged lungs. Clemente Biondetti... got the coupé by default. The notion of aging, heroic underdog Nuvolari... facing the rain, snow and ice of the Alpine passes while his principal adversary, the patrician Biondetti, cruised along in presumed luxury, prompted a national orgy of sympathy.'[7]

The cars began to be dispatched at midnight and went on at minute intervals, as in 1947, until 4.30 in the morning. The expected time of the first cars had been announced the day before: Verona 12.47am, Vicenza 1.21am, Padua 1.44am, Rovigo 2.13am, Ferrara 2.37am, Ravenna 3.21am, Forli 3.40am, Rimini 4.10am, Pesdaro 4.35am, Scheggia Pass 5.31am, Terni 6.51am, Rome 7.00am, Civitavecchia 8.47am, Grosseto 10.01am, Livorno 11.19am, Pisa 11.29am, Florence 12.14pm, Raticosa Pass 12.40pm, Bologna 1.10pm, Modena 1.16pm, Reggio Emilia 1.27pm, Tortona 2.45pm, Alessandria 2.55pm, Asti 3.11pm, Turin (autostrada) 3.36pm, Milan (autostrada) 4.36pm and Brescia 5.20pm.

Alberto Ascari (Maserati) took an early lead and at Padua he was averaging 145kph (90.1mph). He led Consalvo Sanesi (Alfa Romeo) by 1m 9s and Nuvolari by 1m 50s. Ascari soon fell back and Cortese (Ferrari) came through but his gearbox began to fail; Sanesi crashed.

At Forli, Taruffi driving a Cisitalia was in front averaging 132kph (82.0mph) but after Forli Nuvolari attacked. Into the Apennine passes – 'he called the twisty sections "my resources"' (Yates) – he gained so much time that at Rome he led overall, having covered 714 kilometres in 5h 40m 22s (averaging 125kph/77.6mph), followed three minutes later by Cortese, then Biondetti. At the Rome checkpoint, Nuvolari's car looked a wreck: the front left mudguard had shaken completely off and the whole bonnet had blown away. At the stop he levered himself out of the cockpit and everybody could see it then: his body movements were those of an old man, tentative, his arms pushing his torso upwards, his face lost in a grimace – of pain? Before he stepped out he seemed to need an instant to regain his balance.

After Rome, both Cortese and Ascari dropped out – Cortese had lost third gear and no doubt the whole gearbox surrendered soon after. Nuvolari was flying: at Florence he led Biondetti by 30 seconds but[8]

He came in... covered with mud and water. Blood was dribbling down his chin. The mechanic started to get out to check the car, but Nuvolari spat out a gob of blood and told him to stay aboard. He took a cursory look around the disintegrating car and got back in. Meanwhile two other cars had come into the control. They were free to leave before him, but when the drivers recognised him they refused to go, on the grounds that the crowd around Nuvolari's car must have held him up. They could not convince themselves that they had the right to leave before him. They waited until he was well on his way, several minutes down the road, before they would start.

Somewhere after Florence, as Yates writes:

... he overcooked it on a bend and spun into a ditch, damaging the rear suspension and breaking [co-driver] Scapinelli's seat loose from its mountings. Undeterred he negotiated the fearsome Futa and Raticosa passes.

The *Auto Italiana* caught the mood of the day:

He snaked... towards Florence, the steep and difficult Futa, Bologna and the wide roads of the Po valley. A sprinkling of rain, a heavy shower and then a downpour followed Nuvolari as if trying to cool his ardour. Nothing [could do that]. Nuvolari went on and the gap behind him got larger and in all the towns in Italy where a loudspeaker was able to give news of the great run, hundreds of thousands of listeners seemed to go mad.

Inevitably the worsening conditions made the mountain roads slippery and a Maserati went off the road, killing the mechanic. Meanwhile Nuvolari came down out of the mountains to Bologna, where he now led Biondetti by 29 minutes. He moved along the straight, flat road to Modena and then on to Reggio-Emilia. Near there a spring failed and the Ferrari cruised to a halt.

It was by definition a legendary moment, and the final proof that you don't really ever get the girl, the money and the fame all in the moment. It has also been – following the theme which has echoed gently down the whole of this book – a subject of conflicting testimonies.

Yates says that 'furious, Tazio Nuvolari climbed out, ending the last titanic drive of his incomporable career.' Purdy says the '56-year-old Nuvolari sat beside the road, weeping, until a village priest came along and took him home and put him to bed.' *Auto Italiana* says Nuvolari 'checked that the break was irreparable. He did not swear: he asked only for a bed to rest in.'

From his very first motorbike race at Cremona on 20 June 1920 all the way to here – 2 May 1948 – he'd earned a rest, all right.

* * * * *

Intermezzo

It has been said there's a pathos in old age, and I suppose there is. Tazio Nuvolari was not, in 1948, old in any accepted sense today but all those years of breathing fumes had damaged his lungs and he seemed old.

Two weeks after the Mille Miglia he drove a Cisitalia in the Monaco Grand Prix, qualifying on the sixth row of the grid (of eight). He was eighth on lap 8 but retired on lap 16. A broken piston was given as the reason.

He was fourth overall in the Grand Prix of Bari, but he was sharing a Ferrari Tipo and handed it over to his co-driver after three laps. He was second at Mantua, in a race named after his sons. He went into the lead while Ascari, Cortese, Villoresi and Felice Bonetto pursued: we may imagine that they made sure it was a good show. Certainly Bonetto took the lead from him and certainly Nuvolari regained it. His health wouldn't permit him to drive beyond lap 8. He was seventh in the French Grand Prix at Rhiems, sharing the driving again.

By now Crombac was getting pit passes because, as he points out, the organisers of races only issued the positions every 20 laps or so and 'if a team wanted to know where it was they had to have someone doing a lap chart. Not everybody could but I learnt how. This is where I met Nuvolari, at Rhiems. He didn't do the full race because he was already very, very sick.

I was invited to come and do the lap chart for a guy who was running in the small races – the curtain-raiser – a fellow called De'saugé, who knew Nuvolari. We were wandering round the paddock waiting for practice and he saw Nuvolari. He said "hello, Tazio" and he introduced me. Tazio extended his hand and shook mine. I didn't wash my hand for a couple of days! I was 19, I was completely smitten by motor racing and for me he was the greatest. Before the war there is no doubt he was the greatest driver. In fact I can prove it by quoting René Dreyfus. I saw a lot of Dreyfus after the war and one day I did ask him "who was the quickest in your day?" He answered "the one we all feared was Tazio." Therefore to shake his hand – me just a lap charter – was something fantastic. I think he may have spoken a little bit of French, I didn't speak Italian but in any case I wouldn't have spoken to him because he was the big star and I was the young fan. You don't speak to these guys, you just listen to them with bated breath!'

In 1949, Nuvolari only competed once (Marseilles, when he handed the Maserati over to his co-driver after a single lap) but journeyed to Britain, as Neil Eason Gibson recounts:

> *... to drive at Silverstone for William Lyons*[9] *in what was called a production race in those days. After a while in the car he was taken ill and he ended up in an hotel in Brackley in bed. My father* [a prominent motor sport figure] *was basically the interpreter and wanted to make sure he was all right. We ended up in his bedroom where he was in bed with a hairnet on. I knew quite a few Italians who wore a hairnet to keep their hair in place at night so they don't get it all ruffled and messy. Lurani used to wear a hairnet – I stayed with him once in the north of Italy and he came down for breakfast in the morning wearing one!*
>
> *Nuvolari had charisma, definitely, even lying there in bed. I think some of his victories were due to the fact that people were beaten before the start. The only one who seemed to fight against him at his peak was Varzi.*
>
> *A lot of people said you could never learn the Mille Miglia course but I should think Nuvolari* [was so intuitively good that he] *knew it without having to learn it. I certainly don't think he was a wild man at any time because he knew his capabilities.*

I remember the last historic Mille Miglia I went to some years ago and there was an elderly gentleman sitting on the kerb – I think a Grand Prix driver from the 1930s who might even have driven in the Mille Miglia when Nuvolari did. He was wearing the gold badge that Nuvolari gave to friends. It wasn't until I'd got on the plane home that I suddenly realised the badge suggested what this driver might have been.

It was a badge of honour, still conferring – mute, against the tide of the years – intimacy and status, and keeping memory safe.

He drove a time or two more, at the Targa Florio in April 1950 where the Cisitalia broke down or, as some reports had it, he broke down; and at a Palermo hill climb where he won his class and was fifth overall. His presence attracted several thousand spectators who still had eyes for only him.

That was it.

Then he rested.

12

Man on the Unbroken Horse

I STARTED this book by insisting that no attempt was being made to compare the great drivers of different eras. I only claimed that, among all those who have made any kind of a study of the subject, when the talk does turn to Fangio and Clark and Senna and Schumacher, Nuvolari is always there, too. I hope, by now, that you understand why.

Nuvolari lives, or rather his memory lives, and that means this chapter can begin in the present.

I asked Neil Eason Gibson why he has an obsession about him. He replied:

> *I wouldn't say it's an obsession. When I started reading books about motor sport, and the reviews in magazines and articles, they always came across as written by people who couldn't understand why this one person had such a grasp of how to drive, or how people accepted him as being their better at motor sport. Rodney Walkerley,[1] who did that interview at Albi with Nuvolari, used to say that you could not explain why he did what he did. He just did it!*

The Mayor of Mantua, Gianfranco Burchiellaro, suggests that Nuvolari lives on not only because of the 'pages of history he wrote – however exciting they were – but also for his social work. During his life he did a great deal in road-safety for young people. It's important, maybe essential, that sports people and other competitive people who stand out must be linked to society. That is why I say that today Tazio Nuvolari is linked. He represents the highest expression of a pioneer in motor racing, and as that he has become part of the historical and cultural context of Mantua.'

Moving from the present, I want to draw in several aspects of the past.

There is always an element of mystery about the truly great ones in any human activity but arguably more so in those who master machinery, and even more so if that machinery is simultaneously delicate, dangerous and unimaginably fast. You have to wonder how it can be that hundreds of millions of people drive, many thousands have driven competition cars, several hundred have driven Grand Prix cars but only a tiny number – say less than ten – have been able to elevate it to a level unattainable to all the rest.

It cannot be simply physical – Nuvolari small, Fangio verging on the portly, Schumacher almost lean – because, we must assume, those hundreds who have driven Grand Prix cars *all* had fast reflexes, good co-ordination, excellent eyesight, were all more or less fit, and so on. There is no suggestion that the great ones had any decisive physical advantage over the rest.

Clearly stamina plays an important part, more then than now because the races were so long and the conditions so rugged, but again we must assume that others had as much of it as Nuvolari, or almost as much. If they hadn't they couldn't have done the races.

In terms of comparison, man to man, I suspect bravery plays a less significant part (although Ken Purdy will be querying that in a moment). Mike Hailwood, who's dad Stan had been in the 1933 TT at Ards, once wrote that no man is fearless. Accepting that – because Mike was himself regarded by others as fearless, so he knew – we must assume that all racers have a certain level of bravery, and perhaps an excess of it might be a dangerous thing. We shall be hearing testimony in a moment that much of what Nuvolari did with a racing car seemed the product of bravery pitched into recklessness, but it wasn't that at all. This man *thought*.

No, the difference between the few and the many must be in the mind, must be more mental than physical: personality, desire, judgement, strategy and the instinctive *feel* for the machinery which was so clearly visible at Ards, adjust-adjust-adjusting. That one man's limit may be so different to another's in a corner, when they are both competent and in identical cars, can only be this feeling – this mental balance translated to the physical. The moment of truth for any driver is when his teammate out-drives him regularly in an identical car.

Evidently Nuvolari had exceptional balance, even though we have treated the saddle-vaulting at school with caution. We have just heard him explaining, at Albi in Walkerley's Riley, about holding all the forces of a car in balance. He once said that 'he could tell to a kilo the amount of weight on any wheel of a car in any situation, cornering, accelerating, braking, drifting, whatever.'[12]

This is strangely reminiscent of the sort of thing Senna could do: in karting he once pointed out that one of the tyres lacked a tiny amount of pressure and initially the team disbelieved him. They were wrong. Moreover Senna could do a five-lap run in testing and then recount, corner by corner, what all four wheels had been doing. The people who worked with him found this difficult to believe at the time, and some still do, just because it is so unattainable – that word again – to even good Grand Prix drivers.

It is also strangely reminiscent of Clark. Technicians, comparing the tyre wear of the top drivers of his era, discovered that some drivers wore the fronts out faster than the rears, or the left front faster than the right front. When they examined Clark's they discovered the wear was *precisely* the same on all four. It meant he had the car perfectly balanced at all moments. They had never seen this before and, I'll wager, never saw it again. Clark was an instinctive driver and was probably unaware of this perfection in any conscious, thinking way – he did it because it must have *felt* right, and in that he is instantly united with Nuvolari and Senna.

The difference between the few and the many may well be, too, in technique: what you do in any given set of circumstances and how you do it. Enzo Ferrari *(The Enzo Ferrari Memoirs)* found that out when he went with Nuvolari as a passenger.

> *At the first bend, I had the clear sensation that Tazio had taken it badly and that we would end up in the ditch. I felt myself stiffen as I waited for the crunch. Instead we found ourselves on the next straight with the car in a perfect position. I looked at him. His rugged face was calm, just as it always was, and certainly not the face of someone who escaped a hair-raising spin. I had the same sensation at the second bend. By the end of the fourth or fifth bend I began to understand.*
>
> *In the meantime, I had noticed that through the entire bend Tazio did not lift his foot from the accelerator and that, in fact, it was flat on the floor. As bend followed bend, I discovered his secret. Nuvolari entered the bend somewhat earlier than my driver's instinct would have told me to. But he went into the bend in an unusual way: with one movement he aimed the nose of the car at the inside to where the curve itself started. His foot was flat down and he had obviously changed down to the right gear before going through this fearsome rigmarole.*
>
> *In this way he put the car into a four wheel drift, making the most of the thrust of the centrifugal force and keeping it on the road with the traction of the driving wheels. Throughout the bend the car shaved the inside edge, and when the bend turned into the straight the car was in the normal position for accelerating down it, with no need for any corrections.*

To modernise this, and give you a variation of such sensitivity, I offer you what Gerard Ducarouge[3] was telling me the other day, about when Senna won in the wet in Estoril in 1985: while the others floundered and spun off Senna was driving *the equivalent of a dry race*. Senna's feel permitted this, and it enabled him to apply his technique on top of his mental strength. Watch Schumacher in any wet race and you see the same: one time in Spain, Schumacher rode a thunderstorm with his car in such absolute control that it can only have been abnormal feel. He overtook several cars on the first lap quite normally, although because the visibility was so bad he had no idea how many.

Eason Gibson, however, does point to a very basic difference between then and now which strengthens Nuvolari's claim to be included among the ultimate greats of the sport:

> *It comes down to the fact that he did things with a car at a time when motor sport was dangerous, very dangerous. There was an article recently by Tony Brooks[4] asking how you can compare Fangio and Schumacher. He said you can't because, when Fangio was driving, motor sport was dangerous, as it said on the signs. Nowadays you might as well throw the signs away because Grand Prix racing is not dangerous. He said he'd asked Fangio what was the difference between then and now, and Fangio said 'I lost 33 people in motor racing when I raced.' That is the difference – and in Nuvolari's day it was more dangerous still.*

This might seem to contradict my point about bravery but it doesn't because the drivers of the 1930s to the 1960s, maybe even 1970s, all confronted very real danger every time they got into a car and – certainly in the 1930s – were inhibited from excessive risk: the cars and circuits would give back lethal answers if you asked them those questions. Let's leave them all as brave men.

Eason Gibson does feel that Nuvolari 'did things which, in theory, should have taken you straight off the course. I've been over the Mille Miglia route twice and I think of the Raticosa Pass if it was raining, the cloud had come down, there wasn't tarmac – and he drove in the dark. The only other one who could drive like that was Rosemeyer, who could see in the fog.'

In fact, Bernd Rosemeyer was another outstanding driver of the 1930s and evidently had a freakish ability to see not only through fog but spray in wet races, too. That's another story.

In an interview with *Sports Illustrated* Nuvolari explained how methodical he was in preparation, strategy and technique. It dispelled the notion of devil-may-care absolutely.

The first thing you do, he said, was embark on a complete examination of the circuit – this was before he took a car out – to gauge the correct gearing: fast circuit – high; slower circuit because of many corners – low; compromise circuit between the two – medium. That done, he did take the car out and practised as much as he could even before he reached the qualifying sessions. The practice was both learning and rehearsing: by constant repetition, he came to know every metre of the circuit intimately, experimenting with his braking points and gear changes and points of acceleration. He said that *only* by this practice ritual could he come to know the maximum speed he could take a corner without losing control. He saw such a loss of control not in terms of danger but of time lost.

He also took the opportunity to watch the opposition doing their laps, perhaps picking up ideas for his own driving, certainly noting who was on form.

This done, he felt a calmness. He'd eat well and sleep well.

Ken Purdy expands on this when he writes of how Nuvolari was 'a great student' of the nature of track surfaces and in practice experimented with what we call 'lines' – the optimum lines a racing car should take for maximum speed round a circuit. Evidently Nuvolari took this a stage further and conducted experiments by putting wheels off – to see what would happen, and store that information in case it happened during the race.

Purdy refines this by adding that Nuvolari occupied himself with 'bumps' and anything unusual about the surfaces. If he gave you a ride, 'even in a little Fiat sedan,' he'd demonstrate how these bumps could be *used* [my italics] to help the car change direction. This was a 'great revelation' even to those who fancied themselves as drivers.

To *Sports Illustrated* Nuvolari gave a revealing glimpse into his character. He was never nervous before a race, he said, although he might be during practice if the car wasn't right or the session was delayed for some reason. He can't have meant nervous but irritated and impatient. On the day of the race he was 'perfectly calm' and certainly experienced no nerves during the race – his concentration on the driving, of course, precluded emotions. The concentration involved watching all the cockpit dials as he watched cars front and back – especially any car coming up to challenge.

Like most racing drivers he could never remember which lap he was on, so every time he went past his pit he looked for the board they held out to him. That gave him the lap, other relevant information and when to pit. He added that the timing of the pit stops had been decided before the race. Once he did pit – and remember the pit stops were long then, sometimes minutes – he made a point of relaxing, lit a cigarette and had a drink. (Mischievously, no doubt. He explained to the American reporter 'no, nothing alcoholic!') He did say that he habitually carried a thermos flask in the cockpit so he could have a cool drink if he felt like it.

This suggests a meticulous approach – genius has an infinite capacity for taking pains, as we know – but throws little or no light on the mystery of his greatness.

Since Nuvolari's day, sporting performances that can be measured have improved to an astonishing degree. Consider: 1932, the year Nuvolari won Monaco. The Olympic Games were held in Los Angeles and the marathon won in a time of 2h 31m; in Sydney 2000 that had been reduced to 2h 10m – 21 minutes. What does that translate to? Four *miles*. And so it goes everywhere you look.

Why should the sports you can't measure – cricket, soccer and so on – be exceptions? No one can watch even a clip of tennis from Wimbledon in the 1930s and avoid wincing at what even mediocre modern players would do to the *winners* then.

If you get into these arguments, you always come up against the proviso that the modern players have superior equipment, training, diet, fitness and a psychological understanding of what these days is called motivation. Hence their superiority. (My own feeling is that if you are prepared to discharge yourself from hospitals in order to risk your life, or continue to drive a car which is on fire, you don't need any lessons from a sports psychologist about motivation.)

During the same period technology has made the modern car much easier to drive. Were there not rumours that one team had taken a car at racing speed round Silverstone not so long ago by remote control, no driver in there at all? And we constantly hear bleating and groaning that this technology has removed the skill of the driver. Nuvolari's magic has been replaced by the microchip. Maybe Schumacher's claim to greatness rests not on the staggering statistics he has amassed but on something even more impressive: his creation of ways to dominate a generation of opponents while all were held within the constraints of the technology. In theory that ought to have made such domination impossible. In broad terms, a car can be programmed to deal with a circuit automatically, and one of Senna's complaints was that the technology exercised a levelling. The ordinary driver could take a corner much as the great driver could, because the *technology* was taking the corner in both cases.

Nuvolari had minimal assistance of this nature – well, none! – and some of the incidents we've seen in the book remind us forcibly of that: the black soap to repair the fuel tank at Le Mans, then chewing gum; the tool boxes they carried and, in one flickering black and white image – not Nuvolari – a car is being refuelled with coal from sacks.

What Nuvolari did is arguably superior to anything since, *because* the technology was rudimentary and the roads were rudimentary too. In order to gain an insight in to the conditions that he faced I drove out of Bologna retracing the Mille Miglia route.

You start on flat land, lush and verdant, but soon enough after a village or two you're rising. The 50 kilometres or so of road is smooth as it twists and turns up what is now a gentle slope. Women taking their children to school in modest little saloons clip along at 70 or 80kph, no bother at all. Higher up the road becomes bleaker as the vegetation thins, the trees and the bushes are hardier, and sudden vistas of valleys spread themselves below. There is still nothing alarming. You reach the Raticosa Pass at the top, almost a thousand metres above sea, and the road remains smooth. There's a plain restaurant to one side, nothing much to the other except a junction. You do need to force your imagination to see what it must have been and why so many describe it in terms of awe, this same Raticosa.

The descent from the pass altered everything because the route through one village was being resurfaced, a detour in operation. The detour pitched traffic onto the old country lanes: narrow, rendered blind by hedgerows and copses of trees, muddy, switchback, rough, uneven.

If Nuvolari was doing 70 or 80kph an hour over these, he was a hell of a driver – especially in stiff cars with awful brakes, and especially, too, because the Mille Miglia could not be run on perfectly closed roads. He didn't know what was coming at him, or across him, round the next corner any more than I did. Now imagine him doing it at night.

And the magnificent madness that I mentioned at the very beginning? That was not carelessly risking his life, as so many people writing about him have insisted, but a contempt for any manner of physical setback which any rational person would have accepted: racing the motorbike swathed in bandages, discharging himself from hospitals to race cars, pushing the car at Monaco *after he'd continued steering it standing up to avoid the flames* – and all that with the race lost; driving a car towards the point of disintegration in the Mille Miglia and, made wretched and weak by illness, forcing it to the point where it did begin to disintegrate.

One time Senna crashed at Monaco, an unforced error, and was still sobbing about it in his apartment at 9.00 that evening. It happened near the entrance to the tunnel, 56 years after Nuvolari passed precisely this way with the Alfa Romeo on fire. The need to win is a very deep thing. I believe Senna would have fully understood that Nuvolari *had* to ignore the flames and *had* to push the car because, within himself, he could never surrender – or live with himself if he did. That is magnificent madness. 'Someone in Italy told me once,' Eason Gibson says, 'that if you watched Nuvolari he always seemed to be steering at something *which nobody else could see.* Maybe that's it: read ahead, see a problem which might arise and correct – position the car or whatever – before it does *so you don't have the problem.* The brakes in those days were so bloody terrible that you might go in this direction or that direction if you used them. Nuvolari's solution? Not to touch the brakes! Amazing…'

René Dreyfus[5] says that Nuvolari 'was the kindest of men, completely unpretentious, wonderful company. In the Italian Grand Prix in 1935, you know, I handed my car over to him after his own had failed, and he finished second. Afterwards he refused any of the prize money, said it should all go to me. "It was your car, and you allowed me to race it," he said. "That was all I wanted." There has never been anyone like Nuvolari.'

I've included this anecdote because, although it is delightful in itself and worth including just for that, it is something more. It counters the notion that Nuvolari liked money more than a principled person might. More broadly it reflects the whole of our story because it reveals, yet again, how contradictory the evidence for Nuvolari's character is. I have tried to pick a path through it without ever losing sight of the small, leathery man with the strong forearms and toothy grin who comes to us, still, as largely a stranger.

Dreyfus added that 'perhaps Rudolf Caracciola was technically the best – the most complete – but the greatest without any doubt was Nuvolari. In his case you had the impression of a man on an unbroken horse – but instead of fighting it he let it run free. With him, there was no accepted 'line' around a circuit: he would turn into a corner early, aim at the apex, put the power down hard and do the steering with the throttle using his hands only for small corrections. It was his speed out of the corners which was so exceptional. We all tried to copy his technique but no one can borrow another man's instinct. Only Tazio could drive like Tazio. What you have to remember about those times is that the cars had almost no grip, almost no brakes. Therefore cornering speeds were set very much more by the driver than by the car. I was also a member of the Scuderia Ferrari at that time and thought I was a pretty good driver but Tazio would pass me in corners, travelling at a completely different speed – as if he were on a dry track, and for me it was raining…'

Yes, Clark anywhere, Senna at Estoril, Schumacher in Spain…

Hans Ruesch captures an aspect quite different to all this, and curiously enough it is one rarely discussed. It is normality.

> *Most of the time in racing is spent talking, sitting in the pits talking, talking, talking. And of course we all talked. Nuvolari was a perfectly normal person. He often had his wife along and his wife was very, very nice. He was a car nut. Nothing else interested him. He had a fixed idea and it was just racing. I can give you one interesting example of a conversation with Nuvolari. I was wearing a helmet – an iron helmet, French and from World War One for a soldier. Special crash helmets did not exist and very few people wore helmets of any kind.*

Anyway, the conversation was in Alessandria, a road race near Genoa. All the crazy racers were there – and Nuvolari. We were speaking about this: should we wear a helmet or not? Nuvolari said it's impossible, you can never wear a helmet, absolutely not, only a little linen skullcap like a Balaclava. He didn't feel right in a helmet. He said 'I must sense the wind.' I understood that, too, and, because of what Nuvolari said, I decided to get rid of my helmet. From the next race on, I would wear only a Balaclava like him.

In the practice at Alessandria I had an accident. I was thrown out of the car, the car went up into the sky, and I hit my head on a milestone. My metal helmet had a big dent in it and I was completely stunned. I lay there in the grass, my mechanics came and they all thought I was dead. After a moment or two I was perfectly OK again but I saw the dent in the helmet and from that day on I never abandoned it.

We are back trying to sort the fact from the myth. Cholmondeley-Tapper[6] is interesting on that.

Nuvolari... was often called in his own country the 'Son of the Devil' – fearless – but from my acquaintance with him I found this catch phrase inaccurate. He would make no secret of his dislike of any particularly dangerous section of a course, and, in spite of what sometimes appeared to be extremely abandoned driving, he did in fact know exactly what he was doing, and possessed sound judgment and a thorough knowledge of his capabilities.

He always sat well back in the cars he drove, so as to allow complete freedom of arm movement when cornering, and unless hard pressed he would rarely use brakes to the full, retarding speed by slewing his car across the track on corners. His methods were not always understood, and he left a perplexed inquirer on one occasion when, after winning a TT race on an MG in Ireland, he was asked what he thought of its brakes, and replied that he could hardly tell, as he had never used them fully.

Contrary to what one might expect, Nuvolari was a very safe driver on the public roads, and although he liked to travel fast where possible, he used his private cars carefully. When I knew him, he owned a Lancia Augusta of which he thought very highly, although it was not even the latest model from the Lancia factory.

Piero Taruffi[7] discusses technique and does a little era vaulting. 'Comparing the style of Nuvolari with that of Varzi – talking in terms of drift angles and percentages – I would say that Varzi generally cornered at 15–16 degrees drift angle... while Nuvolari more often took corners at 18–22 degrees. The net result was almost the same. Varzi's method gave higher speed on the road after the corner, and was lighter on tyres; Nuvolari's favoured overtaking on the way in, and saved time when a series of corners came after a fast straight. It was also lighter on brakes.'

Taruffi had a way of awarding marks for cornering – entry, during, exiting – and 'comparing Ascari and Fangio I would give [them higher] markings than those of Nuvolari and Varzi. This is because pre-war cars were less precise in their construction than modern ones, and did not allow the same results to be achieved. For this reason I do not feel inclined to draw direct comparisons between the two sets of drivers, as I am often asked to do, nor shall I extend the comparison to include present-day drivers [1964], who are continually coming closer to the limit, partly because the technique of driving is now far more widely understood, but mainly because the cars they drive have progressed enormously in manageability, precision and cornering power.'

It's an age-old argument about relative merits and, because the vault from Nuvolari across Fangio and Senna to Schumacher is so wide and deep, it remains conjectural, almost a matter of personal preference rather than judgement. Perhaps the best we can say is that, as Sir Jackie Stewart insists, you can only be the best in your own era and, beyond that, nobody knows.

Yet there is something utterly compelling about Nuvolari and his legend, something more than hero worship from afar. It's something to do with very great intuitive skill being forged with meticulous approach and then brought to an immortal climax. There's a quality about the whole of his career which hovers between conjuring, faith-healing and mind over matter.

Ken Purdy dismisses talk of a pact with the devil and black magic, and sums up what he believed Nuvolari had: a lifetime's experience, courage so intense he found the possibility of death 'insignificant', and a skill built on 'abnormally, almost freakishly fast reaction.' Purdy quotes one expert who said: 'Nuvolari's reaction in emergency was so nearly instantaneous as to appear pure instinct, bringing him unscathed from a situation that wrecked other drivers. His truly amazing skill was demonstrated over and over again by his sensational performance with cars which lacked the speed of his rivals.'

Every day takes us further away from Nuvolari. Yet as Neil Eason Gibson says there is little danger of him being forgotten – 'Not as long as we've got good people who may never have met or seen him but want to write about him and talk about him. As long as that goes on I don't think he will disappear. People will always want to speculate about who was the greatest.'

The greatest: that word keeps coming back.

Nuvolari went to hospital in Mantua on 3 June 1953. He knew recovery was no longer possible[8] and he 'told his friends that the man they had come to see was dead. He was alone anyway: most of those he had raced against were gone, dead at the wheel to the last man': Rosemeyer who'd brought him to Auto Union, one way or another; Varzi, who remains an elegant mystery of a man; Wimille whom Nuvolari had punted so unceremoniously out of the way; Sommer who'd circled Le Mans while the lights of night flickered and he waited so eagerly to take over; Dick Seaman, the Englishman lost in the Reich; Ascari senior, beset by the superstitions his son Alberto inherited and took to his own grave; Borzacchini of the Tripoli share-out; Archangeli…

Past and present are united in this: when it's all happening, the scale of the races – teams, cars, officials, spectators – is so vast, and the races themselves wring so much from each passing second, that you think somehow the grim reaper could never take all of this away and leave only silence and memory.

It was impossible to be at Le Mans in 1933, just as it is impossible to be there today, and think sometime it will all be gone, *everything;*

impossible to see the hundreds of thousands thronging the Mille Miglia – noisy, gesticulating, a whole country caught in the immense communal emotion of it – and see them all gone; impossible to be at Monte Carlo as the cars go hunting in a pack up the hill, in front of so many rich residents and poorer visitors, and think that even this cannot withstand the reaper.

But it has all gone into silence and memory now.

That is why we are back where we began, with Nuvolari still coming to us in black and white photographs and flickering film taken from the middle distance. But I hope that, now we are near the end of our story, we are closer to the man and can appreciate what the film truly represents.

When Nuvolari died, John Cooper wrote a touching and elegant farewell in *The Autocar's* issue of 21 August 1953. Here it is.

> *Nobody who ever saw Tazio Nuvolari drive – as I count myself fortunate to have done – could ever forget him. The 'Flying Mantuan', as he was affectionately known, with his small wiry build, his nut-brown hatchet face and white teeth, his red helmet, yellow pullover and gay scarf, made an irresistible spectacle, pulling faces, working at the wheel, almost dancing from side to side in the cockpit as he hurled the car round corners at hair-raising speeds, defying all the accepted rules of line or style. No – there will never be another Nuvolari and I shall always think of him as incomparable, the greatest of them all.*

There's the word again. It will be staying.

Notes

Introduction

1. *Car Magazine,* April 1997.
2. Piazza Broletto, 9 – 46100 Mantua.
3. *Tazio Nuvolari, Il Mantovano Volante,* Studio Max-Pol S.n.c, available from the museum.
4. *Omnibus of Speed,* in the chapter 'Nuvolari: The Devil from Mantua'.
5. Taruffi, *Works Driver.*
6. Yates, *Enzo Ferrari: the Man and the Machine.*
7. Knickers is an American abbreviation for knickerbockers, which, according to the *Concise Oxford Dictionary,* are 'loose-fitting breeches gathered at the knee or calf.' So there.
8. Cholmondeley-Tapper, *Amateur Racing Driver.*
9. Moretti, *When Nuvolari Raced.*
10. Ibid.
11. *Nuvolari* by Count Lurani. I am grateful to Neil Eason Gibson, long-time motor racing activist, for this portrait of Lurani: 'He used to race before the war. In fact he drove an Aston Martin at the 24 hours of Pescara and raced Alfa Romeos. He was one of the MG team when they did the Mille Miglia – he spent most of the time being the co-driver. He felt that he was a gift to motor sport in Italy. He was very proud of his ancestry and he was scared stiff of his mother, who dominated him completely until she died – she was a challenge to anybody! He nearly bowed to her when she was having a go at him. When she died he lost his direction a bit.

    'She was not poor. They had this castle just north of Monza [and if you were staying there] he took people out to a little village and put you off Italian food by giving you olives and garlic! You had to eat it as soon as it was made because it went off in an hour. You never spoke to anyone afterwards because you'd knock them out with the garlic. Powerful stuff!

'He was part of historic motoring for years, he was just a character. He spent his time going round races in Europe. I'm not sure whether he bought the cars he raced or was lent them because of who he was in Italy. He was not a bad driver. He was attractive to young women and I think he was married three times.

'He was a stickler for accuracy on some things. At Monza for a run of the historic championship, Lurani was there making sure the Italian cars coming in were legal – he let off a fog horn to tell one driver his 1932 Alfa wasn't! This little chap looked at Lurani, said "yes sir, yes sir" – and he left.'

12 I went to interview Ruesch in his apartment in Milan: a fascinating man, irascible, very self-certain, and yet an olde worlde charm about him. It turned out that he was very passionately involved in *Civis,* the organisation for medicine without vivisection. As a matter of principle, he would not accept that *any* experiments on animals had yielded *any* benefit and, further, claimed in the most trenchant way that if I mentioned *Civis* in *any* publication, the publishers would be so frightened of offending multinational corporations they'd strike it out.

Wrong, sir. I just have and the publishers just haven't.

Chapter 1

1. Nicolò Paganini (1782–1840) was a composer and violinist 'considered by many the greatest of all time' according to the website www.paganini.com/nicolo/nicindex.htm. 'His playing of tender passages was so beautiful that his audiences often burst into tears, and yet he could perform with such force and velocity that at Vienna one listener became half crazed and declared for some days that he had seen the devil helping the violinist.'

2 Moretti, *When Nuvolari Raced.*

3 There is a typically Italian confusion over the name Castel D'Ario itself – should it be Casteldario? Moretti gives both on successive pages! Lurani gives it as a single word, and so does the museum booklet. The Michelin guide to Italy gives it as two. I have gone for two, because that's what the road sign says when you get to it.

4 Moretti, op. cit.

5 Yates, *Enzo Ferrari: The Man and the Machine.*

6 Moretti, op. cit.

7 Sheldon, *A Record of Grand Prix and Voiturette Racing.*

8 *Chronicle of the Twentieth Century,* entry datelined 26 April 1915. 'The worst fears of Germany and Austria about Italy, their Triple

Alliance partner, have been realised. Italy will come in on the Allied side.'

9 Moretti, op. cit.

10 Yates, op. cit.

11 www.kaleden.com/articles/682.html

12 Moretti, op. cit.

13 Desmond, *The Man with Two Shadows.*

14 Hodges, *The French Grand Prix.*

15 Yates, op. cit.

16 Yates, op.cit.

Chapter 2

1 *The Motor.*

2 Nixon, *Racing the Silver Arrows.*

3 *The Motor.*

4 To show how misleading subsequent accounts can be, Lurani wrote that 'At dawn, with smaller cars all away, Nuvolari's Alfa left.'

5 *The Motor.*

6 From 1927 to 1930 the Mille Miglia route was the opposite of what it was afterwards.

7 *The Motor.*

8 Ibid.

9 *The Autocar.*

10 Renato Balestrero, Italian amateur driver. O.M. was a Milanese company, founded in 1899, which had a factory at Brescia.

11 *The Autocar.*

12 *The Motor.*

13 Lurani.

14 Ibid.

15 *The Motor.*

16 *The Motor.*

17 *The Autocar.*

17 Yates.

18 This is the only mention I can find of tyre problems.

20 *The Motor.*

21 *The Autocar.*

22 Mille Miglia = 1,000 Italian miles, which = 1,018.42 British/American miles.

23 *The Autocar.*

24 *Motor Italia.*

25 It is not clear which race Neubauer is talking about. He described Nuvolari and Varzi as 'also rans' in the race he watched, and that cannot have been 1930. In 1931 Nuvolari retired with engine

trouble on lap 3 and Varzi didn't compete. Nuvolari didn't compete in 1932 and won, as we shall see, in 1933. All this casts doubt, again, on what Neubauer wrote in his autobiography.

26 Coppe del Miglia, *l'Auto Italiana,* 20 April 1931.

27 This seems contradictory, but in fact Caracciola's exhaust had broken and repairs lasted 10 minutes. Assuming he had recovered just enough to get past them he would still be behind on the staggered time.

28 Taruffi, *Works Driver.*

Chapter 3

1 Temple Press Books, 1964.

2 *L'Equipe.*

3 *The Autocar.*

4 Sir Malcolm Campbell was a racing driver but much better known for his attempts on the world land speed record in Bluebird. He broke it in 1923, 1924 (twice), 1925, 1927, 1928, 1931, 1932, 1933 and 1935 (twice). The latter took it to 301mph (484kph) over the flying mile.

5 *The Autocar.*

6 Ibid.

7 Hodges.

8 *The Autocar.*

9 Ibid.

10 Ibid.

11 *L'Equipe.*

12 Caracciola, *A Racing Driver's World.*

13 *L'Equipe.*

14 Hodges.

15 *Motor Sport.*

16 Caracciola, op. cit.

17 Cholmondeley-Tapper, *Amateur Racing Driver.*

18 Dreyfus, *My Two Lives.*

19 Stevenson, *Driving Forces.*

20 Moretti, *When Nuvolari Raced.*

21 Taruffi, *Works Driver.*

22 Taruffi, op. cit.

23 *L'Auto Italiana,* 10 July 1932, quoted in Moretti.

24 Taruffi, op. cit.

25 Moretti, op. cit.

Chapter 4

1 *The Motor.*

2 Hodges, *Monaco Grand Prix.*

3 *L'Equipe.*
4 Caracciola, *A Racing Driver's World.*
5 *The Autocar.*
6 *L'Equipe.*
7 Ibid.
8 Ibid.
9 *The Motor.*
10 Ibid.
11 *L'Equipe.*
12 *The Motor.*
13 *The Autocar.*
14 *The Motor.*
15 Ibid.
16 Dumb iron, 'the curved side-piece of a motor vehicle chassis, joining it to the front springs' (Concise Oxford English Dictionary).
17 *The Motor.*
18 Ibid.
19 *The Autocar.*
20 Hodges, op. cit.
21 I laid my fears about the finish on Doug Nye, the noted and impeccable historian. He pondered it, saw the contradictions of the long-accepted versions and murmured several times 'now that *is* an interesting question.' He rummaged among photographs and concluded that it was not at all clear but felt his colleague David Weguelin, the noted and impeccable film-maker, might have footage of the finish and that would solve it. Weguelin certainly did have footage of Varzi winning it but on an incline. We pondered that the coverage would naturally concentrate on the finish and the chequered flag, and momentous events happening at this moment elsewhere – like Nuvolari pushing towards the pits far out of sight – simply wouldn't have been covered because the cameras weren't there. It was (probably) as simple as that...

Chapter 5

1 *Sports Illustrated,* July 1937.
2 In *When Nuvolari Raced.*
3 When I read the Capps reconstruction on the Atlas F1 site it astonished me because it was based on original research and convincingly contradicted just about everything I'd read on the race. Courtesy of Atlas F1's Goren Biranit, I reached Capps and asked him about it. You've already heard in the chapter how he felt the received version 'didn't track, didn't fit with what we know about Nuvolari.'

He read a lot of articles – 'in English, particularly' – and felt something was wrong but 'you can't put your finger on it. In the back of my mind I had something from the early or late 1960s, an article in *Motor Sport* that Bill Boddy wrote. That was all I could remember.'

Boddy had entertained doubts about the accuracy and authenticity of the supposed fix and was sure 'some of the drivers weren't doing what people had said they'd done. I probably did my piece on lap times and the finishing order and reports I'd read of the race. My piece wasn't built on Neubauer's book at all. It's an interesting thought that a journalist who wasn't there can sometimes find out more about what happened than those who were!' What struck Boddy hard was that Nuvolari fixing a race seemed inconceivable. He sensed *something* had been going on in Tripoli, he understood how much money was at stake, and it might have been a 'sort of fix' though not in the hard, direct sense of that term.

Bill Boddy is no bad judge, and his feature article articulated (forgive the pun) the doubts Capps would have. Capps says: 'The first person that I know of that sat down and asked "*what in the world really happened?*" was the wonderful Betty Sheldon, Paul's wife. [He of the indispensable volumes covering the early Grands Prix races.] She's got a very good command of Italian and she went back digging. In Volume 3 at the end of the 1933 season they put in an article and this was the first time I had seen it. I'd *known* it but not seen anybody write it! She was the one who finally got all of us to come to our senses.'

Sheldon's book appeared in 1992 and, in a special 'chapterette', Betty wrote two pages which constitute, without doing a word count, slightly more than Neubauer. She set out the basic structure of the arrangement and examined the claims objectively. She went back to the contemporary Italian publications – always a worthwhile exercise because they are reports of current events and, by definition, cannot contain any distortions of hindsight. She pointed out that Santini in his book *Nuvolari* claimed Varzi had told him the true story and nothing that Santini and Varzi say 'conflicts with information from other independent sources.' She adds that 'in contrast to Varzi, increasing knowledge casts ... doubts about Nuvolari's motives.' She wonders aloud why Canestrini did not write about the 'arrangement' in *Gazzetta dello Sport* when other publications were writing about it. Was Canestrini 'too deeply involved financially?'

Whatever, the groundwork had been laid.

'Once I saw that,' Capps says, 'I started going back with some people on the Nostalgia Forum [at Atlas F1.] We dug up the Bill

Boddy article, we dug up some other things, we found the original stuff and it all started clicking into place. Once we had resolved those issues we assembled the article. In fact a more complete version is on Leif Snellmann's site. [Just tap Leif Snellmann into your search engine and you'll find this and much more]. It was just a simple matter of fitting the pieces together – but there are a lot of pieces and some of them are contradictory. I rewrote the article about 800 times, went through and through and through, and my conclusion is that we probably never will know everything.

'There was, however, no doubt once we had looked at it – after we had gone back to the Italian sources – that this was completely legal at the time. They built a syndicate and it didn't matter which one of the three won. All they were saying was '*we will distribute the prize money as we wish because we have won it.*' No collusion about backing off. It was a legal syndicate. There is no evidence they approached anybody else – including Louis Chiron. I think it's wonderful he got banned [subsequently, for being involved] for something he wasn't even at!

'There *was* no collusion and it was emphatic, time after time in the contemporary articles, that Varzi and Nuvolari were racing, they were going at it hammer and tongs – which is how they normally did go at it. There was respect but no love between the two.

'That was another clue. The one person that Nuvolari would never let up for – never, ever – would be Varzi. And another clue if you think of how reliable Canestrini was on a scale of 1 to 10 – well, about the coin toss, I'd say 1.'

Overall, 'you have to keep in mind Nuvolari had a lifestyle that was not cheap. He was the Jackie Stewart of his time. He understood his worth – all he had to do was show up to draw the crowds – and he drove a hard bargain for starting money with organisers. He was very upfront about it, he never played games. He said '*this is it, I don't negotiate*'. Of course he did ... but he was worth it. Even in America he had a great following. There were two places that knew he existed: New York and Los Angeles, big immigrant communities and where the racing communities were, too. Well, three places: Indianapolis as well.'

4 Atlas F1.

5 Yates.

6 Nixon's version (*Racing The Silver Arrows)* is that 'not long after his arrival in Tripoli, Marshal Balbo was approached by a dentist, who suggested reviving the Grand Prix, this time in conjunction with a state lottery.'

7 Yates.

8 Capps at Atlas F1.
9 op. cit.
10 op. cit.
11 op. cit.
12 Yates.
13 Capps op. cit.
14 Quoted in Moretti, *When Nuvolari Raced.*
15 Nixon op. cit.
16 See www.brooklandstrack.co.uk
17 Taruffi, *Works Driver.*
18 www.brooklandstrack.co.uk

Chapter 6

1 AOC, *24 Heures du Mans.*
2 *Motor Sport.*
3 Ibid.
4 *L'Equipe.*
5 *Motor Sport.*
6 Automobile Club de l'Ouest.
7 *The Motor.*
8 *The Autocar.*
9 *L'Equipe.*
10 *The Autocar.*
11 Ibid. AOC, op. cit.
12 *The Motor.*
13 *The Autocar.*
14 *Motor Sport.*
15 Ibid.
16 Fraichard, *The Le Mans Story.*
17 *Motor Sport.*
18 *The Autocar.*
19 Fraichard op. cit.
20 Ibid.
21 Yates.

Chapter 7

1 Eyston was well-known for taking part in speed records on the German autobahns in an MG. Whitney Straight was an American who became heavily involved in motorsport and later became chairman of Rolls-Royce.
2 *The Autocar.*
3 *Ireland's Saturday Night* was a continuation of the *Belfast Telegraph* and the first part of its report was lifted from the *Telegraph.*

4 Lurani, *Nuvolari.*
5 I am indebted to the video *Strictly TT,* a Spence Brothers film, for what the circuit looked like.
6 The company made a 'pre-selector' gearbox, forerunner of the automatic gearbox of today.
7 Richard Hough, *Tourist Trophy* (Hutchinson, London, 1957), quoted in *When Nuvolari Raced.*
8 Hough op. cit.
9 *The Chronicle.*
10 Ibid.
11 *The Belfast Telegraph.*
12 *Motor Sport.*
13 *The Autocar.*
14 *Motor Sport.*
15 *The Autocar.*
16 *The Autocar.*
17 *The Motor.*
18 *The Autocar.*
19 In the video *Strictly TT.*

Chapter 8

1 Mays, *Split Seconds.*
2 Günter Molter, *Automobile Magazine,* March 1991.
3 Interview with author. In one of William Boddy's columns in *Motor Sport* decades later, a Mr H.J. Thomas, writing from Holland, said he had seen a wall plaque at the Eifeler Hof saying who had stayed where in 1935. Neubauer was in room 28, Caracciola 27, Fagioli 29, Von Brauchitsch 26. Nuvolari apparently stayed elsewhere.
4 Mays, op. cit.
5 Taruffi, *Works Driver.*
6 Neubauer, *Speed was my Life* – not forgetting how unreliable Neubauer's book is.
7 Lurani, *Nuvolari.*
8 The matter of Nuvolari's car at the Nürburgring is an intriguing one, in view of what he was able to make it achieve. Hans Berends, a motor racing historian, has pondered it in some detail. He sent me this:

'After due consideration I've come to the conclusion that, apart from Nuvolari's undoubted wizard qualities (only equalled by Fangio on same circuit in 1957) we must take a close look at the technical aspects.

'It must be realised that the Tipo B 3-litre was at its peak development-wise: this car, which was Jano's masterpiece (he contests this), was four years old in design but also contained four years of development. And development is crucial in the motor car business.

'Now we take Mercedes Benz: this car was a 2-year-old design and not at all perfect. The trouble is that being objective on Mercedes Benz is not the easiest thing – one tends to be overly impressed by the 'blood & thunder,' huge organisation and sophisticated design. When in 1954 Mercedes Benz came back to racing everybody expected miracles and Coventry-Climax withdrew their V-8 engine fearing that they couldn't hold a candle to the Mercedes Benz 8-cylinder inclined engine with fuel-injection, etc. etc. In the end they found that the power of the Mercedes Benz engine was nothing like they feared.

'Back to 1935: the Mercedes Benz design, especially the roadholding (i.e. chassis conception), left a lot to be desired. The swing-axle rear suspension wasn't up to the job and the power of the engine resulted in exceptional tyre-wear, which called for numerous pit stops – not forgetting the fuel consumption.

'These factors were at Mercedes Benz's disadvantage at the Nürburgring, and in retrospect we can safely say that Nuvolari held all the trump cards – which seemed most unlikely at the time, I grant you.

'Then Mercedes Benz called in [Technical Director Rudolf] Uhlenhaut who redesigned the car and had a very close look at the chassis/suspension – a De Dion rear end was installed and that made a lot of difference.

'And finally the financial aspects: Mercedes Benz had virtually unlimited means and Alfa Romeo was in the hands of the receiver, while Scuderia Ferrari was a modest set-up.

'This comparison is l00% of my own making but I'm perfectly confident having put my finger on the soft spot.'

In another letter Mr Berends writes:

'The Scuderia Ferrari had a secret weapon which was brought to the Nürburgring. This was the 'out-bored engine to surpass them all': 77mm bore with 100mm stroke, which gave 3.8 litres and 330bhp. Scuderia Ferrari had the gravest doubts about this unit, but in the end put it into the chassis and it worked. So as you see the car was very much 'one-off'.

'In 1937 Kenneth Evans bought the car from Scuderia Ferrari but of course didn't get the engine – he got a 2.9-litre unit. The rest remained the same – no wonder the car was slower than before.

'At the Nürburgring, Nuvolari's Tipo B was very 'hush-hush' and it even seems that the bonnet was sealed (or even padlocked shut).

'Of course after the race there was a terrible excitement and before going on the rostrum Nuvolari asked his chief-mechanic *'dov'è la macchina?'* ('where's the car?'). After being assured that the car was safely tucked away, he was at ease. This was overheard by a Dutch reporter and I never saw or heard this mentioned. In my opinion this single question provides the clue.'

9 Lurani, op. cit.
10 Neubauer.
11 Lang.
12 Mays, *Split Seconds.*
13 Mays, op. cit.
14 *Motor Revue*, Stuttgart, 1968.
15 *The Autocar.*
16 Posthumous, *German Grand Prix.*
17 *The Autocar.*
18 *The Motor.*
19 *The Autocar.*
20 Ibid.
21 Lurani, op. cit.
22 *Motor Revue.*
23 Lurani, op. cit.
24 Ibid.
25 Cholmondeley-Tapper, *Amateur Racing Driver.*
26 B.Bira, *Bits and Pieces.* Bira, a Siamese prince and Anglophile, was also a fabled pre-war motor racing privateer.

Chapter 9

1 Owen, *Alfa Romeo.*
2 Our old friend Count Lurani has given a heart-rending account of Nuvolari leaving his dying son to go and compete in the Vanderbilt Cup, complete with death-bed vow to bring back a cup for him. 'The doctor,' Lurani writes, 'announced that the crisis would be reached at any moment, and that in any case he could not last long.' Nuvolari sailed on the *Rex* 'next day' and 'while at table one night' a waiter gave him a note that there was a radio call for him. 'With a dull ache in his heart,' Nuvolari heard a 'faint, distant voice' telling him Giorgio had 'passed quietly away a few hours previously.'

Lurani then goes on to describe how, in the race, Nuvolari 'shot into the lead and was never caught.' He describes how George Vanderbilt presented him with the cup and more, all in the florid style we have come to expect.

The problems with this need elaborating. The Vanderbilt Cup of

1936, which Nuvolari shot off and won, took place on 'Columbus Day on 12 October,' as Lurani writes.

Giorgio died on 26 June 1937.

Lurani's account make some semblance of sense if he had been talking about the Vanderbilt Cup of 1937, which Nuvolari went to and which was held on 5 July – other reports confirm that Giorgio died while Nuvolari was on the boat. But Nuvolari retired on lap 16, when his car caught fire. That Lurani has hopelessly confused the two races casts extreme doubt on the credibility of his account, and any verbatim quasi-dialogue is even more dubious.

Finn comments that, when reading the chapter, he was 'a bit surprised' to see, in the words above, 'the Lurani story about the death of Nuvolari's son. Lurani made a muddle of it, which we have known for years. In fact, I still have an exchange of correspondence between us from 1959 wherein Lurani admits to getting the story facts confused. He was supposed to change it for the second edition of his book, which never came out.'

I am sure Finn, and other students of motor racing history, have long been aware of how discredited aspects of Lurani's book are but others may well not be. I say this for a reason. At the beginning of my research I bought a copy and it cost £125 ($190) because it is both scarce and still regarded as a primary source. The only warning I'd had – long before I bought the book – was from Pino Allievi, respected Grand Prix reporter on *Gazzetta dello Sport* (who has a son called Tazio). When I mentioned one of Lurani's descriptions, he made snorting noises of derision down the phone and said 'don't trust that book.'

3 Santini, *Nuvolari.*

4 *The New York Sun.*

5 Finn, *American Road Racing, the 1930s.*

6 The race programme, kindly provided by Don Capps.

7 The 8c-35 was the 1935 car, superseded by the V12 which would be used for the race.

8 *Corriere della Sera.*

9 *New York Sun.*

10 *Corriere della Sera.*

11 *New York Sun.*

12 Finn op. cit.

13 Ibid.

14 Ibid.

15 Relief drivers were not unknown but weren't used by anybody, as far as I can tell, in the 1936 Vanderbilt.

16 The word in the headline is 'PREPOTENZA', which is not easy to

translate straight into English. Ms Gadeselli, translating, said it was somewhere between 'impertinence and cheek.' The Penguin Concise Italian Dictionary gives 'arrogance, insolence.' You get the general idea, however.

17 Moretti, *When Nuvolari Raced.*
18 Nuvolari interview in *Sports Illustrated.*
19 Neubauer, *Speed was My Life.*
20 Nixon, *Racing the Silver Arrows.*
21 Lang, *Grand Prix Driver.*
22 Adolf Hühnlein, described as German motor sports führer, a portly and self-important man who, it seems, was a believing Nazi, did not profit unduly from that and died during the war.

Chapter 10

1 Nixon, *Racing the Silver Arrows.*
2 Sometimes in German documents von Brauchitsch is referred to without the von. Wherever this happens I have left it as originally written.
3 Caracciola, *Racing Driver's World.*
4 Grids could be decided by drawing lots, as we have seen.
5 Arnold Wychodil, a Sudeten German – the northern area of Czechoslovakia which was historically, culturally and linguistically German. Wychodil would likely have spoken Czech and Slovak.
6 This Vienna race is mentioned in Mercedes's documents but I have no reference to it anywhere else. Whatever it was going to be, the darkness claimed it.
7 Mercedes had clearly planned a different route for their return journey, although why doesn't seem at all clear.
8 Caracciola, op. cit.
9 The film is part of *Racing Mercedes Part Two (1937–1939)* © Bill Mason Films/David Weguelin Productions 2001 (Motorfilms). Weguelin says he is certain it is of the convoy arriving because some of the pedestrians are looking at it, which they wouldn't be if it was just a Mercedes saloon on its own. He adds that having a camera on the front of the car is rare – he could think of only one other instance, at Tripoli – but often the photographers travelled with the team and in that context filming the arrival in Belgrade is not surprising.
10 Manfred von Brauchitsch, *Kampf um Meter und Sekunden.*
11 Nixon, op. cit.
12 Lang, op. cit.
13 www.kolumbus.f1/leif.snellman/db.htm
14 Oddly, Lang claimed to have spent nights listening to the radio after

driving from the team's Nottingham hotel before the Donington Grand Prix: it was the time of the 1938 Munich crisis. We know that, in fact, Mercedes were only at the hotel for one night. Events must have distorted Lang's memory, and perhaps done the same at Belgrade.

15 These words are from the commentary on *Racing Mercedes,* written by the late Bill Mason. Weguelin insists that Mason was a most meticulous man about his facts and, whenever challenged, could justify them – sometimes even by producing the most obscure sources. With Weguelin's kind permission, I have used the words for that reason – and for the fact that any strategic withdrawal would have gone through Hühnlein. Whether Hühnlein cleared it with Hitler is another matter.

16 Lang, op. cit.

17 Von Brauchitsch, op. cit.

18 Lang op. cit.

19 Lang ibid.

20 Camphor, a 'volcanic substance with aromatic smell and bitter taste' (Concise Oxford English Dictionary) used to keep moths away from stored sheets and clothing. People of a certain generation can smell it still down all these years. I can.

21 Why von Brauchitsch would have left love letters at the Caracciolas is a complete mystery.

22 When Amanda Gadeselli had finished translating this letter, she expressed mild astonishment that it had been written at all. She explained that Italy does not have a culture of replying. For example, if you apply for a job you won't get an acknowledgement. 'If they're interested they'll ring you up, if not it goes straight in the bin!' However, reflecting, she concluded that in those days, when phones were not so common, it may have been different and 'in any case, Nuvolari had travelled extensively and would have understood, even if you might not have bothered replying to something from an Italian, it would be rude with a letter like this one from Auto Union.'

Chapter 11

1 Cimarosti, *The Complete History of Grand Prix Motor Racing.*

2 Taruffi, *Works Driver.*

3 *The Autocar.*

4 Ibid.

5 *The Autocar.*

6 Yates, *Ferrari: the Man and the Machine.*

7 Ibid.

[8] Purdy, *Omnibus*.

[9] Sir William Lyons (1901–1985), founder of Jaguar Cars.

Chapter 12

[1] See Chapter Eleven.

[2] Purdy, *Omnibus*.

[3] Ducarouge, a leading Grand Prix car designer of the 1980s.

[4] Brooks, a Grand Prix driver between 1956 and 1961, a gentle man and a gentleman who saw that motor racing was not everything in life. He once explained to me that cars were dangerous when he raced and, as a consequence, bumping and barging did not exist because the consequences could well have been fatal. This makes Nuvolari giving Wimille's car a whack even more remarkable.

[5] Dreyfus in an interview with Nigel Roebuck.

[6] Cholmondeley-Tapper, *Amateur Racing Driver*.

[7] Taruffi, *Works Driver*.

[8] Purdy, *Omnibus*.

Statistics

Car races except where stated. (b) = bikes; R = retired; ic = in class; DNS = did not start; NK = not known; 1= =first equal; DNQ = did not qualify

1920			
20 June, Cremona (b)	Della Ferrera		R
1921			
20 Mar, Verona	Coppa Verona	Ansaldo Tipo 4	1
22 May, Brescia		Ansaldo Tipo 4	2 (ic)
7 Sept, Brescia	Flying km	Ansaldo Tipo 4	9 (ic)
11 Sept, Brescia	GP 'Gentlemen'	Ansaldo Tipo 4	R
1922			
4 June, Pinerolo	4,000km	NK	R
16-17 Sept, Milan-Naples (b)	4th Raid Nord-Sud	Sarolea 500cc	R
15 Oct, Brescia		Ansaldo Tipo 6AS	2 (ic)
5 Nov, Mantua (b)		Harley Davidson 1000cc	1
18 Mar, Genoa (b)		Fongri 500cc	3 (ic)
1923			
3 Apr, Perugia (b)		Norton 500cc	R
15 Apr, Cremona (b)		Sarolea Tipo 23D 500cc	R
22 Apr, Mantua (b)		Norton 500cc	R
6 May, Cremona (b)	MC D'Italia GP	Sarolea 500cc	R
6 May, Cremona		Diatto	R
13 May, Parma (b)	Parma-Poggio	Garelli 350cc	2 (ic)
20 May, Parma (b)		Garelli 350cc	1 (ic)
27 May, Alessandria (b)		Norton 500cc	4 (ic)
1 June, Busto Arsizio (b)		Norton 500cc	1
10 June, Varese (b)		Indian 1000cc	4 (ic)
17 June, Ravenna (b)		Indian 1000cc	4 (ic)
1 July, Como (b)		BSA 500cc	R
8 July, Treviso (b)		Indian 1000cc	1
9 July, Treviso (b)		Indian 1000cc	1
22 July, Rimini (b)	Coppa dell'Adriacato	Indian 1000cc	R
5 Aug, Biella (b)		Indian 1000cc	2 (ic)
12 Aug, Torino (b)		Indian 1000cc	1
26 Aug, Bologna (b)		Indian 1000cc	1
8 Sept, Monza (b)	Coppa delle Nazioni	Indian 500cc	DNS
7 Oct, Messina (b)		Indian 1000cc	1 (ic)
21 Oct, Barcelona	Penya Rhin GP	Chiribiri Tipo Monza	5
29 Oct, Barcelona (b)		Moto Borgo 500cc	NK
4 Nov, Barcelona	Voiturette GP	Chiribiri Tipo Monza	4
25 Nov, Brescia		Chiribiri Tipo Monza	R

1924			
13 Apr, Rapallo		Bianchi Tipo 18	1
20 Apr, Mantova (b)		Norton 500cc	1
30 Apr-4 May, Milan (b)	Tour of Italy	Bianchi 350cc	23
25 May, Ravenna		Chiribiri Tipo Monza	1 (ic)
29 May, Ravenna		Bianchi 350cc	R
1 June, Rovigo		Chiribiri Tipo Monza	2
9 June, Cremona (b)		Norton 500cc	1
9 June, Cremona		Chiribiri Tipo Monza	1 (ic)
15 June, Padova (b) (2 races)		Norton 500cc	R/2
29 June, Como (b)		Bianchi 350cc	12 (ic)
6 July, Varese (b)		Bianchi 350cc	R
13 July, Pontassieve (b)		Norton 500cc	2 (ic)
20 July, Rimini (b)		Bianchi 350cc	R
3 Aug, Alessandria (b)		Norton 500cc	1
6 Sept, Monza (b) (2 races)		Bianchi 350cc	6
		Norton 500cc	R
28 Sept, Parma (b)		Norton 500cc	2 (ic)
23 Nov, Rapallo (b)		Norton 500cc	4 (ic)
1925			
24 Feb, Rome (b)		Bianchi 350cc	1 (ic)
22 Mar, Rapallo (b)		Bianchi 350cc	3 (ic)
5 Apr, Brescia (b)		Bianchi 350cc	5 (ic)
17 May, Perugia (b)		Bianchi 350cc	4 (ic)
24 May, Ravenna (b)		Bianchi 350cc	R
31 May, Padua (b)		Bianchi 350cc	1 (ic)
12 July, Como (b)		Bianchi 350cc	1 (ic)
9 Aug, Rimini (b)		Bianchi 350cc	2 (ic)
13 Sept, Monza (b)	GP des Nations	Bianchi 350cc	1 (ic)
I Nov, Bologna (b)		Bianchi 350cc	1
11 Nov, Milan Velodrome (b) (2 races)		Bianchi 350cc	1-2
1926			
7 Mar, Rome (b)		Bianchi 350cc	1
21 Mar, Recanati (b)		Bianchi 350cc	2
1 Apr, Rome (b)	Reale Premio Roma	Bianchi 350cc	2 (1 ic)
2 May, Turin (b)		Bianchi 350cc	3 (ic)
16 May, Stuttgart		Bianchi 350cc	R
23 May, Ravenna		Bianchi 350cc	R
27 June, Padua (b)		Bianchi 350cc	R
11 July, Como (b)		Bianchi 350cc	3 (1 ic)
25 July, Pietrasanta (b)		Bianchi 350cc	R
15 Aug, Rimini		NK	2 (1 ic)

19 Sept, Monza (b)		Bianchi 350cc	1 (ic)
26 Sept, Milan–Lodi (b)		Bianchi 350cc	1 (ic)
5 Oct, Ferrara (b)		Bianchi 350cc	1
10 Oct, Florence (b) (2 pursuits)		Bianchi 350cc	1-2
17 Oct, Bologna (b) (2 pursuits)		Bianchi 350cc	1-1
24 Oct, Mantua (b) (pursuit)		Bianchi 350cc	1
13 Nov, Mantua (b)		Bianchi 350cc	R

1927

26-27 Mar, Brescia	Mille Miglia	Bianchi Tipo 20 Sport	5 (ic)
17 April, Lugo (b)		Bianchi 350cc	1
24 April, Macerata (b)		Bianchi 350cc	1
8 May, Ravenna (b)		Bianchi 350cc	R
15 May, Stradella (b)	GP Moto Club d'Italia	Bianchi 350cc	R
22 May, Perugia (b)		Bianchi 350cc	R
29 May, Perugia		Bugatti Type 35	3 (ic)
5 June, Verona (b)		Bianchi 350cc	1
12 June, Rome–Parioli	GP Reale di Roma	Bugatti Type 35	1
19 June, Bologna		Bugatti Type 35C	R
26 June, Vercelli (b)		Bianchi 350cc	1 (ic)
3 July, Treviso		Bugatti type 35	2 (ic)
10 July, Geneva–Meyrin (b)		Bianchi 350cc	3 (ic)
24 July, Como (b)		Bianchi 350cc	1 (ic)
31 July, Reconati (b)		Bianchi 350cc	1
7 Aug, Livorno (b)		Bianchi 350cc	R
14 Aug, Livorno		Bugatti Type 35	2 (ic)
18 Sept, Monza (2 races)	GP of Milan	Bugatti Type 35C	R
(b)	GP of Nations	Bianchi 350cc	2
9 Oct, Brescia		Bugatti type 35	1

1928

11 Mar, Tripoli	Tripoli GP	Bugatti type 35C	1
25 Mar, Verona		Bugatti Type 35C	1
31 Mar – 1 Apr, Brescia	Mille Miglia	Bugatti Type 43C	6 (ic)
22 Apr, Alessandria		Bugatti Type 35C	1
6 May, Palermo	Targa Floria	Bugatti Type 35C	R
13 May, Messina		Bugatti Type 35C	1 (ic)
27 May, Torino (b)		Bianchi 350cc	R
10 June, Rome	GP Reale di Roma	Bugatti Type 35C	R
17 June, Como (b)		Bianchi 350cc	3 (ic)
24 June, Cremona		Bugatti Type 35C	2 (ic)
29 June, Rome (b)		Bianchi 350cc	R
4 Aug, Pescara	Coppa Acerbo	Bugatti Type 35C	4
19 Aug, Livorno		Bugatti Type 35C	2 (ic)

9 Sept, Monza	GP of Europe	Bugatti Type 35C	3
23 Sept, Monza (b)	GP of Nations	Bianchi 350cc	1
9 Dec, Rapallo (b)		Bianchi 350cc	1
1929			
21 Mar, Tripoli	GP of Tripoli	Bugatti Type 35C	2 (ic)
13-14 Apr, Brescia	Mille Miglia	O.M. Tipo 665 SMM	9 (ic)
26 May, Rome	Reale GP Roma	Bugatti Type 35C	R
9 June, Florence		Alfa Romeo Tipo 6C	6 (ic)
23 June, Como (b)		Bianchi 350cc	1
21 July, Livorno		Alfa Romeo 6C 1750SS	2 (ic)
15 Sept, Monza	GP di Monza	Talbot GP 1500	2
22 Sept, Monza (b)	GP of Nations	Bianchi 350cc	R
29 Sept, Cremona		Talbot GP 1500	R
13 Oct, Ferrara (b)		Bianchi 350cc	1
27 Oct, Palermo (b)		Bianchi 350cc	1
24 Nov, Rapallo (b)		Bianchi 350cc	1
1930			
12-13 Apr, Brescia	Mille Miglia	Alfa Romeo Tipo 6C	1
20 Apr, Alessandria		Alfa Romeo	R
4 May, Palermo	Targa Floria	Alfa Romeo Ripo 6C	5
18 May, Rome (b)	Reale Primo Roma	Bianchi 350cc	R
25 May, Rome	Reale GP Roma	Alfa Romeo Tipo P2	R
8 June, Pavia (b)		Bianchi 350cc	1 (ic)
15 June, Trieste		Alfa Romeo Tipo P2	1
29 June, Cuneo		Alfa Romeo P2	1
6 July, Como (b)		Bianchi 350cc	1
13 July, Treviso (morning)		Alfa Romeo Tipo 2	1
13 July, Forli (afternoon) (b)		Bianchi 350cc	R
Livorno (b)	Coppa del Mare	Bianchi 350cc	1 (ic)
27 July, Livorno (b)	Coppa del Mare	Bianchi 350cc	1 (ic)
3 Aug, Livorno	Coppa Ciano	Alfa Romeo Tipo P2	R
10 Aug, Linthal, Switzerland	Klausen Hillclimb	Alfa Romeo Tipo P2	1 (ic)
17 Aug, Pescara	Coppa Acerbo	Alfa Romeo Tipo P2	5
24 Aug, Belfast	Tourist Trophy	Alfa Romeo Tipo 6C	1
7 Sept, Monza	GP di Monza	Alfa Romeo Tipo P2	R
14 Sept, Monza (b)	GP of Nations	Bianchi 350cc	R
28 Sept, Brno (Czech)	Circuit of Masaryk	Alfa Romeo Tipo P2	R
12 Oct, Florence		Alfa Eromeo Tipo 6	2
23 Nov, Rapallo (b)		Bianchi 350cc	5 (ic)
1931			
15 Feb, Verona		Alfa Romeo Tipo 1500SS	1
11-12 Apr, Brescia	Mille Miglia	Alfa Romeo Tipo 8C	9

26 Apr, Alessandria		Alfa Romeo Tipo 8C	R
10 May, Palermo	Targa Floria	Alfa Romeo Tipo 8C	1
24 May, Monza	GP d'Italia	Alfa Romeo Tipo A monoposto	1
7 June, Rome	GP Reale di Roma	Bugatti Type 35C	R
21 June, Montlhéry	GP de ACF	Alfa Romeo Tipo 8C	11
28 June, Genoa		Alfa Romeo 8C	1=
12 July, Spa	GP of Belgium	Alfa Romeo Tipo 8C	2
19 July, Nürburgring	GP of Germany	Alfa Romeo Tipo 8C	4
2 Aug, Livorno	Coppa Ciano	Alfa Romeo Tipo 8C	1
9 Aug, Bologna		Alfa Romeo Tipo 6C	1
16 Aug, Pescara	Coppa Acerbo	Alfa Romeo Tipo A 12C	3
22 Aug, Belfast	Tourist Trophy	Alfa Romeo Tipo 8C	R
6 Sept, Monza	GP of Monza	Alfa Romeo Tipo A 12C	R
27 Sept, Brno		Alfa Romeo Tipo 8C	R
4 Oct, Florence		Alfa Romeo Tipo 8C	1
1932			
9-10 April, Brescia	Mille Miglia	Alfa Romeo Tipo 8C	R
17 Apr, Monaco	GP of Monaco	Alfa Romeo Tipo 8C	1
8 May, Palermo	Targa Floria	Alfa Romeo Tipo 8C	1
5 June, Monza	GP d'Italia	Alfa Romeo Tipo B 'P3'	1
19 June, Genoa		Alfa Romeo Tipo 8C	3
3 July, Rheims	GP of France	Alfa Romeo Tipo B 'P3'	1
17 July, Nürburgring	GP of Germany	Alfa Romeo Tipo B 'P3'	2
24 July, Avellino		Alfa Romeo Tipo 8C	1
31 July, Livorno	Coppa Ciano	Alfa Romeo Tipo B 'P3'	1
7 Aug, Linthal (Switz)	Klausen Hillclimb	Alfa Romeo Tipo 8C	6
14 Aug, Pescara	Coppa Acerbo	Alfa Romeo Tipo B 'P3'	1
29 Aug, Bolzano		Alfa Romeo Tipo 8C	2 (ic)
4 Sept, Brno		Alfa Romeo Tipo B 'P3'	3
11 Sept, Monza	GP di Monza	Alfa Romeo Tipo B 'P3'	3
25 Sept, Marseilles	GP of Marseilles	Alfa Romeo Tipo B 'P3'	2
1933			
26 Mar, Tunis	GP of Tunis	Alfa Romeo Tipo 8C	1
8-9 Apr, Brescia	Mille Miglia	Alfa Romeo Tipo 8C	1
23 Apr, Monaco	GP of Monaco	Alfa Romeo Tipo 8C	R
30 Apr, Alessandria		Alfa Romeo Tipo 8C	1
7 May, Tripoli	GP of Tripoli	Alfa Romeo Tipo 8C	2
21 May, Berlin	Avus race	Alfa Romeo Tipo 8C	3
28 May, Nürburgring	Eifel race	Alfa Romeo Tipo 8C	1
4 June, Nîmes (Fr)	GP of Nîmes	Alfa Romeo Tipo 8C	1
11 June, Montlhéry	GP of France	Alfa Romeo Tipo 8C	R
17-19 June, Le Mans	24 Hours	Alfa Romeo Tipo 8C	1

25 June, Barcelona	GP of Penya Rhin	Alfa Romeo Tipo 8C	5
2 July, Rheims		Alfa Romeo Tipo 8C	R
9 July, Spa (Belg)	GP of Belgium	Maserati Tipo 8CM	1
30 July, Livorno	Coppa Ciano	Maserati Tipo 8CM	1
6 Aug, Nice	GP of Nice	Maserati Tipo 8CM	1
15 Aug, Pescara	Coppa Acerbo	Maserati Tipo 8CM	2
27 Aug, Marseilles	GP of Marseilles	Maserati Tipo 8CM	R
2 Sept, Belfast	Tourist Trophy	MG K3 Magnette	1
10 Sept, Monza	GP of Italy	Maserati Tipo 8CM	2
24 Sept, San Sebastian	GP of Spain	Maserati Tipo 8CM	R
1934			
2 Apr, Monaco	GP of Monaco	Bugatti Type 59S	5
8 Apr, Brescia	Mille Miglia	Alfa Romeo Tipo 8C	2
22 Apr, Alessandria		Maserati Tipo 8CM	R
27 May, Berlin	Avus race	Maserati Tipo 8CM	5
3 June, Nürburgring	Eifel race	Maserati Tipo 8CM	R
17 June, Barcelona	GP of Penya Rhin	Maserati Tipo 8CM	R
1 July, Montlhéry	GP of France	Bugatti Type 59S	R
8 July, Rheims		Maserati Tipo 8CM	R
15 July, Nürburgring	GP of Germany	Maserati Tipo 8CM	4
22 July, Livorno		Maserati Tipo 8CM	3
12-13 Aug, Pescara	24 hour race	Alfa Romeo Tipo 8C	R
15 Aug, Pescara	Coppa Acerbo	Maserati Tipo 8CM	2
19 Aug, Nice	GP of Nice	Maserati Tipo 8CM	R
26 Aug, Bern	GP of Switzerland	Maserati Tipo 8CM	R
2 Sept, Biella		Alfa Romeo Tipo 8C	R
9 Sept, Monza	GP d'Italia	Maserati Tipo 6C-34	5
23 Sept, San Sebastian	GP of Spain	Maserati Tipo 6C-34	3
30 Sept, Brno	Masaryk race	Maserati Tipo 6C-34	3
14 Oct, Modena		Maserati Tipo 6C-34	1
21 Oct, Naples		Maserati Tipo 6C-34	1
1935			
24 Feb, Pau (Fr)	GP of Pau	Alfa Romeo Tipo B 'P3'	1
22 Apr, Monaco	GP of Monaco	Alfa Romeo Tipo B 'P3'	R
5 May, Tunis	GP of Tunis	Alfa Romeo Tipo B 'P3'	R
12 May, Tripoli	GP of Tripoli	Alfa Romeo Bimotore	4
20 May, Bergamo		Alfa Romeo Tipo B 'P3'	1
26 May, Berlin (heats)	Avus race	Alfa Romeo Bimotore	6
9 June, Biella		Alfa Romeo Tipo B 'P3'	1
23 June, Montlhéry	GP of France	Alfa Romeo Tipo B 'P3'	R
30 June, Barcelona	GP of Penya Rhin	Alfa Romeo Tipo B 'P3'	3
7 July, Turin		Alfa Romeo Tipo B 'P3'	1

28 July, Nürburgring	GP of Germany	Alfa Romeo Tipo B 'P3'	1
4 Aug, Livorno	Coppa Ciano	Alfa Romeo Tipo B 'P3'	1
15 Aug, Pescara	Coppa Acerbo	Alfa Romeo Tipo B 'P3'	R
18 Aug, Nice	GP of Nice	Alfa Romeo Tipo B 'P3'	1
25 Aug, Bern	GP of Switzerland	Alfa Romeo Tipo B 'P3'	5
1 Sept, Bolzano		Alfa Romeo Tipo B 'P3'	2
8 Sept, Monza	GP d'Italia	Alfa Romeo Tipo 8C-35	R
16 Sept, Modena	GP di Modena	Alfa Romeo Tipo 8C-35	1
22 Sept, San Sebastiabn	GP of Spain	Alfa Romeo Tipo 8C-35	R
29 Sept, Brno	Masaryk race	Alfa Romeo Tipo 8C-35	2
1936			
13 Apr, Monaco	GP of Monaco	Alfa Romeo Tipo 8C-35	4
10 May, Tripoli	GP of Tripoli	Alfa Romeo Tipo 12C-26	8
7 June, Barcelona	GP of Penya Rhin	Alfa Romeo Tipo 12C-36	1
14 June, Nürburgring	Eifel race	Alfa Romeo Tipo 12C-36	2
21 June, Budapest	GP of Hungary	Alfa Romeo Tipo 8C-35	1
28 June, Milan	GP di Milano	Alfa Romeo Tipo 12C-36	1
26 July, Nürburgring	GP of Germany	Alfa Romeo Tipo 12C-36	R
2 Aug, Livorno	Coppa Ciano	Alfa Romeo Tipo 12C-36	R
15 Aug, Pescara	Coppa Acerbo	Alfa Romeo Tipo 12C-36	R
23 Aug, Bern	GP of Switzerland	Alfa Romeo Tipo 12C-36	R
13 Sept, Monza	GP d'Italia	Alfa Romeo Tipo 12C-36	2
20 Sept, Modena		Alfa Romeo Tipo 12C-36	1
12 Oct, New York	Vanderbilt Cup	Alfa Romeo Tipo 12C-36	1
1937			
18 Apr, Turin		Alfa Romeo Tipo 12C-36	DNS
9 May, Tripoli	GP of Tripoli	Alfa Romeo Tipo 12C-36	R
13 June, Nürburgring	Eifel race	Alfa Romeo Tipo 12C-36	5
20 June, Milan	GP di Milano	Alfa Romeo Tipo 12C-36	1
5 July, New York	Vanderbilt Cup	Alfa Romeo Tipo 12C-36	R
25 July, Nürburgring	GP of Germany	Alfa Romeo Tipo 12C-36	4
15 Aug, Pescara	Coppa Acerbo	Alfa Romeo Tipo 12C-37	R
22 Aug, Bern	GP of Switzerland	Auto Union Type C	5
12 Sept, Livorno	GP d'Italia	Alfa Romeo Tipo 12C-36	7
26 Sept, Brno	Masaryk race	Alfa Romeo Tipo 12C-36	5
1938			
21 May, Pau	GP of Pau	Alfa Romeo Tipo 308	DNS
24 July, Nürburgring	GP of Germany	Auto Union Type D	4
14 Aug, Pescara	Coppa Acerbo	Auto Union Type D	R
21 Aug, Bern	GP of Switzerland	Auto Union Type D	8
11 Sept, Monza	GP d'Italia	Auto Union Type D	1
22 Oct, Donington	Donington GP	Auto Union Type D	1

1939			
21 May, Nürburgring	Eifel race	Auto Union Type D	2
25 June, Spa	GP of Belgium	Auto Union Type D	R
9 July, Rheims	GP of France	Auto Union Type D	R
23 July, Nürburgring	GP of Germany	Auto Union Type D	R
20 Aug, Bern	GP of Switzerland	Auto Union Type D	4
3 Sept, Belgrade (Yu)	GP of Belgrade	Auto Union Type D	1
1946			
12 May, Marseilles	GP of Marseilles	Maserati Tipo 4CL	R
30 May, Paris	Resistance Cup	Maserati Tipo 4CL	R
9 June, Paris	Paris-St Coud GP	Maserati Tipo 4CL	R
23 June, Como		Fiat 1100S speciale	R
30 June, Modena		Fiat 1100S speciale	R
14 July, Albi (Fr)	GP of Albi	Maserati Tipo 4CL	1
21 July, Geneva	GP of Nations	Maserati Tipo 4CL	4
1 Sept, Turin		Maserati Tipo 4CL	R
3 Sept, Turin	Coppa Brezzi	Cisitalia Tipo D46	13
8 Sept, Venice		Fiat 1100S speciale	R
22 Sept, Asti (heats)		Fiat 1100S speciale	R
29 Sept, Milan		Maserati Tipo 4CL	R
6 Oct, Mantua	Coppa Albert e Giorgio Nuvolari	Cisitalia Tipo D.46	2
1947			
13 Apr, San Remo		Fiat 1100S speciale	R
21-22 June, Brescia	Mille Miglia	Cisitilio Tipo 202-MM	2
6 July, Forli		Ferrari Tipo 125S	1 (ic)
13 July, Parma		Ferrari Tipo 125S	1
24 Aug, Livorno		Ferrari Tipo 125S	R
14 Sept, Venice		Cisitalia Tipo D.46	3
1948			
1-2 May, Brescia	Mille Miglia	Ferrari Tipo 166S	R
16 May, Monaco	GP of Monaco	Cisitalia Tipo D.46	R
30 May, Bari	GP of Bari	Ferrari Tipo 166/F.2	4
13 June, Mantua	Coppa Alberto e Gorgio Nuvolari	Ferrari Tipo 125S	R
18 July Rheims	GP of France	Maserati Tipo 6C-2000	7
1949			
22 May, Marseilles (final)	GP of Marseilles	Maserati Tipo 6C-2000	DNQ
1950			
2 Apr, Palermo	Targa Floria	Cisitalia-Abarth Tipo 204.A	R
10 Apr, Palermo	Hillclimb	Cisitalia-Abarth Tipo 204.A	5

BIBLIOGRAPHY

Beaumont, Charles and William F. Nolan *Omnibus of Speed* Stanley Paul, London, 1961.
'Bira, B.' (Prince Birabongse of Thailand) *Bits and Pieces* G.T. Foulis & Co Ltd, 1943.
Brauchitsch, Manfred von *Kampf um Meter und Sekunden* Verlag der Nation, Berlin, 1955.
Caracciola, Rudolf *A Racing Driver's World* Motoraces Book Club, Cassell, London, 1963.
Chakrabongse, Prince Chula *Dick Seaman, Racing Motorist* G.T. Foulis & Co Ltd, London, undated.
Cholmondeley-Tapper, T.P. *Amateur Racing Driver* Motoraces Book Club, G.T. Foulis & Co, London, 1966.
Cimarosti, Adriano *The Complete History of Grand Prix Motor Racing* Aurum, 1986.
Desmond, Kevin *The Man with Two Shadows* Proteus Books, 1981.
Dreyfus, René with Beverly Rae Kimes *My Two Lives* Aztex Corporation, 1983.
Ferrari, Enzo *The Enzo Ferrari Memoirs* Hamish Hamilton, 1963.
Finn, Joel E. *American Road Racing – the 1930s* Garnet Hill Publishing Company, Inc., 1995.
Fraichard, Georges *The Le Mans Story* The Sportsman's Book Club. London, 1956.
Franceschi, Gianni *Tazio Nuvolari Museo* Sasa editore, 1998.
Hodges, David *The Monaco Grand Prix* Temple Press Books, 1964.
——— *The French Grand Prix* Temple Press Books, 1967.
Lang, Hermann *Grand Prix Driver* G.T. Foulis & Co Ltd, London, 1954.
Lurani, Count Giovanni *Nuvolari* Cassell, London, 1959.

Mays, Raymond *Split Seconds* G.T. Foulis & Co Ltd, London, 1951.
Mercer, Derrik (Editor-in-Chief) *Chronicle of the Twentieth Century* Longman, 1988.
Moity, Christian/Jean-Marc Teissedre and Alain Bienvenu *25 Heures du Mans 1923–1992* Editions D'Art Barthélemy, Automobile Club de l'Ouest, Besançon, 1992.
Moretti, Valerio *When Nuvolari Raced...* Autocritica Edizioni, Milan 1992/Veloce Publishing Plc., Godmanstone, Dorset 1994.
Neubauer, Alfred *Speed was My Life* Barrie and Rockliff, London, 1960.
Nixon, Chris *Racing the Silver Arrows* Osprey Publishing Limited, London, 1986.
Owen, David *Alfa Romeo: Ninety years of success on road and track* PSL, 1993.
Posthumous, Cyril *The German Grand Prix* Temple Press Books, 1966.
Ruesch, Hans *The Racers* Ballantine Books, New York, 1953.
Rosemeyer, Elly Beinhorn and Chris Nixon *Rosemeyer!* Transport Bookman Publications, Isleworth, Middlesex, 1989.
Santini, Aldo *Nuvolari: Il Mantovano Volante* Rizzoli, Milan, 1983.
Sebastian, Ludwig *Hinter Drohnenden Motoren* EKZ-Einband, 1958.
Sheldon, Paul *A Record of Grand Prix and Voiturette Racing, Volume 1* St Leonard's Press, 1987.
Stevenson, Peter *Driving Forces* Bentley Publishers, Cambridge, MA, 2000.
Taruffi, Piero *Works Driver* Temple Press Books, London, 1964.
Unique Motor Books *Mille Miglia 1927–1957* Unique Motor Books, undated.
Yates, Brock *Enzo Ferrari* Bantam Books, London, 1992.

Index